Federated Learning

Federated Learning: Unlocking the Power of Collaborative Intelligence is a definitive guide to the transformative potential of federated learning. This book delves into federated learning principles, techniques, and applications, and offers practical insights and real-world case studies to showcase its capabilities and benefits.

The book begins with a survey of the fundamentals of federated learning and its significance in the era of privacy concerns and data decentralization. Through clear explanations and illustrative examples, the book presents various federated learning frameworks, architectures, and communication protocols. Privacy-preserving mechanisms are also explored, such as differential privacy and secure aggregation, offering the practical knowledge needed to address privacy challenges in federated learning systems. This book concludes by highlighting the challenges and emerging trends in federated learning, emphasizing the importance of trust, fairness, and accountability, and provides insights into scalability and efficiency considerations.

With detailed case studies and step-by-step implementation guides, this book shows how to build and deploy federated learning systems in real-world scenarios – such as in healthcare, finance, Internet of things (IoT), and edge computing. Whether you are a researcher, a data scientist, or a professional exploring the potential of federated learning, this book will empower you with the knowledge and practical tools needed to unlock the power of federated learning and harness the collaborative intelligence of distributed systems.

Key Features:

- Provides a comprehensive guide on tools and techniques of federated learning.
- Highlights many practical real-world examples.
- Includes easy-to-understand explanations.

Chapman & Hall/CRC Artificial Intelligence and Robotics Series
Series Editor: Roman Yampolskiy

Unity in Embedded System Design and Robotics
A Step-by-Step Guide
Ata Jahangir Moshayedi, Amin Kolahdooz, Liao Liefa

Meaningful Futures with Robots
Designing a New Coexistence
Edited by Judith Dörrenbächer, Marc Hassenzahl, Robin Neuhaus, Ronda Ringfort-Felner

Topological Dynamics in Metamodel Discovery with Artificial Intelligence
From Biomedical to Cosmological Technologies
Ariel Fernández

A Robotic Framework for the Mobile Manipulator
Theory and Application
Nguyen Van Toan and Phan Bui Khoi

AI in and for Africa
A Humanist Perspective
Susan Brokensha, Eduan Kotzé, Burgert A. Senekal

Artificial Intelligence on Dark Matter and Dark Energy
Reverse Engineering of the Big Bang
Ariel Fernández

Explainable Agency in Artificial Intelligence
Research and Practice
Silvia Tulli David W. Aha

An Introduction to Universal Artificial Intelligence
Marcus Hutter, Elliot Catt, and David Quarel

AI: Unpredictable, Unexplainable, Uncontrollable
Roman V. Yampolskiy

Transcending Imagination:
Artificial Intelligence and the Future of Creativity
Alexander Manu

Responsible Use of AI in Military Systems
Jan Maarten Schraagen

AI iQ for a Human-Focused Future
Strategy, Talent, and Culture
Seth Dobrin

Federated Learning
Unlocking the Power of Collaborative Intelligence
Edited by M. Irfan Uddin and Wali Khan Mashwan

For more information about this series please visit:
https://www.routledge.com/Chapman--HallCRC-Artificial-Intelligence-and-Robotics-Series/book-series/ARTILRO

Federated Learning
Unlocking the Power of Collaborative Intelligence

Edited by M. Irfan Uddin and
Wali Khan Mashwani

CRC Press is an imprint of the
Taylor & Francis Group, an **informa** business

A CHAPMAN & HALL BOOK

Designed cover image: www.shutterstock.com

First edition published 2025
by CRC Press
2385 NW Executive Center Drive, Suite 320, Boca Raton FL 33431

and by CRC Press
4 Park Square, Milton Park, Abingdon, Oxon, OX14 4RN

CRC Press is an imprint of Taylor & Francis Group, LLC

© 2025 selection and editorial matter, M. Irfan Uddin and Wali Khan Mashwani; individual chapters, the contributors

Reasonable efforts have been made to publish reliable data and information, but the author and publisher cannot assume responsibility for the validity of all materials or the consequences of their use. The authors and publishers have attempted to trace the copyright holders of all material reproduced in this publication and apologize to copyright holders if permission to publish in this form has not been obtained. If any copyright material has not been acknowledged please write and let us know so we may rectify in any future reprint.

Except as permitted under U.S. Copyright Law, no part of this book may be reprinted, reproduced, transmitted, or utilized in any form by any electronic, mechanical, or other means, now known or hereafter invented, including photocopying, microfilming, and recording, or in any information storage or retrieval system, without written permission from the publishers.

For permission to photocopy or use material electronically from this work, access www.copyright.com or contact the Copyright Clearance Center, Inc. (CCC), 222 Rosewood Drive, Danvers, MA 01923, 978-750-8400. For works that are not available on CCC please contact mpkbookspermissions@tandf.co.uk

Trademark notice: Product or corporate names may be trademarks or registered trademarks and are used only for identification and explanation without intent to infringe.

ISBN: 978-1-032-72432-4 (hbk)
ISBN: 978-1-032-73897-0 (pbk)
ISBN: 978-1-003-46658-1 (ebk)

DOI: 10.1201/9781003466581

Typeset in Times LT Std
by Deanta Global Publishing Services, Chennai, India

Dedication

To my two wonderful sons Aaban Uddin and Imad Uddin.
"This book, like your iPad history, is proof that not all screen time is wasted. May your lives be filled with knowledge, kindness, and learning."

– Love, Papa

Contents

Preface		ix
About the authors		xi
List of Contributors		xii

1	**Introduction to Federated Learning** Vaneeza Mobin	1
2	**Foundations of Deep Learning** Sajid Ullah	23
3	**Chronicles of Deep Learning** Syed Atif Ali Shah and Nasir Algeelani	40
4	**User Participation and Incentives in Federated Learning** Muhammad Ali Zeb and Samina Amin	56
5	**A Hybrid Recommender System for MOOC Integrating Collaborative and Content-based Filtering** Samina Amin and Muhammad Ali Zeb	78
6	**Federated Learning in Healthcare** Muhammad Hamza	94
7	**Scalability and Efficiency in Federated Learning** Alyan Zaib	111
8	**Privacy Preservation in Federated Learning** P. Keerthana, M. Kavitha, and Jayasudha Subburaj	127
9	**Federated Learning: Trust, Fairness, and Accountability** Sana Daud	145
10	**Federated Optimization Algorithms** S. Biruntha, S. Rajalakshimi, and M. Kavitha	160
Index		177

Preface

In the domain of artificial intelligence (AI), collaboration is needed among the few models for edge devices. Therefore, federated learning is rising as a groundbreaking approach that can unlock the power of collective intelligence residing inside individual models. In this book, we provide a comprehensive overview of different federated learning techniques, their applications in different domains, and the future directions of federated learning and collaborative intelligence.

Traditional AI models are based on processing a large amount of data at a centralized location and hence there are issues such as security, privacy, and processing power. Federated learning is a new alternative to centralized processing, enabling collaborative model training on edge devices promoting data security and privacy. Local data remains on the edge device and only the shared parameters of the model are shared with the centralized model hence the privacy of the data remains intact, and the techniques provide the benefits of collaborative learning.

Chapter 1 by Vaneeza Mobin provides an overview of federated learning techniques. The chapter explains the basic details of federated learning such as what it is, its benefits, challenges (privacy, security), and real-world examples. It also discusses the future of federated learning and how it could change machine learning in distributed systems.

Chapter 2 is on the foundations of deep learning by Sajid Ullah and describes the foundations of the federated learning techniques. This chapter unlocks the secrets of deep learning, exploring the building blocks of modern AI. It examines three key areas: 1) the elaborate structures of neural networks, 2) how activation and loss functions work together to optimize models, and 3) the training process powered by gradient descent and backpropagation algorithms. The chapter is a comprehensive overview of deep learning techniques enabling students and practitioners to have a deeper understanding of this transformative technology.

Chapter 3 by Syed Atif Ali Shah and Nasir Algeelani is an extension of Chapter 2 and provides further details of deep learning and federated learning. The advancements in deep learning have revolutionized machine learning and have provided mechanisms for processing real values and probabilistic comparisons. It can effectively provide decision-making and can resemble human-like solutions to problems and make informed decisions. This is a new direction for AI techniques that are adaptive and powerful.

Chapter 4 by Muhammad Ali Zeb and Samina Amin provides details of user participation and incentives in federated learning. The chapter explains deep learning and natural language processing techniques to analyze text from social media platforms such as X (formerly Twitter). The chapter demonstrates that older techniques used for sentiment analysis are less effective and federated learning can provide an effective solution. The chapter also explores transfer learning techniques providing efficiency to deep learning solutions.

Chapter 5 by Samina Amin and Muhammed Ali Zeb is based on recommendation techniques and the integration of collaborative and content-based filtering. With the vast amount of content in MOOCs, choosing the right courses can be overwhelming. This chapter proposes a hybrid recommender system using both content-based and collaborative filtering to suggest the best courses for individual learners. It considers not just course content but also learner preferences, skills, and past behavior. The chapter delves into how recommender systems work in MOOCs, explores popular evaluation metrics, and emphasizes the additional use of e-learning filtering to personalize learning recommendations.

Chapter 6 by Muhammad Hamza is based on federated learning applications in healthcare. Federated learning offers a promising approach to healthcare by analyzing medical data (records, images, sensors) while preserving privacy. Unlike traditional machine learning methods that require central data sharing, federated learning trains model collaboratively on decentralized devices, protecting individual privacy. This leads to better predictions, precision, and accuracy compared to traditional machine learning with similar (or even better) results. Implementing federated learning globally in healthcare can improve decision-making, ensure equal access to quality care, and bring fairness to treatment.

Chapter 7 by Alyan Zaib provides the details of scalability and efficiency in federated learning. It discusses the efficiency and scalability of federated learning algorithms to process large amounts of data. It discussed the concepts of group learning by optimized methods for information sharing and resource sharing. The challenges of using different edge devices with different capabilities and limitations are discussed.

Chapter 8 by P. Keerthana, M. Kavitha, and Jayasudha Subburaj is about privacy preservation techniques in federated learning. The chapter focuses on privacy preservation in federated learning along with their technical details. The protection of sensitive information residing on edge devices is ensured by the framework developed in the chapter offering more robust solutions.

Chapter 9 by Sana Daud is about trust, fairness, and accountability in federated learning. The chapter discussed these issues in the Internet of things with more focus on trust and fairness by developing new evaluation metrics beyond just privacy. A new framework is explained using the principles of fairness, privacy, robustness, accountability, explainability, and federation.

Chapter 10 by S. Biruntha, S. Rajalakshimi, and M. Kavitha is on the optimization techniques in federated learning. Different optimization techniques to overcome the issues of device diversity and heterogeneity are discussed. The techniques presented in the chapter improve the efficiency and effectiveness of federated learning without any compromise on data privacy and security.

The book has addressed fundamental issues, their solutions, techniques, algorithms, applications, and future directions of federated learning. The chapters are written with detailed explanations and easy language for the readers to follow the concepts and apply the concepts in their domain. All those who are interested in getting insights into federated learning will find the book interesting and comprehensive.

Finally, I would like to thank all the book contributors. These include the authors of the chapters, reviewers, editors, proofreaders, and all those who gave suggestions to improve the book and make it a comprehensive guide for the readers. We hope that you will find the book a useful read and can adapt the book for your teaching, research, or practical applications.

About the authors

M. Irfan Uddin is currently working as a faculty member at the Institute of Computing, Kohat University of Science and Technology, Kohat, Pakistan. He has received his academic qualifications in computer science and has worked as a researcher on funded projects. He is involved in teaching and research activities related to different diverse computer science topics and has more than 18 years of teaching plus research experience. He is a member of IEEE, ACM, and HiPEAC. He has organized national and international seminars, workshops, and conferences. He has published over 100 research papers in international journals and conferences. His research interests include machine learning, data science, artificial neural networks, deep learning, convolutional neural networks, recurrent neural networks, attention models, reinforcement learning, generative adversarial networks, computer vision, image processing, machine translation, natural language processing, speech recognition, big data analytics, parallel programming, multi-core, many-core, and GPUs.

Wali Khan Mashwani received an M.Sc. degree in mathematics from the University of Peshawar, Khyber Pakhtunkhwa, Pakistan, in 1996, and a Ph.D. degree in mathematics from the University of Essex, UK, in 2012. He is currently a Professor of Mathematics and the Director of the Institute of Numerical Sciences, Kohat University of Science and Technology (KUST), Khyber Pakhtunkhwa, Pakistan. He is also the Dean of the Physical and Numerical Science faculty at Kohat University of Science and Technology, Khyber Pakhtunkhwa, Pakistan. He has published more than 100 academic papers in peer-reviewed international journals and conference proceedings. His research interests include evolutionary computation, hybrid evolutionary multi-objective algorithms, decomposition-based evolutionary methods for multi-objective optimization, mathematical programming, numerical analysis, and artificial neural networks.

Contributors

Nasir Algeelani
Air University
Islamabad, Pakistan and
Al-Madinah International University
Kuala Lumpur, Malaysia

Samina Amin
Kohat University of Science and
Technology
Khyber Pakhtunkhwa, Pakistan

S. Biruntha
Assistant Professor / AIDS
Dr NGP Institute of Technology
Coimbatore, India

Sana Daud
Kohat University of Science and
Technology
Khyber Pakhtunkhwa, Pakistan

Muhammad Hamza
Kohat University of Science and
Technology
Khyber Pakhtunkhwa, Pakistan
Sri Krishna College of Engineering
and Technology,
Coimbatore, India

M. Kavitha
Sri Krishna College of Engineering
and Technology
Coimbatore, India

P. Keerthana
Sri Krishna College of Engineering
and Technology
Coimbatore, India

Vaneeza Mobin
Kohat University of Science and
Technology
Khyber Pakhtunkhwa, Pakistan

S. Rajalakshimi
Sri Krishna College of Engineering
and Technology
Coimbatore, India

Syed Atif Ali Shah
Air University
Islamabad, Pakistan and
Al-Madinah International University
Kuala Lumpur, Malaysia

Jayasudha Subburaj
Sri Krishna College of Engineering
and Technology
Coimbatore, India

Sajid Ullah
Kohat University of Science and
Technology
Khyber Pakhtunkhwa, Pakistan

Alyan Zaib
Kohat University of Science and
Technology
Khyber Pakhtunkhwa, Pakistan

Muhammad Ali Zeb
Kohat University of Science and
Technology
Khyber Pakhtunkhwa, Pakistan

Introduction to Federated Learning

Vaneeza Mobin

1.1 BACKGROUND AND MOTIVATION

In the area of big data, machine learning has emerged as a powerful technique for driving a conclusion from massive amounts of data. The centralized nature of conventional machine learning approaches raises concerns about data security and privacy. Data becomes more sensitive and as it is dispersed across multiple devices and organizations more privacy approaches to machine learning are needed. In order to solve these issues the federated learning (FL) paradigm allows for cooperative model training without the requirement for centralized data storage. In federated learning several devices are established called clients that use their local data to train a shared model without exchanging the raw data, a central service receives the entire train model and combines them to create a global model update and this process is repeated until the global model coverage. Compared to the conventional centralized machine learning technique federated learning has the following benefits [1]:

- As federated learning keeps the training data dispersed across central devices and it preserves user privacy, the central server and clients never receive the raw data.
- Only the model update, not the raw data itself, is sent using federated learning thus lowering the communication overhead when compared to the centralized training.
- Federated learning permits on-device training which lowers network congestion to enhance the application response and performance.
- Federated learning enables cooperative learning across many devices and organizations enabling them to exchange knowledge and enhance their performance model without jeopardizing data privacy.

DOI: 10.1201/9781003466581-1

Due to these advantages, FL is a viable option for a variety of applications, especially in industries such as healthcare, banking, and mobile computing where data privacy is most important. For example, federated learning can be used to create fraud detection systems for financial institutions or train customized keyboard prediction models on mobile devices. The development of federated learning is fueled by rising demand for machine learning solutions that protect privacy as well as expand the availability of distributed computing resources [1].

1.2 THE RISE OF COLLABORATIVE INTELLIGENCE

Federated learning is a paradigm shift that opens the door to collaborative intelligence in the rapidly developing field of artificial intelligence. In order to achieve shared objectives and solve the challenging issues this notion imagines a symbiotic relationship between humans and artificial intelligence systems, in which each entity offers its special skills. With its enormous potential cooperative intelligence completely changes a number of industries including healthcare, banking, education, and transportation.

Envision a healthcare system in which medical practitioners and high-power diagnostic tools work together to create individual treatments that are customized to meet the special needs of each patient. Thinking of a financial market where human traders and Artificial Intelligence (AI) collaborate to make wise investment choices using each other specialties.

Federated learning is essential to the development of collaborative intelligence as it offers a safe and effective environment in which human specialists and AI systems may work together. Federated learning makes it possible for AI models to learn from data that is separate across several devices and organizations which helps to create a collective intelligence that is more powerful than what can be achieved by AI systems or by humans working alone [2].

A key component of collaborative intelligence is data privacy which is addressed by the federated learning's decentralized structure. Federated learning ensures that sensitive data stays under the ownership of its owner by maintaining decentralized training data on client devices. Participation in cooperative intelligence programs is encouraged and trust is fostered by this privacy-preserving strategy. Federated learning encourages accountability and openness in AI decision-making. This is because federated learning collaborative model updates can be accessed and reviewed openly. This allows the stakeholder to see any biases and review the reasoning behind artificial intelligence–driven decisions. Building trust in artificial intelligence systems and guaranteeing their responsible and ethical use depend on this transparency.

We anticipate a boom in collaborative intelligence applications that revolutionize a range of industries and enhance our daily lives as federated learning technology develops and becomes more widely used. With the help of collaborative intelligence, we will be able to solve complicated problems more skillfully and open up previously unthinkable opportunities. Let's think about the possible effect of collaborative intelligence on science research to train the artificial intelligence models on shared data sets a global network of scientists might accelerate discoveries and achievement in a variety of disciplines of study or picture of the future in which human translators and AI power language translation technology working in unison to promote the international understanding and dissolve the obstacles to communications [2].

Cooperative intelligence has far-reaching consequences that transcend technology and touch on many facets of society. Envision an individual learning system that adjusts to the unique learning style and speed of every student driven by artificial intelligence algorithms collaborating with educators to deliver tailored education. Now alternatively take into account social media sites that use federated learning to identify and stop online harassment creating a safer and friendlier online community. As we approach the dawn of a new era in artificial intelligence, collaborative learning suggests a time when user and AI collaborate peacefully and use their combined intelligence to improve the world.

1.3 PRINCIPLES AND BENEFITS OF FEDERATED LEARNING

Federated learning has revolutionized the area of machine learning as federated learning offers decentralized privacy-preserving techniques for group model training without transferring the raw data. Federated learning allows the use of multiple devices, and organizations prefer it as a client as it allows the use of local data to train a global model. This is compared to traditional centralized machine learning which collects data in one location. This decentralized method preserves the fundamental principle of data protection while enabling the development of innovative applications by tackling the important problem of data security and privacy.

1.3.1 The Principles That Underpin Federated Learning's Success

Federated learning is based on the following set of fundamental principles:

- *Decentralized data storage:* The first principle of federated learning is decentralized data storage. In order to ensure that private information is still distributed among client devices federated learning rejects decentralized data storage. By lowering the likelihood of unauthorized access and data breaches the centralized approach effectively protects user privacy.
- *Local model training:* The second principle of federated learning is local model training. Unlike centralized training we send the data to the central server for model training, this approach enables each client to train the model using local data. This local training approach reduces the communication

overhead, protects data privacy, and facilitates one-device training enhancing application response and performance.
- *Model update aggregation:* The third principle of federated learning is model update aggregation. Federated learning gathers and combines model updates from several clients to combine the raw data from the client. These model updates are sent to a central server where they contain the information gleaned from local training.
- *Privacy-preserving communication:* The fourth principle of FL is privacy-preserving communication. Federated learning uses encryption techniques to protect the model changes during central server connection in order to maintain data confidentiality to ensure that unauthorized parties cannot access the underlying raw data, only encrypted updates are shared.
- *Collaborative learning:* The fifth principle of federated learning is collaborative learning. Federated learning creates a cooperative learning atmosphere where clients train a common model together through the utilization of collective knowledge. Federated learning maintains data privacy while facilitating the creation of a resilient and broadly applicable model [3].

1.3.2 Reaping the Benefits of Federated Learning

Due to its decentralized and privacy-preserving nature, federated learning has a number of advantages that influence machine learning features, such as:

- Federated learning limits data exposure and maintains data decentralization, successfully protecting user privacy.
- The second benefit of FL is that, unlike centralized training which entails exchanging massive volumes of data, federated learning decreases the communication overhead by only transmitting model updates, mitigating the risk of data breaches, illegal access, and potential abuse of sensitive data. This decrease in data transferred results in better scalability and cheaper communication expenses.
- Federated learning makes distributed training possible across separate organizations and devices and facilitates effective model training on dispersed datasets. This distribution method leverages the collaborative knowledge from several data sources to increase the scalability and performance of the model.
- Federated learning models benefit from the variety of data that is dispatched from different users. Federated learning models can be trained on a range of data distribution which increases the performance and generalizability in real-world applications.
- Federated learning minimizes data exchange and ensures data privacy which compiles with laws such as GDPR. Through this compliance, enterprises may leverage the power of machine learning while complying with data privacy regularization.

- Federated learning allows for one-device training in which the model is trained directly on the client device. This one-device approach lowers the latency and enhances application response, especially in a context with limited resources.
- Federated learning makes it possible for several entities to collaborate on model training which permits knowledge exchange and model improvement. Organizations can pull their knowledge and resources thanks to this cooperative strategy all without sacrificing data privacy.
- Federated learning gives the data owners the ability to manage their data and take part in model training without sacrificing their privacy by maintaining data sovereignty through decentralized governance.
- Another benefit of federated learning is that it promotes trust and transparency in the machine learning process and makes it possible to create personalized and localized models that are suited to particular user requirements and data distribution through the utilization of local data.
- Federated learning reduces the possibility of improper use of data by controlling data exposure and encouraging openness throughout the training process. As a result of decreased exposure there is a lower chance of privacy violation which guarantees the ethical development and implication of machine learning models [3].

1.4 THE EVOLUTION OF MACHINE LEARNING IN DISTRIBUTED SYSTEMS: A JOURNEY TOWARDS FEDERATED LEARNING

The history of machine learning (ML) in the setting of distributed systems is a charming one, replete with ever-present creativity and flexibility. Decentralized learning on local devices has developed from its humble origins in centralized systems to its cutting-edge form. It is characterized by extensive discoveries and paradigm-shifting improvements. This timeline now not only displays the growing complexity of facts and processing demands, but also the ongoing intention of higher performance, scalability, and privacy [4].

1.4.1 Early Days: Centralized Systems and Limited Data

The early tiers of device machine learning in decentralized systems had been typified by way of centralized techniques. All of the data became stored on a central server that functioned because of the version trainer. Although this approach was easy to undertake, it had numerous hazards. First of all, performance deterioration and bottlenecks resulted from the statistics' increasing bulk, which critically confined its scalability. Second, the requirement to store personal records raised sizable privacy worries since it shared the records with unauthorized access and hackers.

1.4.2 Rise of Distributed Machine Learning: Addressing the Challenges

To overcome these limitations, researchers advanced the idea of distributed systems gaining knowledge of DML (distributed machine learning). The potential to teach models on records allotted across numerous devices became possible with this paradigm shift, which paved the manner for great breakthroughs. DML progressed scalability by way of lowering processing time and boosting productivity by way of dividing the learning technique across more than one node. Additionally, it reduced learning times and increased performance by way of distributing the burden, which led to quicker inference. In order to address privacy issues, DML also reduced the need for centralized data storage and advanced statistics protection and reduced the likelihood of safety breaches [3].

1.4.3 Two Primary Architectures Emerged in DML

There are two primary architectures in distributed machine learning: peer-to-peer and central server architecture.

In parameter server architecture a worker node trains the local models using their respective data subsets while a central server maintains the global model parameters. These local model modifications were then sent to the server which used them to update the global parameters, this process repeated until the model coverage [5] (Figure 1.1).

The parameter server consists of:

- A server group that can facilitate the running of multiple algorithms in the system.
- A server manager who is responsible for maintaining a consistent view of the server group.
- A worker group that is typically assigned for an application, the worker group communicates with the server group for pulling of parameters and pushing of gradients.

Peer-to-peer architecture did not include a central server, instead to share data and adjust the model parameters all nodes were in direct connection with one another, this approach might be easier to administrate and implement but it might also be less successful [6] (Figure 1.2).

The development of machine learning in distributed systems underwent changes that made it possible to address more complicated and large-scale issues which resulted in important breakthroughs across a range of industries. Many fields such as recommendation systems, computer vision, and natural language processing have benefitted from this paradigm change.

Introduction to Federated Learning 7

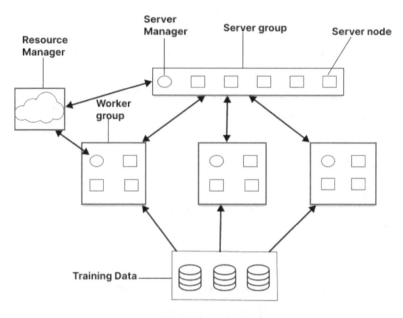

FIGURE 1.1 Parameter server architecture

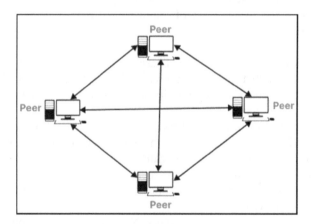

FIGURE 1.2 A simple peer-to-peer network

1.4.4 Recent Developments: The Rise of Federated Learning

Federated learning (FL) has attracted great interest these days as a disruptive deep learning method. This particular method focuses on training machine learning models using data to gain awareness of trends from individual devices or edge devices. This decentralized technique offers numerous advantages over traditional DML.

8   Federated Learning

- *Improved privacy:* Since data in no way leaves the tool, FL offers superior privacy safety for sensitive information. This is mainly necessary for applications used in industries concerned with data privacy, such as banking and healthcare.
- *Enhanced scalability:* FL is ideal for models that deal with vast quantities of data due to the fact it can effortlessly cope with large volumes of data by utilizing the processing power of millions of devices in the network.
- *Reduction in communication costs:* FL lowers communication exchange by only sending targeted model updates as opposed to entire updates, which is beneficial for devices with limited resources.

FL has the power to essentially change how machine learning models are used and trained. It lets us benefit from the extensive volumes of information that devices generate while safeguarding and securing information. This opens up fascinating possibilities for tailored packages, collaborative learning, and allotted intelligence [4].

1.4.5 Beyond Federated Learning: The Future of ML in Distributed Systems

The area of distributed machine learning is always evolving as new strategies and advancements are made. Apart from FL, numerous different elements are impacting the future of DML:

- *Graph neural networks (GNNs):* These state-of-the-art algorithms have the ability to research from graph-representable information, which opens up new packages in social community analysis, recommender systems, and other associated domains.
- *Reinforcement learning (RL):* This is an exciting area of federated learning that can educate retailers on how to make decisions in complex environments. Its uses consist of robotics, gaming, and self-sufficient systems.
- *Transfer learning:* By allowing us to use understanding from one task to some other, this powerful tactic improves the efficacy and precision of system studying models.
- *Emerging distributed systems designs:* New designs such as blockchain and fog computing are being researched that will improve the scalability, protection, and security of the user's machine learning structures [4].

These improvements show how distributed machine learning is changing. As time goes on, the focus will shift to developing algorithms which are safer, economical, and ensure privacy while utilizing the large amounts of data and computing power to be had in dispersed settings. This focus can improve many elements of our lives and yield beneficial, unique, and practical solutions across a huge spectrum of fields.

1.5 ADVANCEMENTS LEADING TO FEDERATED LEARNING: A JOURNEY FROM ISOLATION TO COLLABORATION

With the appearance of federated learning (FL), which substitutes decentralized, cooperative techniques for local models, machine learning has experienced a sizable transformation. This shift was made feasible because of the advancements listed below, all of which are essential to FL's fulfillment.

1.5.1 The Convergence of Communication and Computing Power

Two key enhancements that FL relies upon are extended transmission bandwidth and broader availability of processing assets. Cutting fees, improvements in community infrastructure and excessive-pace net connections have extensively improved transmission bandwidth. This has made it feasible for devices and the central server to switch model updates efficaciously, which is a necessary precondition for FL. Concurrently, the developing utilization of wearables, smartphones, and other facet devices has created a big worldwide network of computational resources. As a result, FL has progressed in overall performance and expanded model schooling by means of utilizing the pooled computing ability of numerous devices [7].

1.5.2 Securing Collaborative Learning in a Decentralized World

FL's success depends on its potential to collaborate and share information without compromising customers' privacy or non-public safety. This difficulty has been resolved in part with the aid of advances in cryptography and secure verbal exchange protocols. Homomorphic encryption and secure multi-celebration computation (SMC) are strategies that assure data safety and privacy even in decentralized settings. They make it viable for group learning without revealing the underlying unprocessed data [8].

1.5.3 From Centralized to Decentralized Optimization

Centralized optimization techniques are utilized by conventional devices gaining knowledge of algorithms to address and combine all facts on a central server. However, FL turns into unfeasible and unsustainable as it includes scattered data across numerous devices. To clear up this issue, researchers have evolved efficient allotted optimization algorithms and decentralized studying methodologies. These strategies ensure the convergence of the worldwide model whilst enabling the synchronization of mastering throughout several devices, even in the face of verbal exchange lag and tool heterogeneity.

1.5.4 Open-Source Frameworks: Democratizing Federated Learning

The creation of open-source FL frameworks such as PySyft, Flower, and TensorFlow Federated (TFF) has accelerated FL's popularity and development. These frameworks make FL algorithm deployment and implementation less complicated with the aid of an intuitive user interface and multiple functions that allow accessibility to a wider audience.

1.5.5 Addressing the Growing Demand for Privacy-Preserving Learning

The public's increased awareness of data privacy and protection vulnerabilities has fueled the search for alternative processes that address those difficulties. FL addresses this challenge by providing a technique that allows groups to get to know each other without requiring them to share raw data. This privacy-maintaining approach encourages transparency and self-assurance in cooperative learning projects by lowering the dangers related to centralized statistics processing and garages [9].

1.5.6 Hardware and Software Advancements: Tailoring Technology for FL

The advancements in software and hardware platforms designed mainly for dispensed computing and machine learning have further allowed FL. FL algorithms have ended up extra green and carry out higher, which makes them more appropriate for practical uses. This is due to the fact that machine learning models are accomplished on specialized processors, and software program systems that maximize conversation and resource allocation are used.

1.5.7 Fueling FL with Abundant Data

The availability of large and numerous datasets from various fields has simplified the procedure of teaching FL models. These datasets permit the development of reliable and broadly relevant models that work properly in more than a few real-world situations. Moreover, FL is becoming increasingly more well-known, expanding the body of information and creating a positive feedback loop that propels the improvement of more complex models.

1.5.8 Collaborative Effort across Academia and Industry

The capability of FL has been recognized by influential figures in academia and business, leading to a surge in studies and improvement endeavors. This collaborative effort has extended FL's improvement and integration into other programs. Additionally, the FL environment has grown stronger on account of the improvement of specialized equipment and resources in response to the demand from many stakeholders.

1.5.9 Regulatory Landscape and Ethical Considerations

The improvement of information privacy policies, along with the California Consumer Privacy Act CCPA, in the United States, and the General Data Protection Regulation (GDPR), in the EU, has contributed to the creation and acceptance of privacy-preserving techniques which include FL. Due to these policies, which oblige corporations to handle personal facts accurately, FL provides a captivating choice for cooperative learning that conforms to moral and legal standards.

1.5.10 From Isolated Models to Collaborative Ecosystems

The rapid increase of federated learning can be attributed to each of these advances and the increasing need for decentralized and privacy-preserving learning methods. We trust that as FL advances, its effect will increase across different domains, influencing records evaluation, teamwork, and the improvement of the next generation of smart systems.

FL represents a paradigm shift in system studying, prioritizing decentralized, cooperative learning environments over solitary models. A wide variety of industries, such as finance, schooling, healthcare, and smart cities, may be completely changed by this shift. Through the usage of distributed devices' of mixed intelligence and data protection and privacy, FL has the capability to provide new opportunities and create extra intelligent and collaborative infrastructure.

1.6 UNRAVELING THE CHALLENGES OF FEDERATED LEARNING: FROM THEORY TO REAL-WORLD IMPLEMENTATION

Federated learning (FL) holds the promise to facilitate privacy-preserving learning; however, before FL may be implemented, some of its challenges need to be addressed. These problems can be divided into four principal areas, all of which require careful consideration and original thinking to resolve.

1.6.1 Communication Overhead: A Bandwidth Balancing Act

FL's core functionality depends on devices and the central server replacing model changes. However, some elements may need additional conversation:

- *Restricted bandwidth:* If a tool has few assets, it could be tough for it to supply updates. Higher fees and longer training times will accompany this. Removing this obstacle requires efficient compression strategies and conversation protocols.
- *Heterogeneity:* When using devices with various processing and network capacities, it may bring about an uneven learning environment wherein a few devices make a contribution greater than others. This may affect the learning model's performance and convergence. Adaptive algorithms and dynamic resource allocation techniques are used to manage this heterogeneity.
- *Privacy concerns:* There is a risk that sharing version updates may cause inadvertent monitoring of the private data of the underlying devices. Secure communication protocols and privacy-preserving techniques such as homomorphic encryption are important to maintain privacy and foster collaboration [3].

1.6.2 Data and Model Heterogeneity: Navigating a Patchwork of Information

The quality of the data utilized in Federated Learning (FL) directly impacts its effectiveness.. However, FL offers precise difficulties due to its decentralized approach:

- *Non-IID data:* Local device data distributions can vary substantially, which may cause models that will be biased toward the majority of data and false in more than a few real-world situations. Methods such as federated learning and federated transfer learning are being researched to mitigate this problem.
- *Model poisoning:* Malevolent actors may additionally try to contaminate the learning data with the intention of altering the model's output. Systems for detecting anomalies and robust defenses are vital to maintaining the integrity of the learning model.
- *Privacy leaking:* Even with privacy-preserving safeguards in place, there is a danger that data will leak due to version modifications. Differential privacy techniques need to be carried out and modified with caution [3].

1.6.3 System and Security Challenges: Protecting the Fortress of Knowledge

Potential vulnerabilities offer complicated environments inside the underlying infrastructure supporting FL:

- *Resource constraints:* Devices regularly have a small amount of processing power and short battery lives, which prevents users from participating and reduces the effectiveness of the training. To get past these restrictions, resource-aware algorithms and effective version designs are vital.
- *Security of the machine:* FL structures need to be resilient to quite a few threats, such as backdoors, information poisoning, and version theft. To ensure device integrity intrusion detection structures and stable hardware control are crucial.
- *Methods for protecting privacy:* It may be computationally costly to put in security techniques such as homomorphic encryption and stable multi-party computing (SMC), which affects system scalability and overall performance. Finding a balance between privacy and performance requires investigating novel and effective privacy-preserving techniques [3].

1.6.4 Legal and Ethical Considerations: Navigating the Moral Compass of Data Collaboration

The ethical and moral implications of FL necessitate careful attention:

- *Data possession and governance:* Precise frameworks and governance protocols are needed to outline data possession, obligation, and access control inside FL systems. Collaborative agreements and facts licensing may be used to establish ethical information sharing.
- *Fairness and bias:* FL models may also increase preexisting data biases, leading to unfair and discriminatory outcomes. Routine tracking and bias avoidance methods are necessary to ensure truthful and equitable results for all users.
- *Explainability and transparency:* It is concerning that the decision-making processes of FL models lack transparency and responsibility. Explainable AI strategies and user-friendly interfaces are necessary to increase self-assurance in and knowledge of FL models [3].

1.6.5 Charting a Course for Successful Implementation

Despite the demanding situations, researchers and practitioners are actively developing techniques to overcome them and enable the full capability of FL. Some promising processes include:

- *Federated learning frameworks:* The open-source TFF (TensorFlow Federated), PySyft (Python Syft), and Flower frameworks offer equipment and datasets to simplify FL implementation and address unusual problems.

- *Advanced algorithms:* Federated learning, federated transfer learning, and adaptive algorithms can be utilized to control data heterogeneity and enhance version generalizability.
- *Security and privacy-related solutions:* Privacy-preserving data exchange protocols, stable hardware control, and differential privacy methods can all be used to defend record confidentiality and system integrity.
- *Legal and ethical frameworks:* Lawmakers, researchers, and stakeholders need to collaborate to develop simple recommendations and standards for data possession and access, justice, and responsibility in FL structures.

Federated learning represents a paradigm change in machine learning by way of providing a privacy-preserving path to collaborative intelligence. By addressing the problems and inspiring unique answers, FL has the capacity to revolutionize how we educate and apply machine learning models. This will attract moral and legal responsibilities while developing new opportunities in a variety of industries. To develop an extra smart and cooperative future, researchers, lawyers, and stakeholders from various backgrounds must work collectively. Let us harness the user's ability together.

1.7 PRIVACY AND SECURITY: THE CORNERSTONE OF FEDERATED LEARNING

Due to data privacy, federated learning has a number of promises for collaborative learning. Federated learning enables a training model on data that are dispersed among different devices or organizations and it can lower the danger of data breach and unauthorized access in contrast to the traditional machine learning models where data is centralized. However, maintaining privacy and security in decentralized data and communication environments calls for careful thoughts and creative solutions [10].

1.7.1 Importance of Privacy in Federated Learning

Data privacy is important in federated learning for several reasons:

- *Safeguarding sensitive information:* Individual data can consist of monetary, geographic, and fitness information. FL reduces the opportunity for undesirable access by ensuring that such facts stay on the user's device.
- *Establishing transparency and trust:* Users are more willing to take part in FL efforts, giving important information and hastening the improvement of new models, once they believe that their data are secured.
- *Respecting regulations:* Organizations are required to abide by privacy laws such as the CCPA and GDPR to handle user data securely. FL offers a way to conform to those regulatory standards and facilitate collaborative learning [10].

1.7.2 Methods for Secure and Confidential Data Sharing in FL

To ensure secure and confidential data sharing in FL several methods are employed:

1. *Secure multi-party computation (SMC):* SMC conceals the underlying information while allowing many members to compute a characteristic over their private inputs. This approach preserves data privacy while enabling collaborative model training.
2. *Homomorphic encryption:* With this cryptographic technique, encrypted data may be computed while not having to be decrypted. In doing so, the central server is able to collaborate and update the global version at the same time as keeping the confidentiality of model updates.
3. *Federated differential privacy (FDP):* FDP offers a statistical guarantee of data privacy by adding noise to model updates before sharing. This method prevents a compromise between privacy and usability, retaining user data while permitting version learning.
4. *Secure aggregation protocols:* During communication between the user and the central server, the protocols assure the authenticity and integrity of version updates. This stops bad actors from tampering with the training model or adding poisoned facts.
5. *Secure hardware control:* These specialized hardware additives provide a steady place to perform sensitive calculations. This may be mainly beneficial in safeguarding version parameters and warding off unwanted access to private data.
6. *Privacy-preserving communication protocols*: These protocols further shield user privacy by encrypting and anonymizing communications between devices and the central server.
7. *Federated learning frameworks:* The improvement of personal and reliable FL systems is made simpler via the integrated protection and privacy skills of open-access FL frameworks such as TensorFlow Federated (TFF) and Python Syft (PySyft).
8. *Legal and ethical frameworks:* To make sure accountable records sharing and persons agree with FL tasks, it is vital to set up simple legal frameworks and moral concepts. Data ownership, access, control, equity, and obligations must all be included with the aid of these frameworks [10].

1.7.3 Future Directions in Privacy-Preserving FL

While vast strides have been made in ensuring privacy and protection in FL, ongoing research and development efforts are crucial to deal with increased demand and adapt to evolving technologies. Some promising future models involve:

- Developing extra efficient and scalable privacy-preserving strategies.
- Exploring new approaches to cope with data heterogeneity and model bias.

- Designing robust protection mechanisms in opposition to attacks.
- Promoting transparency and explainability in FL structures.
- Collaborating with policymakers and stakeholders to set up a simple legal and ethical framework for FL.

The cornerstone of effective federated learning is still privacy. Through the implementation of strong safety and privacy-preserving strategies, FL can facilitate collaborative learning while retaining user confidence and legal issues. We might also expect that FL will play a role in influencing machine learning in the future and open the door to a smarter, cooperative system in which protection and privacy are paramount as studies and machine learning improve.

1.8 APPLICATIONS OF FEDERATED LEARNING ACROSS INDUSTRIES

By facilitating collaborative learning on data dispersed across individual devices, federated learning (FL) is rapidly changing sectors and ensuring privacy and protection while supplying insightful information. Numerous successful programs in a number of disciplines have resulted from this paradigm shift, each demonstrating the adaptability and sizeable nature of FL [11].

1.8.1 Healthcare

- *Precision medicine:* FL analyzes patient data from many hospitals, resulting in more individualized treatment regimens and better patient results.
- *Drug discovery:* FL can expedite the process of finding and developing new drugs by working together to analyze genomic data from various patients.
- *Pandemic forecasting:* Using FL models trained on personal health information, disease epidemics can be predicted and tracked, allowing for prompt intervention [11].

1.8.2 Finance

- *Fraud detection:* To appropriately perceive fraudulent operations FL is used to look at large volumes of monetary transactions throughout more than one institution.
- *Evaluation of creditworthiness:* FL models are capable of examining creditworthiness based on personal financial records without jeopardizing privacy, providing more individualized and inclusive financial offerings.

- *Personalized financial recommendation*: FL is able to customize financial merchandise and investment recommendations by way of analyzing every customer's particular monetary information [11].

1.8.3 Retail

- *Personalized product tips:* Product suggestions that are mainly tailored to every user are made through FL models, which remember each user's browsing and buying records on numerous structures.
- *Inventory manipulation:* By the use of FL models to forecast demand for specific products in diverse places, stock control can be optimized and inventory outs may be minimized.
- *Fraud detection:* While protecting consumer privacy, FL models are capable of perceiving fraudulent interest in online transactions [11].

1.8.4 Automotive

- *Predictive renovation:* By utilizing information from onboard sensors in cars, FL models forecast the likelihood of automobile accidents, reducing safety costs and improving safety.
- *Autonomous driving:* To grow the adaptability and protection of self-driving cars, FL is used to train autonomous riding models on a whole lot of driving statistics from unique users.
- *Optimization of traffic flow:* By analyzing real-time data from linked vehicles, FL models can reduce congestion and improve traffic flow [11].

1.8.5 Manufacturing

- *Predictive maintenance:* By using sensor records from networked devices in numerous factories, FL models assume probable device issues, decreasing downtime and streamlining safety plans.
- *Quality management:* FL models are able to identify and reduce quality concerns by means of studying manufacturing data from special machines and ensuring uniform standards.
- *Process optimization:* FL models are capable of finding and fine-tuning system parameters for extended performance by studying operational statistics from diverse manufacturing lines [11].

1.8.6 Success Stories

- *Apple's quick type keyboard:* This custom-designed keyboard learns every user's specific typing fashion and, through the usage of FL, enhances accuracy and usability.

- *Google Gboard:* Like quick type, Gboard uses FL to customize language models and keyboard predictions for every consumer.
- *Samsung's scene recognition:* This characteristic improves overall digital performance and personal experience by way of using FL to recognize and regulate settings based totally on the person's environment.
- *The meal shipping app:* FL from the company Meituan in China assists in tailoring meal recommendations for specific customers in keeping with their tastes and regional traits.
- *Federated learning from an open-minded platform:* This platform democratizes access to this game-changing generation by means of allowing researchers and developers to work together to build FL models throughout multiple domain names.

There is a bright future for FL. We may anticipate even more cutting-edge applications in a wide range of industries as the technology develops and is more widely used. FL promises to transform how we communicate, learn, and use technology in a variety of contexts, including smart cities, tailored education, and personalized treatment. Together, researchers, developers, and business executives can fully realize FL's potential and create a more connected, intelligent future for everybody.

1.9 FUTURE TRENDS AND ADVANCEMENTS IN FEDERATED LEARNING

By maintaining data security and privacy and facilitating collaborative intelligence, federated learning has already completely changed the way we train and use machine learning models but still with further research and development efforts the feature of federated learning promises more exciting breakthroughs. The following encouraging patterns and future initiatives significantly alter the landscape of federated learning.

1.9.1 Improved Security and Privacy

- *Improvements in differentially private algorithms:* More advanced algorithms that reduce overall performance degradation will offer extra privacy assurances.
- *Breakthroughs in secure multi-celebration computation (SMC):* SMC protocol traits will enhance collaborative mastering of safety and privacy, allowing the usage of extra sensitive records.
- *Advances in homomorphic encryption:* Sophisticated methods of homomorphic encryption will permit calculations on encrypted data without the need for decryption, protecting privacy and facilitating sophisticated model training.

- *Hardware protection answers:* To protect sensitive information and model parameters during FL calculations, hardware control, and devoted processors will provide secure environments [12].

1.9.2 Enhanced Efficiency and Scalability

- *Communication-efficient algorithms:* Algorithms that reduce verbal exchange overhead may be created as a way to make FL more appropriate for large-scale deployment and devices with limited resources.
- *Improvements to machine learning:* As machine learning strategies improve, more complex models can be utilized on edge devices, lowering the need for centralized servers and increasing aid performance.
- *Cross-device federated learning:* FL might be accelerated to facilitate cooperation between many device types, which include wearables, smartphones, and Internet of things sensors, bringing new possibilities for context-aware and custom-designed packages. [12]

1.9.3 Handling Bias and Heterogeneity in Models

- *Federated meta-learning:* This method will increase the overall performance and generalizability of FL models with the aid of permitting them to regulate numerous data distributions throughout devices.
- *Federated transfer studying:* This method aims to relieve data scarcity on personal devices and increase learning performance by making use of know-how from pre-educated models.
- *Fairness-conscious FL algorithms:* To reduce prejudice and discrimination in FL models and guarantee simple and equitable results for all users, new algorithms could be created [12].

1.9.4 Novel Use Cases and Applications

- *Federated learning (FL) in healthcare:* FL could be used to train personalized healthcare models on patient-specific fitness facts, resulting in higher infection prevention, analysis, and remedy plans.
- *Federated learning for autonomous automobiles:* Federated learning (FL) is a promising approach to improve safety and performance in self-driving cars by facilitating collaborative learning of riding policies and environment models among numerous automobiles.
- *Federated learning for smart towns:* Federated learning (FL) could be utilized in smart town packages to optimize resource allocation, power consumption, and visitors travel in real-time by way of reading information from numerous sensors and devices.

- *Federated learning for custom-designed education:* FL will make it possible for adaptive studying structures to tailor the pace and substance of instruction to the precise desires and studying options of every learner [12].

1.9.5 Democratizing Federated Learning

- *Open-source FL frameworks:* Developers and researchers can be capable of creating and enforcing FL applications without a superb deal of technical know-how thanks to easily navigable and available FL frameworks.
- *Platforms for collaboration:* Specific platforms will make it less complicated for stakeholders, developers, and teachers to create collectively, with the purpose of promoting innovation and hastening the introduction of FL programs.
- *Standardization and excellent practices:* Defining unambiguous FL requirements and great practices will assure that safety, interoperability, and ethical ideas are respected in diverse implementations [12–14].

1.10 LOOKING AHEAD: A BRIGHTER FUTURE WITH FEDERATED LEARNING

Federated learning has the potential to convert many facets of our lives by embracing those new traits and tendencies [15, 16]. It offers hope for a time when we are capable of protecting users' privacy while using the mixed intellect of dispersed devices [17, 18]. We may additionally anticipate modern applications, a revolutionary era, and a greater cooperative and smart future for all as the sector of FL develops.

1.11 SUMMARY

This chapter narrates federated learning (FL), a transformative paradigm in machine learning in a context that propelled the rise of collaborative intelligence. It gradually extends to the principles and benefits governing FL. Traversing the emergence of FL, this chapter aims to highlight the evolution of machine learning within distributed systems that set the stage for advancements. Keeping in view the challenges encountered in the implementation of FL, a comprehensive detail of privacy considerations is presented. This chapter engages readers to delve into real-world applications, showcasing early research examples that range from predictive modeling on mobile devices to secure disease prediction.

The chapter concludes by foreseeing future aspects, anticipating revolutionary applications, and ongoing research in personalized healthcare. The instances and research presented in this chapter serve as a testament to the versatility of collaborative intelligence, laying the foundation for a future shaped by the continued evolution of FL in artificial intelligence and machine learning. Readers are invited to learn the insights of collaborative intelligence, FL's applications, and envision its promising trajectory in the ever-evolving landscape of modern machine learning.

REFERENCES

1. Qinbin Li, Zeyi Wen, Zhaomin Wu, Sixu Hu, Naibo Wang, Yuan Li, Xu Liu Bingsheng. "A survey on federated learning systems: Vision, hype and reality for data privacy." *IEEE Transactions on Knowledge and Data Engineering, 35*(4), 3347–3366, 2021.
2. Sawsan AbdulRahman, Hanine Tout, Hakima Ould-Slimane, Azzam Mourad. "A survey on federated learning: The journey from centralized to distributed on-site learning and beyond." *IEEE Internet of Things Journal 8* (7), 5476–5497, 2020.
3. Mohammad Aledhari, Rehma Razzak, Raza M. Parizi, Fahad Saeed. "Federated learning: A survey on enablingtechnologies, protocols, and applications." *IEEE Access 8*, 140699–140725, 2020.
4. Joost Verbraeken, Matthijs Wolting, Jonathan Katzy, Jeroen Kloppenburg, Tim Verbelen, Jan S Rellermeyer. "A survey on distributed machine learning." *Acm Computing Surveys(csur)* 53 (2), 1–33, 2020.
5. Mu Li, David G Andersen, Alexander J Smola, Kai Yu. "Communication efficient distributed machine learning with the parameter server." *Advances in Neural Information Processing Systems 27*, 2014.
6. Leonard Barolli, Fatos Xhafa. "Jxta-overlay: A p2p platform for distributed, collaborative- and ubiquitous computing." *IEEE Transactions on Industrial Electronics 58* (6), 2163–2172, 2010.
7. Mohammed Amine Bouras, Fadi Farha, Huansheng Ning. "Convergence of computing, communication, and caching in Internet of Things." *Intelligent and Converged Networks1* (1), 18–36, 2020.
8. Zhuoran Ma, Jianfeng Ma, Yinbin Miao, Ximeng Liu, Wei Zheng, Xiang Li. "Flexible and Privacy-preserving Framework for Decentralized Collaborative Learning." *GLOBECOM 2020–2020 IEEE Global Communications Conference, 33*(4), 1–6, 2020.
9. Xuefei Yin, Yanming Zhu, Jiankun Hu. "A comprehensive survey of privacy-preserving federated learning: A taxonomy, review, and future directions." *ACM Computing Surveys(CSUR) 54* (6), 1–36, 2020.
10. Viraaji Mothukuri, Reza M Parizi, Seyedamin Pouriyeh, Yan Huang, Ali Dehghantanha, Gautam Srivastava. "A survey on security and privacy of federated learning." *Future Generation Computer Systems 115*, 619–640, 2021.
11. Li Li, Yuxi Fan, Mike Tse, Kuo-Yi Lin. "A review of applications in federated learning." *Computers & Industrial Engineering 149*, 106854, 2020.
12. Subrato Bharati, M Mondal, Prajoy Podder, VB Prasath. "Federated learning: Applications, challenges and future directions." *International Journal of Hybrid Intelligent Ssystems 18* (1–2), 19–35, 2022.
13. A. Khan *et al.*, "Summarizing online movie reviews: A machine learning approach to big data analytics," *Science Program 2020*, 5812715, 2020, doi: 10.1155/2020/5812715.

14. S. Amin et al., "Recurrent neural networks with TF-IDF embedding technique for detection and classification in tweets of dengue disease," *IEEE Access 8*, 131522–131533, 2020, doi: 10.1109/access.2020.3009058.
15. Z. Ullah et al., "Certificateless proxy reencryption scheme (CPRES) based on hyperelliptic curve for access control in content-centric network (CCN)," *Mobile Information System 2020*, 4138516, 2020, doi: 10.1155/2020/4138516.
16. F. Aziz, H. Gul, I. Uddin, G. V Gkoutos, "Path-based extensions of local link prediction methods for complex networks," *Scientific Reports 10* (1), 19848, 2020, doi: 10.1038/s41598-020-76860-2.
17. F. Aziz, T. Ahmad, A. H. Malik, M. I. Uddin, S. Ahmad, M. Sharaf, "Reversible data hiding techniques with high message embedding capacity in images," *PLoS One 15* (5), e0231602, 2020.
18. N. Mast et al., "Channel contention-based routing protocol for wireless Ad Hoc Networks," *Complexity 2021*, 2051796, 2021, doi: 10.1155/2021/2051796.

Foundations of Deep Learning

2

Sajid Ullah

2.1 INTRODUCTION

This chapter, "Foundations of Deep Learning", sets out to give an explanation of the fundamental thoughts guiding this dynamic field within the hastily evolving science of artificial intelligence. Starting by dissecting neural networks and investigating their architectures and functionalities. Additionally, light is shed on the important roles that loss features and activation functions play in optimizing model overall performance. The investigation concludes with a thorough analysis of gradient descent and lower backpropagation, the ideas underlying community optimization.

This chapter's objectives are twofold: first, to demystify the core principles that govern the operation of deep learning models, and second, to empower readers with the information and self-belief to significantly analyze and discover this swiftly evolving area.

2.2 BACKGROUND

The roots of deep learning stretch back in addition than one would possibly suspect, with the seeds of notion sown inside the fertile ground of early artificial intelligence research. In the 1940s, the seminal work of Warren McCulloch and Walter Pitts brought the perceptron a rudimentary version mimicking the binary firing of neurons, laying the inspiration for the interconnected networks that would define deep learning. However, limitations in training and a brief length of skepticism called the "AI winter" forged a shadow over those early efforts [1].

The embers of progress flickered to life again in the 1960s with the work of Alexey Ivakhnenko and Valentin Lapa, who explored polynomial activation capabilities and

DOI: 10.1201/9781003466581-2

laid the basis for multi-layered networks. Yet, realistic demanding situations and computational limitations persevered to hinder tremendous adoption [1].

The authentic renaissance of deep learning arrived within the overdue 1980s and early 1990s with the pioneering work of Geoffrey Hinton, David Rumelhart, and Ronald Williams, who efficiently carried out the backpropagation algorithm to train multi-layered neural networks. This step forward, coupled with advancements in computational strength, fuelled a surge of research and development, propelling deep learning into the coronary heart of the AI revolution [2].

However, the course towards proper adoption was not totally smooth. Critics voiced concerns approximately the lack of interpretability and explainability of deep studying fashions, thinking their reliability for protection-important programs. Additionally, the computational needs of education complicated networks posed a significant hurdle. Despite these demanding situations, the speedy advancement of hardware and the improvement of greater green education algorithms have paved the manner for a golden age of deep mastering. The field has witnessed substantial breakthroughs in diverse domains, from pc imaginative and prescient and natural language processing to self-driving cars and healthcare diagnostics [2].

This chapter delves into the principles underlying those successes, demystifying the complexity of neural networks, activation features, loss functions, and the optimization algorithms that manual their mastering adventure. By expertise those foundational readers gain the gear to seriously determine the full-size and ever-evolving landscape of deep learning, contributing to its accountable and moral development in the years to come.

2.3 NEURAL NETWORKS AND THEIR ARCHITECTURE

Artificial neurons are used to create complex structures called neural networks, which can process several inputs and produce a single output. A neural network's main function is to convert input into usable output. A neural network typically consists of an input layer, an output layer, and one or more hidden layers. An artificial neural network, or ANN, is another name for it. The ANN design is necessary for neural networks to operate precisely like the human brain [2].

In a neural network, every neuron is connected to every other neuron through interactions. The network is capable of identifying and observing each component of the information at hand as well as any potential correlations between the different data elements. Neural networks can search through enormous amounts of data for incredibly intricate patterns in this way [2].

There are two ways that information can be transferred via a neural network:

- *Feedforward network:* Layer by layer, data is fed into the neural network in a feedforward mode. Each layer modifies the input before sending it to the one after it. The input processing procedure is simple and results in a prediction for the output.

Foundations of Deep Learning 25

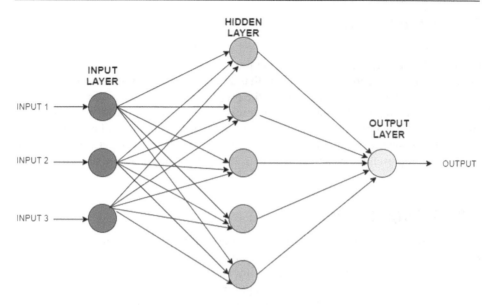

FIGURE 2.1 Architecture of Neural network

- *Feedback networks:* Backpropagation, or feedback, is a little more complex. First, a prediction is made by the network, and the difference between the predicted and actual results is computed. In order to reduce future prediction mistakes, the network's internal parameters (weights and biases) are then systematically adjusted using this error. It is through this iterative process of parameter modification, error computation, and prediction that the network learns and becomes more efficient over time [3] Figure 2.1.

2.3.1 Main Components of Neural Network Architecture

The neural network architecture is made up of input, output, and hidden layers.

2.3.1.1 Input Layer

The first layer of a neural network to receive raw input data is called the input layer. A feature or component of the input data is represented by each neuron in this layer. The dimensionality of the input data determines how many neurons are present in the input layer. Every neuron may represent a pixel in image recognition, for instance. The input layer is the neural network's access factor, and its fundamental job is to switch data from this residue to the layers that come after it for added processing and learning [3].

2.3.1.2 Hidden Layer(s)

The intermediate stages among the enter and output layers of a neural community are known as hidden layers. These layers' neurons carry out intricate calculations, changing the incoming records into a format that aids in the community's correct prediction-making. After receiving entry from the preceding layer, every neuron in a hidden layer gives each input a weight earlier than sending the outcome through an activation characteristic. The potential of the network to study and generalize is basically dependent on the number of neurons in each layer and hidden layers. The network can study hierarchical representations and apprehend complicated patterns in the statistics way to hidden layers [3].

2.3.1.3 Output Layer

A neural community's output layer generates the final results or prediction on the end. Depending on the process at hand, this residue's neuron may additionally range from one for binary classification to numerous for multi-class category, with each neuron representing a class. Activation functions appropriate for the task are usually employed by the neurons in the output layer. The output of a sigmoid function, which is commonly used for binary classification, resembles probability. A softmax function is frequently employed in multi-class contexts to normalize the outputs into a probability distribution across classes. The output layer's job is to offer the final prediction made by the network using the patterns and features that it has learned from the layers that came before it [2].

2.3.2 Types of Neural Networks

Some important neural networks are:

- Convolutional neural network (CNN)
- Recurrent neural network (RNN)
- Long short-term memory (LSTM)
- Generative adversarial network (GAN)

2.3.2.1 Convolutional Neural Network (CNN)

One particular kind of neural network that is used to handle structured grid data, such as photographs, is called a convolutional neural network (CNN). To automatically and adaptively learn the spatial hierarchies of capabilities from the enter; it makes use of convolutional layers. This layout reduces the need for guide function engineering by shooting patterns and spatial correlations within the data, making it beneficial for packages such as photo identification [2].

2.3.2.1.1 Convolutional Neural Network: Architecture

A convolutional neural network consists of four layers: input, pooling, convolutional, and completely linked.

2.3.2.1.1.1 Input Layer The input layer of a convolutional neural network (CNN) is in which the community gets its first entry, which is frequently raw statistics in the shape of a pixel. The input layer of a CNN is made to address information that looks like a grid, in assessment to traditional neural networks. The intensity of the layer shows the number of color channels (three for RGB pixels), and each neuron inside the input layer is equal to a pixel in the entered picture.

Accepting the photo statistics and passing it through the successive convolutional layer in which filters and pooling operations are carried out to extract hierarchical traits from the entered image is the primary job of the input layer. CNNs are capable of efficiently capturing spatial patterns in images because of their grid-like structure [2].

2.3.2.1.1.2 Convolutional Layer Convolutional operations are applied to the input data by the convolutional layer of a convolutional neural network (CNN). To identify patterns, edges, and features in the input image, these procedures entail swiping tiny filters, also known as kernels, across the image [3].

2.3.2.1.1.3 Max Pooling Layer A convolutional neural network (CNN) max pooling layer is a down-sampling process that lowers the input volume's spatial dimensions. Usually, it comes after convolutional layers. Retaining the most pertinent details from a group of values is the main concept. By using max pooling, the network can withstand changes in the location, size, and orientation of its features. Additionally, it lessens the processing burden and assists in avoiding overfitting by concentrating on the most important data in the feature maps [1].

2.3.2.1.1.4 Output Layer Convolutional neural networks (CNNs) use hierarchical characteristics that are taken from the input data to build their final predictions in the output layer. The output layer's configuration is determined by the particular purpose for which the CNN was created.

The final predictions or classifications derived from the traits and patterns that were found out at some point of the CNN's layers are furnished via the output layer [2].

2.3.2.2 Recurrent Neural Network (RNN)

Recurrent neural networks (RNNs) are artificial neural networks designed to research statistics sequences. It is particularly beneficial for obligations in which understanding the temporal relationships and sequence of the records is essential. The fundamental idea behind RNNs is that they have loops, which permit information to stay in one vicinity and be transferred from one stage of the method to the subsequent [3].

2.3.2.2.1 Recurrent Neural Network: Architecture
The architecture of an RNN consists of the following layers.

2.3.2.2.1.1 (Hidden State) Recurrent Neurons The recurrent neurons, now and again referred to as hidden country or reminiscence cells, are the main part of an RNN. These neurons are given an input, generate an output, and preserve an inner country or reminiscence at every step in time (*t*). The network may keep sequential information because the inner kingdom at every occasion step depends upon the internal kingdom at the prior time step and the modern-day input [1].

2.3.2.2.1.2 Input Layer The RNN receives an entry vector (commonly denoted as $x(t)$) at each time step (*t*). This input vector can represent a lot of information formats, together with character time collection facts points, phrases in a sentence, and series factors.

2.3.2.2.1.3 Hidden State Update The process of updating the hidden state in a recurrent neural network (RNN) involves calculating the new hidden state given the current input and the previous hidden state.

Because of the recursive process, RNNs might also capture sequential dependencies in data by keeping a hidden state that holds facts from advanced time steps [2].

2.3.2.2.1.4 Output Layer The recurrent neural network (RNN) output layer produces the very last forecast or output after the records are processed via the recurrent connections. The precise reason for which the RNN was created determines how the output layer must be configured.

The output layer creates the final output, or prediction, for the given enter series with the aid of synthesizing the records processed through the recurrent connections [2].

2.3.2.3 Long Short-Term Memory(LSTM)

An improved method for learning long-term dependencies in sequential data is the long short-term memory (LSTM) type of recurrent neural network (RNN), which was created to address the vanishing gradient issue. To control the information flow, LSTMs feature gates and memory cells [1].

2.3.2.3.1 Long Short-Term Memory: Architecture

2.3.2.3.1.1 Cell State The LSTM network keeps track of a cell state in its internal memory, which is updated and managed by a group of gates. The cell state is appropriate for activities with long-distance dependencies since it may theoretically capture information across lengthy sequences [3].

2.3.2.3.1.2 Hidden State Every time step (ht) in LSTM networks has a hidden state, similar to conventional RNNs. The extra superior LSTM hidden states offer the potential to selectively store or retrieve statistics from the cell state [2].

2.3.2.3.1.3 Gates Three predominant types of gates are utilized by LSTMs to control the data glide: forget, input, and output gates.

- *Forgot gate:*
  A critical part of an LSTM is the forget gate. It determines what records from the nation of the cell need to be retained or destroyed. It makes use of the modern enter in addition to the previous mobile kingdom as input, and it produces values between 0 and 1 with the use of a sigmoid activation function. One (1) suggests "maintain this record", whereas 0 shows to "forget it". This gate makes it possible for LSTMs to deal with sequential entries with long-time period dependencies more efficiently by supporting them in selectively remembering or discarding data [1].
- *Input gate:*
  Determining whether information from the contemporary input and the previous mobile country must be saved inside the mobile is an important function of the input gate in a long short-term memory (LSTM) community. This is how it operates:

  i. *Sigmoid activation:* Two inputs are fed into the input gate: the earlier concealed state and the modern input. These inputs are subjected to a sigmoid activation feature, which generates values between 0 and 1. By serving as gates, these values alter the statistics float. A quantity near 1 indicates "preserve this fact", however, a range of near 0 shows "discard this information".
  ii. *Element-clever multiplication:* Next, the brand new candidate values produced by using the new cell kingdom computation are elevated detail-smart via the sigmoid output. Which quantities of the brand new records ought to be added to the cellular kingdom is determined with the aid of this multiplication.

The enter gate allows LSTMs to deal with lengthy-time period dependencies and apprehend pertinent styles in sequential statistics by means of selectively allowing or blocking off information [2].

2.3.2.3.1.4 Update Cell State In a long short-term memory (LSTM) community, the input statistics, and the prior cellular country are combined to replace the cellular state. For a more thorough clarification, see this:

- *Input gate:* Sigmoid activation is implemented to the present input in conjunction with the formerly hidden nation. To suggest which quantities of the input and earlier cell nation to replace, it generates values between 0 and 1.
- *New cell state:* The current input and the detail-sensible made of the enter gate output and the preceding mobile country are combined, and a tanh activation is carried out. In the range of −1 to at least 1, this generates new candidate values for the cell nation.
- *Updating the cell state:* The new candidate cellular state is expanded detail-wise with the aid of the input gate output. Which additives of the new candidate values must be introduced to the cell country is determined by means of this system.

Subsequently, the output is increased through the fabrication from the previous cellular country and the input gate supplement (1 – input gate output). By preserving long-term dependencies and selectively adding new records, this mixture modifies the mobile kingdom.

2.3.2.3.1.5 Output State Based on the updated cellular kingdom, the output gate in a long short-term memory (LSTM) network determines the following hidden kingdom. This is evidence of the output gate's features:

- *Sigmoid activation:* The input of the output gate consists of the previous concealed country and the current input. These inputs are subjected to a sigmoid activation characteristic, which generates values between 0 and 1. These values govern which quantities of the updated cellular state ought to be found out to the output by acting as gates. A wide variety near 1 indicates "expose these records", whereas a number near 0 suggests "cover this data".
- *Element-wise multiplication:* The updated cellular state that has been tanh transformed is then elevated detail-smart by means of the sigmoid output. The values that cross into the subsequent concealed country are determined by means of this multiplication.

The output gate creates the following hidden nation by selectively revealing pertinent information from the updated cell state. By the use of this technique, LSTMs are able to recognize and extract critical patterns from sequential facts in an effort to produce unique predictions [3].

2.3.2.4 A Generative Adversarial Network (GAN)

A deep learning architecture called a generative adversarial network (GAN) consists of two adversarial-trained neural networks: the discriminator and the generator. New data samples that mimic a particular dataset are produced using GANs [1].

2.3.2.4.1 Generative Adversarial Network (GAN): Architecture

2.3.2.4.1.1 Generator The generator's job is to produce fictitious data samples (such as photos) that resemble the distribution of actual data. It creates data samples that are increasingly better during training using random noise as input. The generator normally consists of one or more layers, and to upgrade the spatial resolution of the data, transposed convolutional layers are frequently used [1].

2.3.2.4.1.1.1 Generator Architecture

- *Input layer:* A Gaussian-like basic distribution sampled from a random noise vector (z) at random.
- *Hidden layers:* A sequence of hidden layers, frequently transposed convolutions, or completely connected layers that gradually convert noise in the input into data that resembles the genuine data.
- *Output layer:* The last layer generates a sample of created data, such as an image.

2.3.2.4.1.2 Discriminator The discriminator's job is to tell authentic data samples from false ones. It assigns a chance that each input is real after accepting data from the generator as well as samples of real data. The discriminator receives training to enhance its capacity to distinguish between authentic and fraudulent data [1].

2.3.2.4.1.2.1 Discriminator Architecture

- *Input layer:* Samples of data, which may be real (taken from the original dataset) or fake (created by a generator).
- *Hidden layers:* The discriminator, like the generator, uses hidden layers to process the input data, frequently utilizing convolutional or fully connected layers.
- *Output layer:* The last layer generates a probability score that shows whether the input is genuine or not. Typically, it generates values between 0 and 1 using a sigmoid activation function.

2.3.2.4.1.3 Training Process (Adversarial Training) During training, a game is played between the generator and the discriminator. The generator tries to offer data that is almost identical to real data in order to deceive the discriminator. The discriminator aims to differentiate between honest and false data. This competitive dynamic causes each network to improve over the years [1].

2.4 ACTIVATION FUNCTIONS AND LOSS FUNCTIONS

2.4.1 Activation Functions

An essential part of deep studying neural networks is activation capabilities. They provide the version of non-linearity, which facilitates apprehending tricky patterns and conveys extra correct forecasts. The following objectives are achieved through activation capabilities in deep learning:

- *Defining non-linearity:*
  A neural network could simply be a linear combination of its input if activation capabilities were not there. The mathematical operations used to affect the output of neurons and introduce non-linearity are called activation capabilities. The network cannot approximate complex, non-linear capabilities in the records without this non-linearity.
- *Facilitating complicated representations:*
  Neural networks can examine and constitute complicated capabilities and hierarchical abstractions in the records with the assistance of activation functions. Edges, textures, forms, and greater superior thoughts in picture

reputation or abstract patterns in natural language processing ought to all be examples of these capabilities.

2.4.1.1 Common Activation Functions

i. **Sigmoid function (logistics activation)**
Sigmoid smoothes input values in the range of 0 to 1. It is frequently employed as an activation function in neural networks to add non-linearity to binary classification issues [5].

- *Output range:* (0, 1)
- *Formula:* $(1 + e(-x))(x) = 1 / (x)$
- Has a history of being utilized in the output layer for binary classification.
- An S-shaped curve that constricts input values to a range between 0 and 1.
- Have vanishing gradient issues, which can slow down deep network training.

ii. **Hyperbolic tangent functions**
Squeezing input values between –1 and 1, it functions similarly to the sigmoid. It is frequently used to manage data that is cantered on zero in LSTMs and RNNs.

- *Output range* :(–1 to 1)
- *Formula:* $\tanh(x) = (e(x) - e(-x)) / (e(x) + e(-x))$
- Its zero-cantered characteristics make it similar to the sigmoid in appearance.
- Also prone to problems with vanishing gradients[4].

iii. **ReLU (rectified linear unit)**
When a ReLU is activated, a positive input is output directly; otherwise, a zero is output. Its popularity stems from how well it promotes sparse representations and how easy it is to use.

- *Output Range*: [0, ∞)
- *Formula*: $\text{ReLU}(x) = \max(0, x)$
- The most used activation function due to its effectiveness and simplicity of use.
- Accelerating convergence during training has been observed empirically.
- However, when certain neurons die, they may experience the "dying ReLU" problem [5].

iv. **Leaky rectified linear unit (leaky ReLU)**
By permitting a tiny, positive gradient for negative inputs, leaky ReLU avoids the dying ReLU issue, in which neurons consistently output zero. It tackles ReLU's shortcomings while handling negative input values.

- *Output Range* : (–∞, ∞)
- *Formula:* Leaky ReLU(x) = x if x > 0, else a * x (where "a" is a small positive constant, typically 0.01)

- Allows a tiny gradient for negative inputs, which solves the "dying ReLU" problem.
- Prevents full neuron inactivation while maintaining non-linearity [5].

2.4.2 Loss Functions

A loss characteristic often referred to as a price function or an objective feature is an important part of the training method for deep neural community models in gadget learning. The inaccuracy or discrepancy among the real target values (the ground reality) and the expected values (the model's output) are what is being measured. This loss feature informs the mastering manner by way of displaying how properly or poorly the version is acting, therefore minimizing it is by far the main objective during training [6]. Let us look closely at loss capabilities:

2.4.2.1 Purpose of Loss Functions

- *Measure error:* Loss features specific to the distinction between the real goal values and the predicted values of the model. The loss will increase in proportion to the error.
- *Guide optimization:* During schooling, the weights and biases of the version are modified to limit loss. These modifications are made by the usage of optimization techniques inclusive of gradient descent, which rent the gradient of the loss with respect to the parameters.
- *Specify the goal:* Depending on the type of job (for example, classification, regression, or generative modeling), the choice of loss function sets the specific learning target of the model.

2.4.2.2 Types of Loss Functions

2.4.2.2.1 Regression Loss Functions
Regression loss functions are utilized when the goal is to predict continuous numeric values.

i. **Mean squared error (MSE) loss:**
   MSE is an additional metric that computes the mean squared discrepancies between the values that were predicted and those that were observed. Although it is more sensitive to outliers than MAE, it penalizes larger errors more severely, which frequently results in training optimization landscapes that are smoother.

   - *Formula:* $MSE = (1/n) * \Sigma (y_i - \hat{y}_i)^2$, where n is the number of data points, $\hat{y}_i$ is the predicted value, and y_i is the true value.
   - Frequently employed for common regression issues.
   - Highlights greater errors and pays attention to outliers [6].

34 Federated Learning

ii Mean absolute error (MAE) loss:
The average absolute disparities between predicted and actual values are measured by the MAE metric. It offers a straightforward, understandable indicator of the average forecast error.
- *Formula:* MAE = (1/n) * Σ $_i$ |– ŷ$_i$|, where n is the number of data points, ŷ$_i$ is the predicted value, and y$_i$ is the true value.
- The average absolute difference between predictions and values is measured.
- In comparison to MSE, less susceptible to outliers [7].

2.4.2.2.2 Classification Loss Functions
These are used for classification tasks where the goal is to assign data points to discrete classes.

i. Binary cross-entropy loss (log loss):
One loss function utilized in binary classification issues is binary cross entropy. It encourages the model to reduce the difference between expected and actual values for each instance by measuring the discrepancy between predicted probability and actual binary outcomes.
- *Formula:* BCE = –Σ (y$_i$ * log (ŷ$_i$) + (1 – y$_i$) * log (1 – ŷ$_i$)), where ŷ$_i$ represents the expected probability of class 1 and y$_i$ represents the true class (0 or 1).
- Used for tasks requiring binary categorization.
- Calculates the difference between expected class probabilities and actual class distributions [7].

ii. Categorical cross-entropy loss (softmax loss):
Tasks involving the classification of multiple classes use categorical cross-entropy. It encourages the model to assign higher probabilities to the proper class for each input by quantifying the difference between the anticipated and actual class probabilities.
- *Formula:* CCE = –Σ (y$_i$ * log (ŷ$_i$)), where y$_i$ is the one-hot encoded true class vector and ŷ$_i$ is the predicted class probabilities vector.
- Used for jobs involving multiclass categorization.
- Punishes incorrect classifications based on the likelihood of the class [7].

2.4.2.2.3 Generative Loss Functions
These are used in generative models such as generative adversarial networks (GANs) and variational autoencoders (VAEs).

i. GAN loss:
A two-part loss function is used by GANs:

1. *Generator loss:* Indicates how effectively the generator produces accurate samples. Usually, it is the negative log chance of tricking the discriminator.

2. *Discriminator loss:* Indicates how successfully the discriminator can tell artificial and genuine samples apart.

ii. **Variational autoencoders (VAEs) loss:**
VAEs use a combination of two losses:

- *Reconstruction loss*: In order to encourage the model to accurately recreate input data, reconstruction loss measures the difference between the input and the rebuilt output.
- *KK divergence loss:* Encourages a structured and continuous latent space by penalizing the model when the distribution of latent variables deviates from a specified standard distribution (often Gaussian) [7].

Depending on the nature of the issue and the type of data being used, the proper loss function must be chosen. In order to choose the best loss function, there are trade-offs between interpretability, robustness, and the peculiarities of the dataset. Different loss functions highlight various aspects of the model's performance. The most appropriate loss function for a given task is frequently chosen with the help of experimentation and domain expertise.

2.5 BACKPROPAGATION AND GRADIENT DECENT

2.5.1 Backpropagation

An essential part of deep learning is getting familiar with a method referred to as lower backpropagation, on occasion called "backward propagation of errors", it is used to teach synthetic neural networks. In order to provide reliable prediction, it is crucial to minimize a targeted loss feature and edit the weights and biases of a neural community [9]. Below is an in-depth explanation of the lower back propagation set of rules:

i. *Forward pass:*
The forward pass is the preliminary degree of lower backpropagation. During this pass, the neural network receives entered records and makes predictions by means of transferring the entry to the output layer with the aid of the layer. By calculating the weighted sum of its inputs and making use of an activation characteristic each layer produces its output. [9]

ii. *Calculate loss:*
The neural network's output is in comparison to the precise goal values following the forward skip. The error or difference between the forecasts and the actual targets is decided using a loss feature, also known as a value characteristic. Depending on the specific task handy, a loss function consisting of

implied squared errors for regression or move-entropy for a category may be chosen [9].

iii. ***Backward pass (backpropagation):***
The number one portion of the backpropagation technique, known as the backward pass, includes calculating the gradients (derivatives) of the loss as one goes from the output layer returned to the input layer, considering the version's parameters (weights and biases) [9].

iv. ***Chain rule of calculus:***
The chain rule of calculus is used to compute the gradients. It states that the derivative of a composite feature is identical to the sum of the derivatives of its factor functions. In the context of neural networks, the gradient of the loss with respect to the parameters of a single layer can be computed by chaining together the gradients from subsequent layers [9].

v. ***Gradient calculation:***
For each layer, the gradients are calculated in two steps:

- *Local gradient calculation:*
The local gradient is the weighted sum derivative of the activation function applied at that layer. This gauges how responsive the layer's output is to variations in the weighted sum.

- *Error propagation:*
The gradient of the loss with respect to the weighted sum is obtained by multiplying the local gradient by the gradient of the loss with respect to the output of that layer (calculated in the preceding layer).

- *Weight and bias updates:*
Each layer's weights and biases are updated in the direction that minimizes loss after computing the gradients. Usually, an optimization algorithm such as gradient descent is used to carry out this update. The learning rate hyperparameter, which controls the step size during optimization, also controls the size of the update.

vi. ***Iterative process:***
Steps 1 through 6 are repeatedly repeated for a predefined number of epochs or until the loss converges to an acceptable level. The model continuously adjusts its parameters to minimize loss as it gains the ability to use the training data to improve its predictions. [8]

vii. ***Stochastic gradient descent (SGD):***
Stochastic gradient descent is a version of gradient descent that is certainly utilized in practice. It is regularly utilized, where gradients are computed for every new release and the usage of a mini-batch of training examples is chosen at random. Adding randomness to the optimization procedure aids in fending off local minima.

An essential neural community education set of rules; backpropagation's effectiveness allows the training of deep and problematic models. It is a key thing of deep gaining knowledge of effectiveness in a number of programs, including reinforcement studying, herbal language processing, and photograph popularity.

2.5.2 Gradient Decent

During training, a neural network's weights and biases are up to date with the usage of the fundamental optimization method called gradient descent. Its essential objective is to limit a sure loss characteristic that measures the discrepancy between the predicted outputs of the version and the actual target values of a dataset. A thorough clarification of the gradient descent algorithm with regards to deep getting to know is supplied beneath [10].

i. *Initialization:*
The version's parameters (weights and biases) are first initialized with small random values throughout the schooling manner. The behavior of the neural community is defined by using those parameters.

ii. *Forward pass*
The forward pass is the technique by means of which input information is transferred through the neural network throughout education. The weighted general of the network's inputs is computed for every layer, and an activation feature is then used to generate that layer's output. Layer after layer, the ahead pass keeps until the favored output is attained. [10]

iii. *Calculate loss:*
The neural network's output is compared to the real intention values once the ahead pass is completed. When comparing anticipated outputs to real goals, an error or disparity is calculated by the usage of a loss feature, additionally referred to as a price function. Mean squared errors (MSE) are a common loss feature in regression and move entropy for class [10].

iv. *Gradient calculation:*
The computation of gradients that is, the derivatives of the loss function with respect to the parameters of the model is the foundation of gradient descent. Gradients demonstrate how changing a parameter would change the loss. Because it allows the derivative of a composite function to be written as the sum of the derivatives of its component functions, the chain rule of calculus is used to calculate gradients. The gradient displays the size and direction of each parameter modification that should be made to the neural network to lessen loss [11–13].

v. *Update parameters:*
The neural network's weights and biases are modified to minimize loss after computing the gradients. To reduce the loss, this update is carried out in the gradients' opposite direction. The hyperparameter that regulates the step size during optimization, the learning rate, also regulates the update size. The modified settings are applied in the next training iteration [14].

vi. ***Iterative process:***
Steps 2 through 5 are repeatedly repeated until the loss converges to an acceptable level or for a predefined number of epochs. The model continuously updates its parameters to minimize loss as it learns to use the training data to improve its predictions [15].

vii. ***Stochastic gradient descent (SGD):***
In practice, stochastic gradient descent (SGD), a variant of gradient descent, is widely used. Instead of creating gradients using the whole dataset for every iteration, SGD chooses a small batch of training examples at random. This frequently speeds up convergence, introduces unpredictability into the optimization process, and helps prevent local minima.

Numerous optimization techniques utilized in deep learning, along with mini-batch gradient descent, adam, RMSprop, and others, are constructed on the concepts of gradient descent [16, 17]. The selection of the optimization approach and hyperparameter, which include learning rate is important while deep neural networks are being skilled. These elements need to be carefully calibrated for a hit model education.

2.6 SUMMARY

In summary, this chapter has explored the complexities of modern synthetic intelligence by targeting important fundamental principles. This chapter has installed the inspiration for a radical draw close of deep learning by revealing the workings of neural community designs, studying the features of activation and loss features, and concluding with a thorough research of gradient descent and again propagation.

As we come to a close, it is clear that corporate know-how of these fundamental principles is crucial for navigating the hastily growing subject of synthetic intelligence. Both novices wishing to enter the vicinity and pro experts wishing to refresh their information can use this excursion of the fundamentals as a stepping stone.

This chapter's desires have been executed by way of giving a thorough, comprehensible, and concise overview. Now, readers can check and apply their knowledge of these concepts. These foundations will simply be essential in figuring out how AI develops in the future and how it affects many exceptional fields as we move forward.

REFERENCES

1. Weibo Liu, Zidong Wang, Xiaohui Liu, Nianyin Zeng, Yurong Liu, Fuad E Alsaadi. "A survey of deep neural network architectures and their applications." *Neurocomputing 234*, 11–26, 2017.
2. Wilamowski, Bogdan. "Neural network architecture and learning." IEEE International conference on Industrial Technology 2003,TU1-T12 Vol.1, 2003.

3. Hooman Yousefizadeh, Ali Zilouchian. "Neural network architecture." *Intelligent Control Systems Using Soft Computing Methodology*, 39–66, 2001, CRC Press.
4. Bin Ding, Huimin Qian, Jun Zhou. "Activation functions and their characteristics in deep neural networks." 2018 Chinese control and decision conference (CCDC), 1836–1841, 2018.
5. Shiv Ram Dubey, S. K. "Activation functions in deep learning: A comprehensive survey and benchmark." *Neurocomputing*, 2022. doi: 10.1016/j.neucom.2022.06.111.
6. Hang Zhao, Orazio Gallo, Iuri Frosio, Jan Kautz. "loss functions for image restoration with neural networks." *IEEE Transactions on computational imaging 3* (1), 47–57, 2016.
7. Simon Kornblith, Ting Chen, Honglak Lee, Mohammad Norouzi. "Why do better loss functions lead to less transferable features?" *Advances in Neural Information Processing Systems 34*, 28648–28662, 2021.
8. Cilimkovic, Mirza. "Neural networks and back propagation algorithm." *Institute of Technology Blanchardstown, Blanchardstown Road North Dublin 15* (1), 2015.
9. Timothy P Lillicrap, Adam Santoro, Luke Marris, Colin J Akerman, Geoffrey Hinton. "Backpropagation and the brain." *Nature Reviews Neuroscience 21* (6), 335–346, 2020.
10. Mandic, Danilo P. "A generalized normalized gradient descent algorithm." *IEEE Signal Processing Letters 11* (2), 115–118, 2004.
11. Yu Xue, Yankang Wang, Jiayu Liang. "A self-adaptive gradient descent search algorithm for fully-connected neural networks." *Neurocomputing 478*, 70–80, 2022.
12. A. Khan *et al.*, "Summarizing online movie reviews: A machine learning approach to big data analytics," *Scientific Programming 2020*, 5812715, 2020, doi: 10.1155/2020/5812715.
13. S. Amin *et al.*, "Recurrent neural networks with TF-IDF embedding technique for detection and classification in tweets of dengue disease," *IEEE Access 8*, 131522–131533, 2020, doi: 10.1109/access.2020.3009058.
14. Z. Ullah *et al.*, "Certificateless proxy reencryption scheme (CPRES) based on hyperelliptic curve for access control in content-centric network (CCN)," *Mobile Information System 2020*, 4138516, 2020, doi: 10.1155/2020/4138516.
15. F. Aziz, H. Gul, I. Uddin, G. V Gkoutos, "Path-based extensions of local link prediction methods for complex networks," *Scientific Reports 10* (1), 19848, 2020, doi: 10.1038/s41598-020-76860-2.
16. F. Aziz, T. Ahmad, A. H. Malik, M. I. Uddin, S. Ahmad, M. Sharaf, "Reversible data hiding techniques with high message embedding capacity in images," *PLoS One 15* (5), e0231602, 2020.
17. N. Mast *et al.*, "Channel contention-based routing protocol for wireless Ad Hoc Networks," *Complexity 2021*, 2051796, 2021, doi: 10.1155/2021/2051796.

Chronicles of Deep Learning

3

Syed Atif Ali Shah and Nasir Algeelani

3.1 DEEP LEARNING

Deep learning is a type of machine learning (ML) that takes input data and produces output. As we discussed in ML, the difference is that it does not need explicit information on features of the input data. Rather it extracts features automatically from data, consequently, it is very data-hungry [1]. Getting more data improves its efficiency and helps it become more accurate. Deep learning algorithms are made up of neural networks. Just like other ML techniques, it has an input layer that collects information to be processed $x_1, x_2,...x_n$, then one or more hidden layers, and finally, an output layer to produce output, i.e., y. Here the hidden layers are more computationally intensive [2]. These hidden layers are responsible for the functioning of the whole model.

3.2 PERCEPTRON

The building block that makes up the neural network is a neuron. So what is the neuron in deep learning? We call it a perceptron and how it works. The idea of a perceptron or a single neuron is very simple. Let us start by talking about and describing the feedforward information feedforward propagation of information.

$$\dot{y} = g\left(\sum_{i=1}^{m} x_i w_i\right) \quad (3.1)$$

Through this model, we define a set of inputs x_1 through x_m. This can be seen in Equation (3.1). Each of these inputs is multiplied by a corresponding weight w_1 through w_n. We can imagine if we have x_1 we multiply by w_1 and x_2 multiplied by w_2 and so on. Take all of these multiplications and add them up. These come together in a summation and then pass this weighted sum through the non-linear activation function to produce a final output which is called ŷ; which can be seen in Equation (3.1). Now we also have another term, which is a biased term. This allows for a shift in the activation function to the left and right. Now on the right side single equation is illustrated as a mathematical formula in Equation (3.2).

$$\dot{y} = g\left(w_0 + X^T W\right) \tag{3.2}$$

It can be rewritten in linear algebra using vectors dot products and matrices, as shown in Equation (3.3). X is a vector of our inputs x_1 through x_m, instead of this is a single number X. X is a vector of multi inputs W is a vector of all of the weights 1 to n.

$$X = \begin{bmatrix} x_1 \\ \vdots \\ x_m \end{bmatrix} \& W = \begin{bmatrix} w_1 \\ \vdots \\ w_m \end{bmatrix} \tag{3.3}$$

We can simply take their weighted sum by taking the dot product between these two vectors. Then we add our bias. Bias is a single number W', then apply the non-linear term. Applying that non-linear term so that the non-linear term transforms that scalar input to another scalar output ŷ.

3.3 ACTIVATION FUNCTIONS

For an activation function there are acouple of different names, first, was the activation function [3]. One common example of a non-linear activation function is called the sigmoid function, shown in Equation (4.4). We can also see one in Equation (3.5), this is a function that takes as input any real number and outputs a new number between zero and one.

$$g = \delta(z) \tag{3.4}$$

$$\delta(z) = \frac{1}{1+e^{-x}} \tag{3.5}$$

It is essentially collapsing our input between this range of 0 and 1. This is just one example of an activation function, but many activation functions use neural networks.

3.4 COMMON ACTIVATION FUNCTIONS

Here are some common ones, and throughout this discussion, we will see these TensorFlow codes. The most commonly used are sigmoid, hyperbolic, and rectified linear units. We will just be using these as a way to kind of bridge the gap between theory and practice. With some of the basic code from TensorFlow, that we will be using in our discussion. TensorFlow code and mathematical formulae are shown in TC 3.1 to TC 3.3 and Equation (3.6) to Equation (3.12), respectively.

$$\delta(z) = \frac{1}{1+e^{-x}} \tag{3.6}$$

$$g(z) = g(z)(1-g(z)) \tag{3.7}$$

tf.nn.sigmoid(z)   TC 3.1

The sigmoid function, as mentioned above, is useful for modeling probabilities. Because like it, it collapses input between zero and one. Since probabilities are modeled between zero and one this is the perfect activation function.

$$\delta(z) = \frac{e^{x} - e^{-x}}{e^{x} + e^{-x}} \tag{3.8}$$

$$g(z) = 1 - g(z)^{2} \tag{3.9}$$

tf.nn.tanh(z)   TC 3.2

$$\delta(z) = \max(0, z) \tag{3.10}$$

$$g(z) = \begin{cases} 1, & z > 0 \\ 0, & otherwise \end{cases} \tag{3.11}$$

tf.nn.relu(z)   TC 3.3

For the end of the neural network if we want to predict probability distributions. In the end, another popular option is their value function, the ReLu. This function is an extremely simple one to compute its piecewise linear and it is very popular. Because it is so easy to compute, it has this non-linearity at $Z = 0$. Less than zero, this function equals zero, and greater than zero it just equals the input. Due to this non-linearity, it is still able to capture all of the great properties of activation functions, while still being extremely simple to compute.

3.5 IMPORTANCE OF ACTIVATION FUNCTION

We need an activation function but the first thing that should come to mind is why we need that activation function. The purpose of activation functions is to introduce non-linearities into the network [4]. This is extremely important in deep learning or machine learning in general. In real life, data is almost always very non-linear. In fact, if we use linear activation functions in a neural network, no matter how deep or wide the network is, no matter how many neurons it has. That is because it uses linear activation functions. We would not introduce a non-linear activation function that allows us to approximate arbitrarily complex functions and draw arbitrarily complex decision boundaries.

Let us understand this with a simple example, values given in Equation (3.12). Imagine a trans network with weights W on the top here, w_0 is 1 and the W vector is 3, –2. This is a trained neural network and to feed a new input to this network how do we compute the output? Remember from before it is the dot product we had our bias and we compute non-linearity there are three steps. Take our basic Equation (3.13) and then put in the corresponding values.

$$\dot{y} = g\left(w_0 + X^T W\right) \tag{3.12}$$

$$\dot{y} = g\left(1 + \begin{bmatrix} x_1 \\ x_2 \end{bmatrix}^T \begin{bmatrix} 3 \\ -2 \end{bmatrix}\right) \tag{3.13}$$

$$\dot{y} = g\left(1 + 3x_1 - 2x_2\right) \tag{3.14}$$

We have $w_0 = 1$ and $w = \begin{bmatrix} 3 \\ -2 \end{bmatrix}$

Finally, we will get Equation (3.15). Take a look at what is going on here what is inside of this non-linear function, the input to the non-linear function?

$$\dot{y} = g\left(1 + 3x_1 - 2x_2\right) \tag{3.15}$$

Well, this is just a 2D line we can plot this 2D line in what we call the feature space. On the X-axis we can see x_1 which is the first input x_2 which is the second input signal

network has two inputs we can plot the line when it is equal to zero. We can see it in the feature space here if we have a new point, a new input to this neural network, and we can also plot this new point in the same feature space [5].

Here are points −1, and 2, we can plot it like this, and we can compute the output by plugging it into Equation (3.15) that we created before this line. If we plug it in we get 1 − 3 − 4 right, which equals −6, that is the input to our activation function. Then we feed it through our activation function here using sigmoid again. For example, our final output is 0.002. What does that number mean, let us go back to this illustration of the feature space again and what does feature space do?

3.6 BUILDING NEURAL NETWORK WITH PERCEPTRONS

The idea behind the perceptron is that it is a single neuron. Let us start by building neural networks from the ground up using one neuron and seeing how this all comes together. There are a few things that we recall from this discussion. There are three steps in computing the output of a perceptron [6]. A dot product at a bias taking non-linearity, three steps with simplified diagram a little bit. To get rid of the bias, remove the weights to keep things simple. To note down here we are writing Z as the input to the activation function so this is the weighted combination essentially of your inputs Y is then taking the activation function with input Z. Using our previous Equation (3.16).

$$z = w_0 + \left(\sum_{j=1}^{m} x_j w_j \right) \tag{3.16}$$

It is the activation function applied to this weighted sum. If we want to define a multi-output neural network now all we have to do is add another perception to this picture.

$$z_i = w_{0,i} + \left(\sum_{j=1}^{m} x_j w_{j,i} \right) \tag{3.17}$$

In Equation (3.17) we have two outputs each one is a normal perceptron as we defined before. Nothing extra and each one is taking all the inputs from the left-hand side computing this weighted sum, adding bias, and passing it through an activation function. This is one where we have a single hidden layer between our inputs and outputs. We called the hidden layer because unlike the input and the output, which are strictly observable or hidden layers learned. Thus we do not explicitly enforce any behavior on the hidden layer and that is why we call it hidden. In that sense, we now have a transformation from the inputs to the hidden layer and the hidden layer to the outputs.

$$z_i = w_{0,i}^{(1)} + \left(\sum_{j=1}^{m} x_j w_{j,i}^{(1)}\right), \dot{y}_i = g\left(w_{0,i}^{(2)} + \sum_{j=1}^{m} x_j w_{j,i}^{(2)}\right) \quad (3.18)$$

We are going to need two matrices and we are going to call them w_1 dot products at a bias for each of the neurons, and then compute an activation function. Consider Equation (3.18), if we look at the single unit, take z_2, for example, it is just the same perception that we saw before. We are going to keep repeating; we took a dot product with the inputs we applied a bias, and then actually. Since it is the one we have not applied for the activation function yet. That shows it is just a dot product plus a bias, so far if we look at it and take a look at a different neuron let us say z_3 or z_4. It was going to be the same, but we are probably going to end up with a different value for z_3 or z_4. The weights leading from z_3 to the inputs are going to be different for each of those neurons. Now, this picture looks a little messy. Let us clean things up a little more and just replace all of these hidden layers and all these lines between the hidden layers with these symbols. Thus, denote fully connected layers where each input to the layer is connected to each output of the layer.

from tf.keras.layers import *	TC 3.4
inputs = inputs$[m]$	TC 3.5
hidden = Dense$\{d2\}(inputs)$	TC 3.6
outputs = Dense$[d2](hidden)$	TC 3.7
model = Model$(inputs, outputs)$	TC 3.8

Another common name for these is dense layers and you can write this in TensorFlow using just four lines of code, starting from TC 3.4 to TC 3.8. Hence this neural network which is a single-layered multi-output neural network can be called by instantiating inputs and feeding those inputs into a hidden layer.

3.7 APPLYING NEURAL NETWORKS

Now we are familiar with perceptron and we know how to compose them to create very complex deep neural networks as well. Let us take a look at how we can apply them. after gaining fundamental knowledge about the neural network and its working, now it is time to step deeper towards implementation. Let us start with a simple two-input

46 Federated Learning

feature model. For the sake of simplicity and to comprehend processes, we will take one feature as the number of lectures attended, and the other feature as the number of hours spent on the final project [7].

Now if we want to find out if we are going to pass or fail the class. We can also apply ourselves to this map we have created. We cannot afford to lecture and spend five hours on our final project and want to know if we are going to pass or fail. We want to build a neural network that is going to learn this. By looking at the old (the previous) people who took the scores and determine whether they pass or fail as well. Then we have two inputs one is 4 and another is 5. These are fed into a single-layer neural network with three hidden units, and we see the final output. The probability that we will pass this class is 0.1 or 10%, which is really bad news. Can we guess why this person, who was in the part of the feature space, was there? It looked like they were actually in a good part of this feature space. It looks like they are going to pass the class. Why did this neural network give such a bad prediction here? The network was not trained, essentially this network is like a baby that was just born it has no idea of what lectures are. It does not know what final labs are nor does it know anything about this world.

3.8 EMPIRICAL LOSS

These are numbers that have been randomly initialized, have no idea about the problem so we got to train it. We have to teach it how to get the right answer. So, the first thing that we have to do is tell the network when it makes a mistake so that we can correct it in the future. How do we do this in neural networks? The loss of the network is actually what defines when the network makes the wrong prediction. It takes the input and predicts the output.

$$J(w) = \left(\frac{1}{n} \sum_{i=1}^{n} (f(x^{(i)};W), y^{(i)}) \right) \quad (3.19)$$

Then the ground truth actual output is grouped with the predicted output. If the predicted output and ground truth output are close to each other, that essentially means that the loss is going to be very low. It did not make a mistake but if the ground truth output is far away from the predicted output that means that it should have a very high loss. It should have a lot of errors and this network should correct that. Now assume that we have data not only from one student but data from many different students who passed and failed the class. Hence we care about how this model applies to not just one student but across the entire population of students. We call this the empirical loss, and that is just the mean of all of the losses for the individual students. We can do it by just computing the loss for each of these students and taking their mean, using Equation (3.19). When training a network what we want to do is not minimize the loss for any particular student but we want to minimize the loss across the entire training set. Now we want to use the different loss because the output of our neural network is different. And defining loss is an art in deep learning.

3.9 MEAN SQUARE LOSS

This is a problem of binary classification, our output is 0 or 1. We already learned that when classifiers are 1 we are probably going to use a softmax output. For those who are not familiar with cross-entropy, this was an idea introduced actually at MIT in a master's thesis here over 50 years ago. It is widely used in different areas such as thermodynamics, and now it is used in machine learning and across information theory [8]. What this is doing here is essentially computing the loss between this 0,1 output and the true output, i.e., the student either passes or fails. Let us assume instead of computing 0 or 1 output, now we want to calculate the actual grade, i.e., usually given in the class. Now it is not 0, 1 it's grade, it could be any number.

$$J(w) = \left(\frac{1}{n} \sum_{i=1}^{n} (y^{(i)} - f(x^{(i)}; W))^2 \right) \tag{3.20}$$

So we have to define the questions. In this example, we are not going to optimize only 0 or 1 loss, but rather optimize any real number, so we use the mean squared error loss; using Equation (3.20), and TensorFlow code is shown in TC 3.9.

$$loss = t.reduce\_mean\big(tf.square\big(tf.subtract\big(model.y, model.pred\big)\big)\big) \quad \text{TC 3.9}$$

That is just computing the squared error so that it takes the difference between what is expected and what the actual output is. Now take this difference and square it and calculate the mean of the entire population.

3.10 TRAINING A NEURAL NETWORK

Now let us put some of this information together because we have learned how to build their networks, and quantify their loss, now we can learn how to use that loss to iteratively update and train the neural network over time. Given some data and essentially what this amounts to. But what this boils down to is that we want to find the weights of the neural network W that minimize this empirical loss. Thus remember again the empirical loss is the loss over the entire training set and we want to minimize that loss and that essentially means we want to find the weights of the parameterization of the network that results [9].

In the minimum loss remember again that W here is just a collection it is just a set of all of the weights in the network. Thus before defining W_0, W_1, and W_2 which are the weights for the first layer second layer third layer, etc; we keep stacking all of these words together.

3.11 LOSS OPTIMIZATION

Here combine them and compute this optimization problem over all of these weights. Again remember our loss function, Equation (3.21), what does a loss function look like?

$$W^* = \left(argmin_w \frac{1}{n} \sum_{i=1}^{n} (f(x^{(i)};W), y^{(i)}) \right) \tag{3.21}$$

It is just a simple function that takes as inputs or weights, and if we have two ways, we can visualize it, using Equation (3.22) and Equation (3.23).

$$W^* = \left(argmin_w J(W) \right) \tag{3.22}$$

Again we can see on the X-axis one wave so this is 1 scalar that we can change and another wave on the Y-axis and Z-axis, this is our actual loss.

$$W = W^{(0)}, W^{(1)}, W^{(2)}, \ldots \tag{3.23}$$

If we want to find the lowest point in this landscape that corresponds to the minimum loss, and we want to find that point so that we can find the corresponding weights that were set to achieve that minimum loss.

So how do we do it if we use this technique called loss optimization through gradient descent? We start by picking an initial point on this landscape and an initial W_0 W_1. Pseudo code and Tensor Flow Code are presented in PC 3.1.

Algorithm

- Initialize weights randomly~ $N(0,\delta^2)$

weights = tf.random_normal(shape, stddev = sigma)

- Loop until convergence
- Compute gradient, $\dfrac{\partial J(W)}{\partial W}$

grads = tf.gradients(ys = loss, xs = weights)

- Update weights, $W \leftarrow W - \eta \dfrac{\partial J(W)}{\partial W}$
- $weights_{new} = weights.assign(weights - lr * grads)$

Return weights *PC 3.1*

We can iteratively repeat this process over and over and over again. Recompute the gradient at each time and keep moving towards that lowest minimum. We can summarize this algorithm known as gradient descent in pseudocode. By this pseudocode in PC 1, we start by initializing a weight and randomly computing this gradient. Then, updating our weights in the opposite direction of that gradient, we used a small amount of data. This can be seen here and this is essentially what we call the learning rate. This is determining how much of a step we take and how much we trust. This way the gradient updates, which we computed.

3.12 GRADIENT DESCENT

How to compute this term? This is a crucial part of deep learning and neural networks. In general computing, this term is essentially all that matters. It is when we try to optimize our network. It is also the most computational part of training and it is known as backpropagation. We will start with a very simple network with one hidden layer and one output. Computing the gradient of our loss concerning [10] W_2 corresponds to telling us how much a small change in W_2 affects our output or loss.

If we consider it as a derivative, we can start by computing this by simply using this derivative using the chain rule, as explained in Equation (3.24).

$$\frac{\partial J(W)}{\partial W_2} = \frac{\partial J(W)}{\partial \dot{y}} * \frac{\partial \dot{y}}{\partial W_2} \qquad (3.24)$$

Backward from the loss through the output, now looks like Equation (3.25).

$$\frac{\partial J(W)}{\partial W_1} = \frac{\partial J(W)}{\partial \dot{y}} * \frac{\partial \dot{y}}{\partial W_1} \qquad (3.25)$$

We keep repeating this. Do the backpropagation all those ways and this gives us the gradient. We have no guarantees that this is not a global minimum. The entire training of stochastic gradient is a greedy optimization algorithm. We are only taking this greedy approach and optimizing only the local minimum, as described in Equation (3.26).

$$\frac{\partial J(W)}{\partial W_1} = \frac{\partial J(W)}{\partial \hat{y}} * \frac{\partial \hat{y}}{\partial z_1} * \frac{\partial z_1}{\partial W_1} \tag{3.26}$$

There are different ways extensions of stochastic gradient descent that do not take a greedy approach. They take an adaptive approach, looking around a little bit. These are typically more expensive to compute stochastic gradients that are extremely inexpensive to compute in practice. That is one of the reasons it is used, the second reason is that in practice local minimums tend to be sufficient.

3.13 NEURAL NETWORKS IN PRACTICE OPTIMIZATION

Insights of training these networks in practice make it incredibly complex and this gets back to the previous question that was raised in practice training neural networks is incredibly difficult. This is a visualization of the lost landscape of a neural network in practice [11]. This is a paper from about a year ago and the authors visualize what a deep neural network's last landscape looks like, you can see many local minimums here. Managing this loss and finding the optimal true minimum is extremely difficult. Now recall the update equation that we defined for gradient descent previously.

$$W \leftarrow W - \eta \frac{\partial J(W)}{\partial W} \tag{3.27}$$

Consider Equation (3.27), here we take our weights and subtract, then move towards the negative gradient. Update our weights in that direction. This is what we call the learning rate, and this is essentially determining how large of a step we take at each iteration. In a practice setting, the learning rate can be extremely difficult and very important for making sure that you avoid local minima again. So if we set the learning rate too slow then the model may get stuck in a local minimum. Like this, it could also converge very slowly even in the case that gets to a global minimum. If we set the learning rate too large the gradient essentially explodes and we diverge from the loss itself. It is also bad to set the learning rate to the correct amount and this can be extremely tedious in practice. Now shall we overshoot some of the local minima and get ourselves into a reasonable local-global minimum? Then converge within the global minima. How can we cleverly do this, one option is that we can try a lot of different possible learning rates to see what works best in practice [12]. In practice, this is a very common technique so many people just try a lot of learning rates and see what works best, let us see if we can do something a bit smarter than that. How about we design an adaptive algorithm we have that learned that adapts its learning rate according to the last landscape? Therefore, this can take into account the gradient at other locations.

3.14 OPTIMIZERS

In the loss, it can take into account how fast we are learning how large the gradient is at that location or many other options. But now since our learning rate is not fixed for all of the iterations of gradient descent we have a bit more flexibility in learning.

- Momentum

    tf.train.MomentumOptimizer **TC 3.10**

- Adagrad

    tf.train.AdagradOptimizer **TC 3.11**

- Adadelta

    tf.train.AdadeltaOptimizer **TC 3.12**

- Adam

    tf.train.AdamOptimizer **TC 3.13**

- RMSprop

    tf.train.RMSPropOptimizer **TC 3.14**

This has been widely studied as well, and there are many different options for optimization schemes. That is present in TensorFlow and our examples of some of them during our discussion. It would be beneficial to try out these different ones from these optimizers and see how they are different. TensorFlow code of different optimizers is presented in TC 10 to 14. Which works best and which does not work, well for our particular problem and they are all adaptive in nature [13].

3.15 MINI BATCHES

So now to continue discussing tips for training these networks in practice, we will focus on the very powerful idea of batching gradient descent and batching data in general.

52 Federated Learning

Algorithm   PC 3.2
- Initialize weights randomly ~ $\mathcal{N}(0,\delta^2)$
- Loop until convergence
   a. Compute gradient, $\dfrac{\partial J(W)}{\partial W}$
   b. Update weights, $W \leftarrow W - \eta \dfrac{\partial J(W)}{\partial W}$
- Return weights

The gradient is very complex to compute. This backpropagation algorithm if we want to compute it for all of the data samples in our training data set, as described in PC 3.2. This may be massive in modern datasets. It is essentially amounting to a summation of all of these data points. In most real-life problems this is extremely computational and not feasible to compute on every iteration. Instead, people have come up with the idea of stochastic gradient descent. That involves picking a single point. In our data set, compute the gradient for that point and then use that to update our grade to update our weights. Now, this is great because computing a gradient of a single point is much easier than computing the gradient over many points. But at the same time, since we are only looking at one point, this can be extremely noisy. Thus, for sure we take a different point each time but still, when we move we take a step in that direction. At that point, we may be going in a step that is not necessarily representative of the entire data set. Is there any middle ground such that we do not have to have a stochastic? It is a stochastic gradient, but we can still be kind of computationally efficient in this sense, instead of computing a noisy gradient of a single point.

3.16 STOCHASTIC GRADIENT DESCENT

Algorithm   PC 3.3
Initialize weights randomly ~ $\mathcal{N}(0,\delta^2)$
Loop until convergence
- Pick batch B data points
   - Compute gradient, $\dfrac{\partial J(W)}{\partial W} = \sum_{k=1}^{B} \dfrac{\partial J_k(W)}{\partial W}$
   - Update weights, $W \leftarrow W - \eta \dfrac{\partial J(W)}{\partial W}$
- Return weights

At this point, we try to get a better estimate by batching our data into mini-batches of data points, the B data points. Now this gives us an estimate of the true gradient by just averaging the gradient from each of these points. This is great because now it's much easier to compute than full gradient descent. Pseudocode is mentioned in PC 3.3.

The order of less than 100 or approximately in that range is a lot more accurate than stochastic gradient descent because we are considering a larger population as well. This increasing gradient accuracy estimation allows us to converge much quicker as well. It means that we can increase our learning rate and trust our gradient more with each step. This ultimately means that we can train faster. However, this allows for massively parallelizable computation, because we can split up batches across their GPU. Send batches all over the GPU compute their gradients simultaneously and then aggregate them back to even speed up even further.

3.17 REGULARIZATION

Here we talk about regularization for deep neural networks. Deepening their regularization is a technique that we can introduce to our networks [14]. That will discourage complex models from being learned. As we have seen before our models must be able to generalize data beyond our training site but also to generalize data in our testing set as well. The most popular regularization technique in deep learning is a very simple idea called dropout. Let us revisit this in a picture of a deep neural network again and drop out during training.

$$tf.keras.layers.Dropout(p = 0.5) \qquad \text{TC 3.15}$$

We randomly set some of our hidden-neuron activations to 0 with some probability. That is why we call it dropping out because we are essentially killing off those neurons. We kill off these random samples of neurons and now we have created a different pathway through the network. For example, we have dropped 50% of the neurons; this means that those activations are set to 0 and the network is not going to rely too heavily on any particular path through the network. But it is going to find whole on the ensemble to different paths because it does not know which path is going to be dropped at a given time. TensorFlow code for dropout is given in TC 3.15.

$$tf.keras.layers.Dropout(p = 0.5) \qquad \text{TC 3.16}$$

We repeat this process at every training iteration now dropping out of 50% of the neurons. As a result, this is essentially a model that creates an ensemble of multiple models through the path of the network and can generalize better to unseen test data. The second technique for regularization is the notion of early stopping [15]. The idea here is also extremely simple. Train in a neural network like before, no dropout, but if just stop training before we have a chance to overfit. We start training and the definition of overfitting is just when our model starts to perform worse on the test set than on the training set. So we can start and we can plot how the losses are going for both training and test sets. We can see that both are decreasing, so we keep training. Now can see that the training the validation of both losses are kind of starting to plateau here. We can keep going but the training loss is always going to decay. It is always going to keep decreasing, especially if we have a network that has such a large capacity to memorize our data. We can always perfectly get a training accuracy of 0 that is not always the case, but a lot of times with deep neural networks. Since they are so expressive and have so many weights, they can memorize the data. If we let them train for too long.

If we continue training as we can see the training site continues to decrease. Now the validation set starts to increase and if we keep doing this to try and continue the idea of early stopping is essential that we focus on this point here and stop training.

When we reach this point we can keep basic records of the model during training. Once we start to detect overfitting we can just stop and take that last model there was occur overfitting before it happens. We do not want to stop too early, we want to let the model get the minimum validation set accuracy, but also do not want to keep training such validation increase.

3.18 CONCLUSION

In conclusion, our comprehensive discussion has unfolded three fundamental components. Initially, we immersed ourselves in an exploration of the essential building blocks of deep learning, centering on the profound significance of the perceptron—a single neuron with transformative potential. Our discourse navigated the intricacies of backpropagation, elucidating not only the process of stacking these neurons into complex deep neural networks but also providing insights into the nuanced art of backpropagating errors through the network layers.

Moving forward, we directed our attention to the critical domain of loss functions, shedding light on their pivotal role in shaping the optimization landscape of neural networks. The discourse emphasized the multifaceted aspects of selecting and fine-tuning loss functions to achieve optimal model performance. Furthermore, our dialogue extended into the practical terrain, where we uncovered a spectrum of details and tricks vital for effective neural network training in the contemporary landscape. Topics such as batching, a strategic approach to managing input data, and regularization techniques to prevent overfitting were discussed in depth. These practical insights underscore the evolving nature of the field and highlight the indispensable nature of continual learning and adaptation.

As we draw the discussion to a close, it is evident that the intricacies of deep learning extend far beyond the theoretical framework. The assimilation of these insights not only enriches our understanding of the subject but also equips us with the tools necessary to navigate the dynamic challenges prevalent in the ever-evolving field of deep learning. This knowledge, encompassing theoretical foundations and practical strategies, forms a solid foundation for anyone seeking not only to enter but to thrive in the dynamic landscape of deep learning.

REFERENCES

1. Y. Hao, "Convolutional neural networks for image classification," *Proceedings - 2021 2nd International Conference on Artificial Intelligence and Computer Engineering, ICAICE 2021*, pp. 342–345, 2021, doi: 10.1109/ICAICE54393.2021.00073.
2. A. Egiazarov, V. Mavroeidis, F. M. Zennaro, and K. Vishi, "Firearm detection and segmentation using an ensemble of semantic neural networks," *Proceedings of the 2019 European Intelligence and Security Informatics Conference*, EISIC 2019, pp. 70–77, 2019, doi: 10.1109/EISIC49498.2019.9108871.
3. S. A. Ali Shah, I. Uddin, F. Aziz, S. Ahmad, M. A. Al-Khasawneh, and M. Sharaf, "An enhanced deep neural network for predicting workplace absenteeism," *Complexity*, vol. 2020, 2020, doi: 10.1155/2020/5843932.
4. X. Yang, "An overview of the attention mechanisms in computer vision," *Journal of Physics: Conference Series*, vol. 1693, no. 1, 2020, doi: 10.1088/1742-6596/1693/1/012173.
5. M. Yang et al., "Integrating convolution and self-attention improves language model of human genome for interpreting non-coding regions at base-resolution," *Nucleic Acids Research*, vol. 50, no. 14, p. E81, 2022, doi: 10.1093/nar/gkac326.
6. M. I. Uddin, S. A. A. Shah, and M. A. Al-Khasawneh, "A novel deep convolutional neural network model to monitor people following guidelines to avoid COVID-19," *Journal of Sensors*, vol. 2020, 2020, doi: 10.1155/2020/8856801.
7. M. Afif, R. Ayachi, Y. Said, E. Pissaloux, and M. Atri, "An evaluation of RetinaNet on indoor object detection for blind and visually impaired persons assistance navigation," *Neural Processing Letters*, vol. 51, no. 3, pp. 2265–2279, 2020, doi: 10.1007/s11063-020-10197-9.
8. M. N. Alhasanat, M. H. Alsafasfeh, A. E. Alhasanat, and S. G. Althunibat, "Retinanet-based approach for object detection and distance estimation in an image," *International Journal on Communications Antenna and Propagation*, vol. 11, no. 1, pp. 19–25, 2021, doi: 10.15866/irecap.v11i1.19341.
9. T. Dou, G. Zhang, and W. Cui, "Efficient quantum feature extraction for CNN-based learning," *Journal of the Franklin Institute*, vol. 360, no. 11, pp. 7438–7456, 2023, doi: 10.1016/j.jfranklin.2023.06.003.
10. A. Pesah, M. Cerezo, S. Wang, T. Volkoff, A. T. Sornborger, and P. J. Coles, "Absence of barren plateaus in quantum convolutional neural networks," *Physical Review X*, vol. 11, no. 4, p. 41011, 2021, doi: 10.1103/PhysRevX.11.041011.
11. S. Atif Ali Shah, A. Hamid, A. Abdel-Wahab, N. Ageelani, and N. Najeeb, "Street-crimes modelled arms recognition technique employing deep learning and quantum deep learning," *Indonesian Journal of Electrical Engineering and Computer Science*, vol. 30, no. 1, p. 528, 2023, doi: 10.11591/ijeecs.v30.i1.pp528-544.
12. Y. Shao, D. Zhang, H. Chu, X. Zhang, and Y. Rao, "A Review of YOLO Object Detection Based on Deep Learning," *Multimedia Tools and Applications*, vol. 44, no. 10, pp. 3697–3708, 2022.
13. H. Boukraichi, N. Akkari, F. Casenave, and D. Ryckelynck, "A priori compression of convolutional neural networks for wave simulators," pp. 1–23, 2023, [Online]. Available: http://arxiv.org/abs/2304.04964.
14. K. Kishor, "Review and significance of cryptography and machine learning in quantum computing," *Quantum-Safe Cryptography Algorithms and Approaches: Impacts of Quantum Computing on Cybersecur*, pp. 159–175, 2023, doi: 10.1515/9783110798159-012.
15. D. Berardini, L. Migliorelli, A. Galdelli, E. Frontoni, A. Mancini, and S. Moccia, "A deep-learning framework running on edge devices for handgun and knife detection from indoor video-surveillance cameras," *Multimedia Tools and Applications*, 2023, doi: 10.1007/s11042-023-16231-x.

User Participation and Incentives in Federated Learning

4

Muhammad Ali Zeb and Samina Amin

4.1 INTRODUCTION

Ensuring the long-term effectiveness of machine learning models for prediction is a challenging task. Data can change over time. Using the models trained on some data for predictions of future data might not be effective due to the changes in future data patterns. Such a scenario is called concept drift. Learning models need to be adaptive to the changes in the data to be effective for long-term prediction. This chapter discusses some of the possible techniques for ensuring the adaptive learning process including the use of federated learning methods.

Using social media platforms to maintain user interest in certain issues or products can be vital for companies and political organizations. This chapter studies the drift in user sentiments and the adaptation of classification models to the changing political narratives on X in response to the framing of certain political issues over time. Framing the political discourse and maintaining the emotions of users can be important for the outcome of political activities such as elections and referendums. Framing is an important element in shaping public perception about an issue or a product. Sharing stories about the world instead of presenting it as knowledge or information, which may or may not include factual elements. These stories are usually framed to build a political narrative around a certain issue. Some political parties might want the user sentiments to peak at the right time, while the opponents affected might want to divert the mass attention by framing a different discourse. Social media can be a useful platform to study how these framing efforts are interpreted by the target audience. Users might support, oppose, or stay objective about the issue being framed, thus associating sentiments with them.

Sentiment analysis can be explained as the computational analysis of emotions, sentiments, and opinions conveyed in online social media content or text [1, 2] or multi-model sentiment analysis [3]. Social media platforms have provided a large opportunity for users to share their views on political issues, business products (items), national and global incidents, and other areas of user interests. These opinions show the collective sentiments of user communities. This chapter investigates the variation in sentiments expressed by users about a certain issue over time and in response to outside incidents using natural language processing (NLP) and traditional deep learning (DL) methods. User sentiments might change over time and therefore most of the existent methods based on static sentiment and topic modeling may not be enough to provide insight into sentiments for a prolonged time. Although privacy needs to be considered when dealing with user-generated data [4], this work focuses on exploring the effect of shaping the political discourse from the variable nature of social media sentiments. The analysis can be used to measure the feedback from users on key political policies and issues. Some works have used summarizing the user opinions about certain topics such as movies [5]. Gamson et al. [6] presented data that users actively pick the content of media within their subject group (topic community) that correlates to the general opinion or places them in a correspondence frame. This is considered a wilful "echo chamber", or a "repillarisation". Some other applications of NLP to text on online social media include disaster prediction [7], disease detection [8, 9, 10], political election [11, 12], and sentiment analysis [13]. Although social network analysis can be explored for studying concept drift in these complex networks using methods such as those presented by Aziz, Gul, and Uddin [14], this chapter explores only the text of the tweets for detecting drifting user opinions.

Several techniques have been explored that can be utilized to analyze the shaping of political issues on social media and how the relationships of users change with certain political topics and entities over time. This chapter studies the changes in language usage patterns by social media users. This chapter focuses on the following main points:

- It studies how to automate the process of sentiment labeling of new data exploring methods in a combination of, and alternative to lexicon-based methods. We study the use of an ensemble of classifiers especially testing the combination of DL and TL techniques with the help of word embedding techniques.
- Negative and positive perceptions depend on the users' approach towards a certain issue and we intend to identify context-based assessment of topics/issues rather than the lexical meaning of the text alone. One person's negative can be another person's positive, and vice versa.
- To automate the process of novel data exploring for sentiment analysis and text categorization in combination with context-based techniques.
- To identify community-based assessment of issues by automating the perception of negative and positive sentiments towards a certain issue.

One challenge identified during the sentiment analysis and categorization was the lack of accessibility to a training set. While in the categorization process, the search keywords were used as representative of the class of each category and most of those texts had those keywords in their texts. Sentiment analysis, on the other hand, can be generalized by the similarity of the meaning of the words frequently used for expressing certain types of sentiments. For example, negative words have been identified in literature into negative lexicons and positive words have been identified into positive lexicons. [15] have explored contextual embedding techniques for the impact analysis of keyword extraction. Different scoring mechanisms are then used to categorize a newly arriving bunch of text into negative, positive, or neutral classes based on the count and frequency of the negative and positive words. Highly biased words may have more weight in the classification of the text into a category. Some of the existing lexicons can, therefore, be used to label novel texts with sentiments with a certain degree of accuracy, as a starting point.

The goal of this chapter is to identify the algorithms that work more efficiently when datasets are small, and many training examples are not available. This work starts with the optimization of some supervised learning techniques with different features. We compare the performance of the state-of-art with some transfer learning techniques. The comparison is performed on traditional models combining them with deep feature extraction methods such as word2vec and doc2vec. Experiments have been performed with some TL models and compared with the results of the traditional techniques. Narrative extraction and classification have been used for experimenting with this set of optimizations. From the experiments, we conclude that given a large dataset with highly distinctive features, most of the traditional models with optimized parameters perform well with classification tasks. With the increased training data, however, DL techniques outperform the traditional models. Deep TL methods perform comparatively better when a small amount of training set is provided.

The rest of the chapter is structured as follows: Section 4.2 provides a brief overview of the background studies on related work. Section 4.3 discusses Natural Language Processing Pipeline and System Design, section 4.4 outlines the deep learning techniques utilized, while section 4.5 discusses results and evaluation.

4.2 LITERATURE REVIEW

There is a wide body of literature about the perceptions and sentiments of people's incidents expressed in social media activities. Some researchers have taken inspiration from the successful modeling of the compositional aspects of the language recently in sentiment analysis. This section presents a review of related work conducted on: 1) sentiment analysis, 2) political framing and narrative extraction and classification, and 3) neural networks language models – distributed representations of text.

4.2.1 Sentiment Analysis

Sentiment analysis has been used over the years for different purposes, such as product recommendations [16], location recommendations [17], user recommendations [18, 19], stress detection [20, 21], and movie recommendations [22]. Various methods have been applied for analyzing sentiments in text, such as probabilistic graphical modeling [23], supervised learning [24], NLP [25], etc. Some researchers have used context-aware topic sentiment modeling. Vanzo et al [27] have considered the conversational context while analyzing sentiments on X.

Hussein et al. [28] presented a survey highlighting the effects of the challenges in the evaluation of sentiment analysis techniques. The comparison is performed from two perspectives. In the first comparison, the relationship between the structure of the sentiment of a review and the challenges in sentiment analysis is considered as an evaluation challenge. This comparison highlights the essential factor of domain dependency as a significant challenge in evaluating sentiment analysis techniques. Negation has also been highlighted as another challenge that might implicitly or explicitly change the meaning of the text based on its structure. The nature of the topic and the structure of the text can be significant challenges in sentiment evaluation.

Another interesting work has been carried out by Heikal et al. [29], where sentiment analysis is predicted for Arabic text using social tweet data with the help of deep learning approaches. Similarly, El Alaoui et al. [30] proposed a novel adaptable approach for sentiment analysis for the 2016 US presidential election using big social media data. Their proposed approach retrieves the users' sentiment and analyses social media posts in real-time. They validated the experimental results of the proposed approach by classifying the tweets data related to the 2016 US election into positive and negative sentiments.

Various methods have been used for short text classification, such as ensemble techniques [31], this chapter focuses on deep neural and transfer learning methods. Although this chapter focuses on the narrative classification generated by political parties for their election campaign and the coverage and response to those narratives on online social media (X), some relevant studies that compare the political campaign messaging and coverage of those campaigns on traditional media are crucial to this work. Performing sentiment analyses of political campaigns in parallel to their traditional and social media coverage may allow us to empirically assess whether media attention can be attracted through negative campaign messaging, a hypothesis studied by [32]. Comparison of the sentiments framed, or the tonality set by the political parties through their messages and the coverage of these campaigns by the news media may enable us to test the "negativity bias" usually presumed by the political parties to have been shown towards them by the news media. Another political aspect is that sentiment analyses can be useful in studying and understanding the effects of negative campaign messaging and negative media coverage on voting behavior.

One such work is performed by Amin, Alharbi, and Uddin [33] for the sake of identification of the political position as indicated by a sentence by applying a recursive neural network (RNN) framework. They have used crowdsourcing to annotate phrases and sentences with political ideologies to demonstrate the importance of modeling subsentential elements. Relationship modeling networks, a deep neural networks–based method, have been recently used for investigating users' social roles in online communities [34] and finding relationships between novels and human characters in the novels [35].

4.2.2 Political Framing and Narrative Extraction

Social media data can be a good resource to study the impact of framing of political issues from political parties and influential personalities. These data provide descriptions of users' perceptions and opinions. Sustained observation of certain issues over longer periods can provide us useful insights into reactions, perceptions, and prevalence of user understanding of these issues. Perseverance might be the key to creating a decisive shift in users' perception of a certain issue. Although some domains use advanced methods to address privacy concerns [36, 37], this work utilizes only the text of the user-generated data and thus tries to avoid using the identity of individual users.

Although, political framing has been studied by some researchers as a phenomenon of social media, particularly X, relatively little work has been done on identifying frames from texts through computational methods. People usually frame their experiences into certain perceptions to make meaningful interactions.

In the literature, political framing has been studied from social and computational perspectives. Social scientists have used some of the existing computational methods to analyze and highlight social and political phenomena taking advantage of the availability of large amounts of social and traditional online media content. The field has benefitted from the use of computational methods for processing and analyzing a large amount of data for studying social patterns. On the other hand, computer scientists studying framing have focused on the development and improvement of computational linguistics and NLP methods to improve the performance of existing classifiers, prediction, and extraction algorithms.

Online social media–based narrative classification is a challenge and has not been explored because of the non-availability of large training datasets and the non-generalized nature of the vocabulary, unlike the sentiment analysis. Most of the existing studies focus on political parties or personalities whose political ideologies and inclinations are already known. The proposed work studies the response of the users to the framing of political issues. The focus here is on studying the adaptation of political sentiments over time using user modeling and online user communities. Although traditional machine learning models are still being used for advanced classification applications such as in Naseem et al. [38], this chapter explores deep learning and transfer learning methods for adapting to concept drift in user sentiments and user narratives over time.

4.3 NATURAL LANGUAGE PROCESSING PIPELINE AND SYSTEM DESIGN

This section presents the NLP pipeline adopted to analyze the given tweet data to classify public sentiment on political rallies or issues from social media content. The proposed framework comprises six modules as follows: 1) data acquisition, 2) data pre-processing and data categorization, 3) feature selection, 4) classification, 5) optimization, and 6) evaluation module. The explanation and validation of the proposed model are discussed in the following subsections.

4.3.1 Data Acquisition

The focus of this work is to analyze the topics of political importance discussed by social media users. We have collected more than 2.4 million tweets through the X application programming interface (API), distributed across multiple topics, such as the Panama Papers, loadshedding, political rallies and gatherings, joint investigation team (JIT) reports, etc. Of the 2.4 million tweets collected, 966,201 were analyzed for sentiments. The breakdown is given in Table 4.1.

4.3.2 Data Pre-Processing

While traditional information retrieval practitioners suggest tokenization, stemming, lemmatization, stop word removal as pre-processing steps [39, 40], social media text usually requires more cleaning in the form of noise removal, removal or interpretation of hashtags, emoticons, abbreviations, links, mentions, replies, likes/dislikes or favoriting activities, and spelling corrections or interpretations [41]. Libraries such as the natural language processing toolkit (NLTK)[1] and Spacy[2] have implementations of

TABLE 4.1 Collection of Tweets Distributed over Panama Papers, Loadshedding, Political Rallies, JIT, PSL, and Dengue

TOPIC	NUMBER OF TWEETS
Loadshedding/Energy	459,757
Panama Papers	517,992
Panama Verdict	274,661
Political rallies, gatherings	784,475
Islamabad lockdown	60,625
PSL final	27,713
Dengue	275,000
Total	2,400,223

traditional as well as modern techniques to cater to the changing landscape of complex text processing. In particular, the problems of overstemming and understemming usually associated with Porter Stemmer[3], which has for decades been used to stem the tokens to their root forms, have been efficiently resolved by these libraries. An example of overstemming would be when a token is stemmed more than it needs to be, converting it to a nonsensical form. For example, Porter Stemmer stems the words universe, universities, university, and universal into "univers", while the intended tokens are universe and university. Similarly, the token datum is stemmed to datu while data and date or stemmed to "dat", an example of understemming.

The data collected during the governance period consists of over 2.4 million uncleaned tweets. After the removal of non-English and duplicate tweets, the remaining tweets are 966,202. 389,836 tweets are about loadshedding, 242,034 are about Panama Papers, 222,625 are about CPEC, 83,829 are about dengue, and 27,877 are about the Panama verdict. We also removed tweets non-relevant to the elections in Pakistan such as loadshedding tweets from South Africa, Nepal, and other countries; and dengue tweets from Sri Lanka and India through keyword search, though some tweets might still be there. Some of the tweets appear to be longer than the specified limit of 140 characters for tweets (280 for more recent tweets). A closer look suggests that hypertext markup language (HTML) encoding has not been converted to text.

In the first step of data preparation, HTML is decoded into general text using the Python library BeautifulSoup. In the second step, "@" mentions are removed from the tweets. Although mentions in tweets might carry useful information about users interacting with each other we are not using this detail in the current analysis and are thus not useful to us. URLs are removed in the third step. Like mentions, URLs can also be useful but have not been used in this analysis. Universal transformation format – 8 byte order mark (UTF-8 BOM) is decoded in the next step. Finally, numbers and # symbols are also removed from the tweets, leaving the text of the hashtags with the # symbol. Contractions such as *have'nt* and *can't* are expanded into have not and cannot since negation words are split into two parts during cleaning and the meaning of the sentence might change. The null entries produced because of the data-cleaning process are removed.

4.3.3 Text Categorization

We show experiments to discover the optimized combination of algorithms and parameters for categorizing the tweets into five classes. The optimized classifier is then configured to estimate the class of newly arriving data. The aim of this study is twofold. In the first phase, algorithms are trained on the data collected in the period preceding an election (July 25, 2018, Elections of Pakistan), roughly ranging from one to five years, depending on the topic being observed and the appearance of the topic on social media. five topics were chosen for this purpose, namely the Panama Papers, the Panama Verdict, loadshedding, the China–Pakistan Economic Corridor (CPEC), and dengue. The training data consists of the period two months before the election. We consider the two months to the election as the campaign period since the elections are announced exactly two months before the scheduled date of elections and the tenure of the government is considered as completed. The data collected for the campaign period is general, and the query words used consist of the major party names, names of political leaders, and locations i.e. province names. The idea is to measure how many of the topics which were around for more than a year or were a major issue at some point during the five years of the incumbent government are reflected in the campaign trail of the political parties. In the second phase of this work, the data from the campaign period is categorized using the optimized classifier trained on the data from the government periods. Here, the government period refers to the duration of government before the elections are announced, in this case, July 2013 to May 2018. This will give us an idea as to which topics prevailed over time and made it to the campaign slogans or manifestoes of the political parties.

4.3.4 Narrative Extraction – Small Training Data

A challenge in supervised learning methods is the non-availability of training data. While some domains such as sentiment analysis can benefit from metadata such as emoticons and lexical meanings, there are areas where the intended meanings of words change with a context or targeted subjects. Political narratives can be a highly subjective area and generalized labeling based on emoticons or lexicons cannot be applied. Most of the learning algorithms perform well on a large amount of training data, adequate determining resources, and proper parameter optimization. A problem is when we have limited training data and manual labeling is expensive and highly prone to bias, especially in tagging political narratives. In this set of experiments, we have shown that although some of the existing algorithms perform better with the availability of an adequate amount of data, they struggle to achieve the same level of accuracy when trained on less amounts of example data. In some cases, the accuracy falls manyfold. The case study for this work is the Panama verdict announced in Pakistan after a legal process triggered by the release of Panama Papers in April 2016. The verdict resulted in the termination of the then Prime Minister of the country and the verdict was widely discussed by both the supporters and opponents of the ousted Prime Minister. The Prime Minister's party framed the Panama Papers and the resulting verdict as a conspiracy, while the opponents framed it as a corruption scandal. We collected tweets related to the issue to analyze the perception of the social media public. A small number of highly polarized tweets were labeled based on the text and hashtags used in the tweet. The labeling process had several challenges such as limited resources due to the lack of access to global labeling sites such as Amazon Turk, hiring of personnel proficient in the area, etc. Hashtags were considered as one possible labeling option but that could not be applied to the entire dataset since a very limited number of tweets used hashtags. Another technique that has been used for labeling a large amount of social media data is using emoticons. Due to the given nature of the topics, using emoticons for labeling was not a feasible option since the number of tweets with emoticons was negligible. Also, the nature of the problem was different from sentiment analysis. An emoticon can be a clear expression of some positive or negative emotion, but it is difficult to extract the political perception of a user from an emoticon. A user using negative lexical words might either be targeting the verdict if she thinks of it as a conspiracy or targeting the prime minister if she thinks of it as proof of corruption. The problem of perception detection, therefore, cannot be generalized such as sentiment analysis. The problem is more relevant to stance detection and framing. We believe that an analysis of the language, part of speech tagging, subjectivity, stance, and intended frame can give us an overall political perception of a user. The focus in this work, however, is on detecting the intended narrative from the text of the tweet. We consider two narratives, corruption and conspiracy, which are eventually used as classes for the tweets. The issue of the Panama Papers was important in the political scenario in Pakistan since the perception it generated resulted in highly polarized general elections and the proposed work will try to assess the impact of the Panama Papers on the general elections held in July 2018.

4.4 DEEP LEARNING TECHNIQUES

4.4.1 Word Embedding Techniques

The text data are embedded in numbers for computation using word embedding techniques. Since machine and deep learning techniques are not able to process text data directly. Alternatively, the text data are converted into number vectors for computation. A word embedding is a count-based approach that generates a matrix of word coincidences to acquire word vectors by performing some dimensionality reduction than the traditional term frequency-inverse document frequency (TF–IDF) [42]. In the proposed method, two embedding techniques *word2bec* proposed by Mikolov et al. [43] and doc2vec (Document to Vector) [44] are used. However, word2vec [43] is a more advanced technique in which words are embedded in a lower-dimensional vector space by utilizing a shallow neural network. The word2vec model results in the number of vectors (dimension) for each word in the corpus to search for the context based on how the word occurs in a sentence. Doc2vec is a word embedding technique in which each document is represented as a vector. Different variants of doc2vec, proposed by Mikolov et al. [43] were used to generate the vectors from each tweet. We fit the vectors with machine, deep, and transfer learning models for further processing. As suggested by Lau and Baldwin [44], the entire dataset was used to train doc2vec due to the unsupervised nature of doc2vec.

Multiple word embedding approaches are developed and TF–IDF is used as a baseline approach. There are word embedding approaches Such as doc2vec, word2vec, fast-text, and glove, etc. In the following subsections, the explanations of the word embedding approaches that are used in this work are discussed as follows.

4.4.1.1 *Word2Vec*

Another word embedding approach used in this work is *word2vec* developed by Mikolov et al. [43] is a more advanced approach in which words are embedded in a lower-dimensional vector space by utilizing a shallow neural network. The word2vec approach results in the number of dimensions to check the semantic and synthetic meaning for each word in the corpus depending on how the word appears in a statement or sentence. In word2vec, all words in the vector space that have a common meaning occur around each other.

These architectures of the word2vec approach such as the *continuous bag-of-words* (CBOW) and *skip gram (SG)* model are utilized in this work. The previous works suggest that the SG model is proposed for a large data size while the CBOW model is mainly designed for medium-sized data. The descriptions of these models are demonstrated as follows.

4.4.1.2 Continuous Bag-of-Words

CBOW attempts to predict the target word dependent on the surrounding context words [8]. To adapt the association between words, it is an essential model that performs better on a small (i.e., medium size) of training data. To understand the perspective of the CBOW model, consider an example tweet: *"all properties leak in Panama"*. The CBOW model will try to learn the surrounding words as shown in Figure 4.1, and then, it will predict *"leak"*, *"spill"*, *"drip"*, or *"escape"* are the most probable words at a randomly chosen closely related to the *leak*. Words such as *"table"* or *"chair"* gain less of the model's attention as it is learned to predict the most probable word (Figure 4.1).

4.4.1.3 Skip Gram

The implementation of the SG technique attempts to perform the opposite of the CBOW implementation [8]. It aims to predict the context words depending on the target word. The surrounding words are determined by the window size.

A tweet example is given in order to comprehend the perspective of the SG implementation such as, *"all properties leak in Panama"*, we choose a window size of two, and the source (target) word is *"leak"*, in this scenario, the context words are (*all, properties, leak, in, panama*), and thus the input and source word combinations or sets can

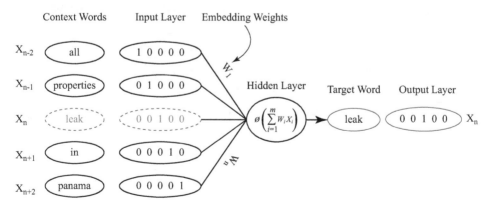

FIGURE 4.1 Architecture of the CBOW model

be *(leak, all), (leak, properties), (leak, in), (leak, panama)*. It is suggested that in the sample windows, the distance of the word to the source word does not play a significant role. However, the context words *(all, properties, in, and panama)* are conserved the same in order to train the model. The SG model is graphically visualized in Figure 4.2, where the word highlighted in red shows the source word, and the context words are also highlighted on the output side (Figure 4.2).

4.4.2 Recursive Neural Network (RNN)

RNN is an architecture of artificial neural networks (ANNs) [33] that can process the syntactic and semantic composition of sentences. Due to the sequential structure of the text corpus, researchers have used a recursive neural network extensively for text mining and classification. An RNN is a network that specializes in processing sequential data in the form of $x^{(1)}, \ldots, x^{(T)}$, assigning more weights to the previous data points of a sequence, thus making it a powerful technique for textual data classification. The consideration of previous nodes allows for better semantic analysis of the structure of a dataset. The scalability of the recurrent neural networks to much longer sequences allows them to be a more practical sequential data classification than the non-sequence-based specialization methods such as convolutional networks. Figure 4.3 depicts the RNN architecture for sequential data.

4.4.2.1 Transfer Learning (Context-Based Learning)

The above models work well when the datasets are large. However, their performance decreases significantly when we do not have a large amount of annotated data. One such challenge is the extraction of narratives from a tweet. Perceptions of political issues can be subjective and thus cannot be generalized on lexicons like sentiment analysis. We use the universal sentence encoder (USE) and neural-net language model (NNLM) [45] to solve the problem of political narrative extraction by labeling a small dataset

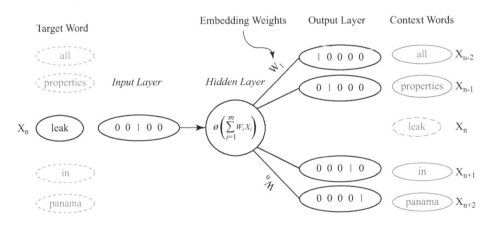

FIGURE 4.2 Architecture of the SG model

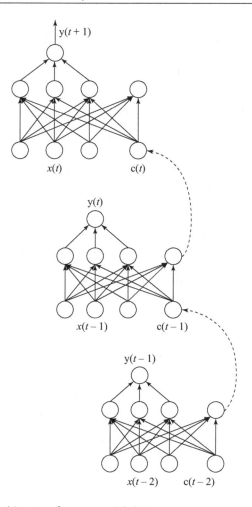

FIGURE 4.3 RNN architecture for sequential data

of 500 tweets. Two classes are used. The tweets that perceive the Panama verdict as part of a conspiracy are labeled as conspiracy tweets, while the tweets considering it as corruption are labeled as corruption. Compared to word embeddings, USE can embed phrases and sentences along with the words. The implementation of the model has been explained in [46]. In this process, a text of variable length is configured as an input, and for an output a 512-dimensional vector is generated. Neural-net language model (NNLM) was proposed by Bengio et al. [45] as a solution to the problem of dimensionality. A distributed representation for words is learned which allows each training sentence to inform the model about an exponential number of semantically neighboring sentences. The mode simultaneously learns a distributed representation for each word along with the probability function for word sequences, expressed in terms of these representations. The model obtains generalization by associating high probability with new word sequences if it is constituted of words that are similar in terms of their distributed representations to the words that form a sentence that has already been seen by the model. For this comparison, we have used a pre-trained model that is trained on the English Google News 200B corpus and computes a vector of 128 dimensions. The model is available on Tensorflow hub[4].

4.4.2.2 Optimization Techniques

Optimizing DL algorithms is a significant challenge. The focus of the optimization for learning algorithms is minimizing an error function (cost function), which can enhance the efficiency of the classifier algorithms. However, the cost function is usually defined as the average over the training phase [8]. We incorporated the following hyperparameters for optimizing the performance of deep learning models for this work.

An optimized text classifier is important for accurately predicting the class of newly arriving text in real-time based on the existing text examples. Multiple challenges are encountered while training learning algorithms for text classification. Text data can have important syntactic and semantic details including or excluding which can significantly affect the outcome of the classifier and the specific NLP task being performed. Some tasks, such as sentiment analysis and political discourse analysis, require a greater insight of the context in which data is generated. A multitude of variables and their combinations, therefore, need to be incorporated to understand and highlight the significant features.

Initially, the algorithms are optimized from two perspectives. The categorization of the tweets data and associated sentiments. The category of a tweet is the query word used to search and collect the tweets' data. The purpose of this optimization is to enable the classifier to classify the newly arriving tweets into a category. This can be an important measure to understand the persistence of discourse over time and events. The algorithms are trained on five categories watched over time and the new data is used as an unseen test set to classify them into these five categories.

4.5 RESULTS AND EVALUATION

This section evaluates the efficiency and potential of the proposed work by classifying political narrative and sentiment analysis in tweets. The results presented are accomplished by performing various experiments following standard evaluation methods [47] to validate all the research objectives. Experiments and results are conducted by using Python (3.6 version) and the Anaconda framework[5]. The word2vec model with 100-dimensional vectors is concatenated to form a 200-dimension vector representation for each word. The tweets are tokenized and a sequential representation of each tweet is obtained where each word is represented as a number and the number of words in each tweet is equal to the length of numbers in sequences. The data is padded by setting the maximum length of each tweet to 55, enabling it to be given to a CNN as an input. Table 4.2 illustrates that the CNNs with word2vec give us the highest accuracy so far, reaching up to 96.73% with Conv1D (Convolutional with 1-Dimension), globalMaxPooling1D (GMP-1D), and ReLU activation function. The accuracy for the large dataset is more in line with the other models.

4.5.1 Results with LSTM

The results with LSTM are like CNN but the algorithm takes much longer. The accuracy for the verdict dataset is 94.13% while for the larger dataset, it is much higher as shown in Table 4.4.

4.5.2 Optimizing the Models Using a Small Dataset

The overall performance of the different machine learning models evaluated above improves with either an increase in the size of the dataset or adequate parameter tuning. A real challenge, however, is when we have a small dataset. Optimizing supervised machine learning models on small training data can be challenging. In this set of experiments, we evaluate different traditional as well as DL models and compare the results with some pre-trained TL models.

4.5.3 Transfer Learning

Universal sentence Encoder (USE): compared to word embeddings, USE can embed phrases and sentences along with the words. The implementation of the model has been explained in [46]. In this process, a text of variable length is configured as an input, and for output a 512-dimensional vector is generated.

4.5.4 Comparison

For the comparison, we used some baselines that do not use TL and the models that configure word-level transfer such as word2vec and doc2vec. Table 4.6 reveals a comparison of the traditional machine learning methods with some of the TL methods we used, along with the word-level transfer models. However, naïve Bayes for multinomial models (NBMM) performs reasonably well for accuracy, precision, and recall. This matches the definition of NB models which are expected to perform better on small datasets [48]. Other models provide linear support vector machine (LSVM) and logistic regression (LR). LR was also tried with word2vec and doc2vec. Both combinations reduce the accuracy of the models. USE gives the overall better recall and f1-score, while the USE-trained gives the best accuracy. The results are in line with the literature such as Joshi et al. [49], which have shown that the sentence-based vector representations perform better than the word-level models.

TABLE 4.2 Sentiment Analysis Word2Vec + CNN – Verdict

MODEL	CONVOLUTION	POOLING	DENSITY	ACTIVATION	WEIGHTS	TRAINABLE	ORDER	ACCURACY
Cnn_01	Conv1D	GlobalMaxPooling1D	256	relu	Embedding_matrix	False	Sequential	94.13
Cnn_02	Conv1D	globalMaxPooling1D	256	relu			Sequential	96.73
Cnn_03	Conv1D				Embedding_matrix	True	Sequential	96.15
Cnn_04					Embedding_matrix	True	Parallel	95.76

TABLE 4.3 Sentiment Analysis Word2Vec + CNN – All Data

MODEL	CONVOLUTION	POOLING	DENSITY	ACTIVATION	WEIGHTS	TRAINABLE	ORDER	ACCURACY
Cnn_01	Conv1D	GlobalMaxPooling1D	256	relu	Embedding_ matrix	False	Sequential	99.89
Cnn_04					Embedding_ matrix	True	Parallel	99.32

TABLE 4.4 Sentiment Analysis Word2Vec+LSTM – Verdict and All Data

DATASET	CONVOLUTION	POOLING	DENSITY	ACTIVATION	DROPOUT	RETURN_SEQUENCES	ORDER	ACCURACY
Vedrict			100	Softmax	0.2	False	Sequential	94.13
All sentiment			100	Softmax	0.2	False	Sequential	99.14

TABLE 4.5 Comparison of TL Models in Terms of Training and Test Accuracy, AUC, Precision, and Recall

MODEL	TRAINING ACCURACY	TEST ACCURACY	TRAINING AUC	TEST AUC	TRAINING PRECISION	TEST PRECISION	TRAINING RECALL	TEST RECALL
nnlm-en-dim128	1	0.63871	1	0.6998	1	0.6	1	0.69863
nnlm-en-dim128-with-training	1	0.658065	1	0.744069	1	0.619048	1	0.712329
use-512	1	0.63871	1	0.735633	1	0.591398	1	0.753425
use-512-with-training	1	0.709677	1	0.757183	1	0.670732	1	0.753425

TABLE 4.6 Comparison of the TL Models With Traditional Learning Models in Terms of Accuracy, Precision, Recall, and f1-Score

CLASSIFIER	ACCURACY	PRECISION	RECALL	F1-SCORE
NBMM	72	72	72	72
LSVM	69	69	69	69
LR	69	69	69	69
w2v+LR	64	64	64	64
d2v+LR	66	66	66	66
USE	72	69	**85**	**77**
NNLM	66	67	69	68
NNLM_train	64	65	65	65
USE-train	**74**	**78**	69	73.5

4.6 CONCLUSION

In this chapter, a detail of the natural language processing pipeline by incorporating new insights (ideas) through innovative methods with optimized techniques is presented. Moreover, the chapter discussed different deep learning models and the techniques for optimization. The dataset designed for this purpose was used to validate each part of the pipeline (including feature extraction or selection, optimization, and sentiment and narrative classification of the users in the political aspect). Sentiment analysis and classification methods with different optimization techniques have been implemented based on the natural language processing pipeline. The performance of each method with optimization techniques has been validated by deploying performance measurement techniques (confusion matric) and their findings have also been presented in this paper.

By offering a thorough examination of deep learning and NLP techniques for narrative classification and sentiment analysis, this chapter aims to close the theoretical and practical gap. It will give readers the skills and knowledge needed to analyze textual narratives across a variety of fields and contexts effectively and derive insightful conclusions.

NOTES

1. https://www.nltk.org/
2. https://spacy.io/
3. https://tartarus.org/martin/PorterStemmer/
4. https://www.tensorflow.org/hub
5. https://www.anaconda.com/distribution/

REFERENCES

1. F. Hemmatian and M. K. Sohrabi, "A survey on classification techniques for opinion mining and sentiment analysis," *Artif. Intell. Rev.*, vol. 52, no. 3, pp. 1495–1545, 2019.
2. K. Ravi and V. Ravi, "A survey on opinion mining and sentiment analysis: Tasks, approaches and applications," *Knowl.-Based Syst.*, vol. 89, pp. 14–46, 2015.
3. Priyavrat, N. Sharma, and G. Sikka, "Multimodal sentiment analysis of social media data: A review," *Recent Innov. Comput. Proc. ICRIC* vol. 2020, pp. 545–561, 2021.
4. Z. Ullah et al., "Certificateless proxy reencryption scheme (CPRES) based on hyperelliptic curve for access control in content-centric network (CCN)," *Mob. Inf. Syst.*, vol. 2020, pp. 1–13, Jul. 2020, doi: 10.1155/2020/4138516.
5. A. Khan et al., "Summarizing Online Movie Reviews: A Machine Learning Approach to Big Data Analytics," *Sci. Program.*, vol. 2020, pp. 1–13, Aug. 2020, doi: 10.1155/2020/5812715.
6. M. Wieringa, D. Van Geenen, M. T. Schäfer, and L. Gorzeman, "Political topic-communities and their framing practices in the Dutch Twittersphere," *Internet Policy Rev.*, vol. 7, no. 2, pp. 1–16, 2018, doi: 10.14763/2018.2.793.
7. A. Hernandez-Suarez, G. Sanchez-Perez, K. Toscano-Medina, H. Perez, J. Portillo, and V. Sanchez, "Using twitter data to monitor natural disaster social dynamics: A recurrent neural network approach with word embeddings and kernel density estimation," *Sensors*, vol. 19, no. 7, 2019, doi: 10.3390/s19071746.
8. S. Amin, M. Irfan Uddin, M. Ali Zeb, A. A. Alarood, M. Mahmoud, and M. H. Alkinani, "Detecting Dengue/Flu Infections based on tweets using LSTM and word embedding," *IEEE Access*, vol. 8, pp. 189054–189068, 2020, doi: 10.1109/access.2020.3031174.
9. S. Amin et al., "Recurrent neural networks with TF-IDF embedding technique for detection and classification in tweets of dengue disease," *IEEE Access*, vol. 8, pp. 131522–131533, 2020, doi: 10.1109/access.2020.3009058.
10. S. Amin, M. I. Uddin, M. A. Zeb, A. A. Alarood, M. Mahmoud, and M. H. Alkinani, "Detecting information on the spread of dengue on Twitter using artificial neural networks," *CMC-Comput. Mater. Contin.*, vol. 67, no. 1, pp. 1317–1332, 2021, doi: 10.32604/cmc.2021.014733.
11. M. Grčar, D. Cherepnalkoski, I. Mozetič, and P. Kralj Novak, "Stance and influence of Twitter users regarding the Brexit referendum," *Comput. Soc. Netw.*, vol. 4, no. 1, 2017, doi: 10.1186/s40649-017-0042-6.
12. S. Ahmed, K. Jaidka, and J. Cho, "The 2014 Indian elections on Twitter: A comparison of campaign strategies of political parties," *Telemat. Inform.*, vol. 33, no. 4, pp. 1071–1087, 2016, doi: 10.1016/j.tele.2016.03.002.
13. K. Jaidka, S. Ahmed, M. Skoric, and M. Hilbert, "Predicting elections from social media: A three-country, three-method comparative study," *Asian J. Commun.*, vol. 29, no. 3, pp. 252–273, 2019, doi: 10.1080/01292986.2018.1453849.
14. F. Aziz, H. Gul, I. Uddin, and G. V. Gkoutos, "Path-based extensions of local link prediction methods for complex networks," *Sci. Rep.*, vol. 10, no. 1, p. 19848, Nov. 2020, doi: 10.1038/s41598-020-76860-2.
15. M. Q. Khan et al., "Impact analysis of keyword extraction using contextual word embedding," *PeerJ Comput. Sci.*, vol. 8, p. e967, May 2022, doi: 10.7717/peerj-cs.967.
16. G. Khanvilkar and D. Vora, "Sentiment analysis for product recommendation using random forest," *Int. J. Eng. Technol.*, vol. 7, no. 3, pp. 87–89, 2018.
17. D. Yang, D. Zhang, Z. Yu, and Z. Wang, "A sentiment-enhanced personalized location recommendation system categories and subject descriptors," in Proceedings of the 24th ACM Conference on Hypertext and Social Media, ACM, Paris, France: ACM, 2013, pp. 119–128.

18. S. Hu, A. Kumar, F. Al-Turjman, S. Gupta, and S. Seth, "Reviewer credibility and sentiment analysis based user profile modelling for online product recommendation," *IEEE Access*, vol. 8, pp. 26172–26189, 2020.
19. C. Musto, P. Lops, M. de Gemmis, and G. Semeraro, "Justifying recommendations through aspect-based sentiment analysis of users reviews," in Proceedings of the 27th ACM conference on user modeling, adaptation and personalization, 2019, pp. 4–12.
20. R. L. Rosa, G. M. Schwartz, W. V. Ruggiero, and D. Z. Rodríguez, "A knowledge-based recommendation system that includes sentiment analysis and deep learning," *IEEE Trans. Ind. Inform.*, vol. 15, no. 4, pp. 2124–2135, 2018.
21. T. Nijhawan, G. Attigeri, and T. Ananthakrishna, "Stress detection using natural language processing and machine learning over social interactions," *J. Big Data*, vol. 9, no. 1, pp. 1–24, 2022.
22. A. Mitra, "Sentiment analysis using machine learning approaches (Lexicon based on movie review dataset)," *J. Ubiquitous Comput. Commun. Technol. UCCT*, vol. 2, no. 03, pp. 145–152, 2020.
23. J. Yadav and R. Tiwari, "Sentiment classification of movie reviews based on probabilistc graphical model," *Int. J. Res. Technol. Stud.*, vol. 2, no. 6, pp. 31–35, 2015.
24. R. P. Mehta, M. A. Sanghvi, D. K. Shah, and A. Singh, "Sentiment analysis of tweets using supervised learning algorithms," in First International Conference on Sustainable Technologies for Computational Intelligence: Proceedings of ICTSCI 2019, Springer, 2020, pp. 323–338.
25. M. R. Hasan, M. Maliha, and M. Arifuzzaman, "Sentiment analysis with NLP on Twitter data," in 2019 international conference on computer, communication, chemical, materials and electronic engineering (IC4ME2), IEEE, 2019, pp. 1–4.
26. L. Abualigah, H. E. Alfar, M. Shehab, and A. M. A. Hussein, "Sentiment analysis in healthcare: A brief review," *Recent Adv. NLP Case Arab. Lang.*, pp. 129–141, 2020.
27. A. Vanzo, D. Croce, and R. Basili, "A context-based model for sentiment analysis in Twitter," *Conf. Comput. Linguist. COLING*, pp. 2345–2354, 2014.
28. D. M. E. D. M. Hussein, "A survey on sentiment analysis challenges," *J. King Saud Univ. - Eng. Sci.*, vol. 30, no. 4, pp. 330–338, Oct. 2018, doi: 10.1016/j.jksues.2016.04.002.
29. M. Heikal, M. Torki, and N. El-Makky, "Sentiment analysis of Arabic Tweets using deep learning," *Procedia Comput. Sci.*, vol. 142, pp. 114–122, 2018, doi: 10.1016/j.procs.2018.10.466.
30. I. El Alaoui, Y. Gahi, R. Messoussi, Y. Chaabi, A. Todoskoff, and A. Kobi, "A novel adaptable approach for sentiment analysis on big social data," *J. Big Data*, vol. 5, no. 1, 2018, doi: 10.1186/s40537-018-0120-0.
31. M. Fayaz, A. Khan, J. U. Rahman, A. Alharbi, M. I. Uddin, and B. Alouffi, "Ensemble machine learning model for classification of spam product reviews," *Complexity*, vol. 2020, pp. 1–10, Dec. 2020, doi: 10.1155/2020/8857570.
32. J. G. Geer, "In Defense of Negativity: Attack Ads in Presidential Campaigns," *J. Polit.*, vol. 71, no. 2, pp. 758–760, 2006, doi: 10.1017/s002238160909063x.
33. S. Amin, A. Alharbi, M. I. Uddin, and H. Alyami, "Adapting recurrent neural networks for classifying public discourse on COVID-19 symptoms in Twitter content," *Soft Comput.*, vol. 26, no. 20, pp. 11077–11089, 2022, doi: 10.1007/s00500-022-07405-0.
34. A. Wang, W. L. Hamilton, and J. Leskovec, "Learning linguistic descriptors of user roles in online communities," in Proceedings of 2016 EMNLP Workshop on Natural Language Processing and Computational Social Science, Austin, TX, 2016, pp. 76–85.
35. M. Iyyer, A. Guha, S. Chaturvedi, J. Boyd-graber, and H. Daum, "Feuding families and former friends: Unsupervised learning for dynamic fictional relationships," in North American Association for Computational Linguistics, 2016, pp. 1534–1544.

36. F. Aziz, T. Ahmad, A. H. Malik, M. I. Uddin, S. Ahmad, and M. Sharaf, "Reversible data hiding techniques with high message embedding capacity in images," *Plos One*, vol. 15, no. 5, p. e0231602, May 2020, doi: 10.1371/journal.pone.0231602.
37. I. Ullah, N. U. Amin, A. Almogren, M. A. Khan, M. I. Uddin, and Q. Hua, "A lightweight and secured certificate-based proxy signcryption (CB-PS) scheme for E-prescription systems," *IEEE Access*, vol. 8, pp. 199197–199212, 2020, doi: 10.1109/ACCESS.2020.3033758.
38. R. Naseem *et al.*, "Performance assessment of classification algorithms on early detection of liver syndrome," *J. Healthc. Eng.*, vol. 2020, pp. 1–13, Dec. 2020, doi: 10.1155/2020/6680002.
39. R. A. Baeza-Yates and B. Ribeiro-Neto, *Modern Information Retrieval*. Boston, MA, USA: Addison-Wesley Longman Publishing Co., Inc., 1999.
40. C. D. Manning and P. Raghavan, "An introduction to information retrieval," 2009, doi: 10.1109/LPT.2009.2020494.
41. S. Amin, M. I. Uddin, M. A. Zeb, A. A. Alarood, M. Mahmoud, and M. H. Alkinani, "Detecting Dengue/Flu infections based on Tweets using LSTM and word embedding," *IEEE Access*, vol. 8, pp. 189054–189068, 2020, doi: 10.1109/ACCESS.2020.3031174.
42. C. P. Medina and M. R. R. Ramon, "Using TF-IDF to determine word relevance in document queries," *Proc. First Instr. Conf. Mach. Learn. Piscataway NJ USA*, pp. 133–142, 2003, doi: 10.15804/tner.2015.42.4.03.
43. T. Mikolov, K. Chen, G. Corrado, and J. Dean, "Efficient estimation of word representations in vector space," *Proc. Int. Conf. Learn. Represent. ICLR Scottsdale Ariz. USA*, pp. 1–12, 2013.
44. J. H. Lau and T. Baldwin, "An empirical evaluation of doc2vec with practical insights into document embedding generation," in Proceedings of the 1st Workshop on Representation Learning for {NLP}, Berlin, Germany: Association for Computational Linguistics, Aug. 2016, pp. 78–86. doi: 10.18653/v1/W16-1609.
45. Y. Bengio, R. Ducharme, P. Vincent, and C. Janvin, "A neural probabilistic language model," *J Mach Learn Res*, vol. 3, pp. 1137–1155, Mar. 2003.
46. D. Cer *et al.*, "Universal sentence encoder for English," in Proceedings of the 2018 Conference on Empirical Methods in Natural Language Processing: System Demonstrations, Brussels, Belgium: Association for Computational Linguistics, Nov. 2018, pp. 169–174. doi: 10.18653/v1/D18-2029.
47. M. Adnan, A. A. S. Alarood, M. I. Uddin, and I. Ur Rehman, "Utilizing grid search cross-validation with adaptive boosting for augmenting performance of machine learning models," *PeerJ Comput. Sci.*, vol. 8, p. e803, Feb. 2022, doi: 10.7717/peerj-cs.803.
48. D. Jurafsky and J. H. Martin, "Naive bayes and sentiment classification," *Speech and Language Processing*, 2016.
49. A. Joshi, S. Karimi, R. Sparks, C. Paris, and C. R. MacIntyre, "A comparison of word-based and context-based representations for classification problems in health informatics," in Proceedings of the 18th BioNLP Workshop and Shared Task, Florence, Italy: Association for Computational Linguistics, Aug. 2019, pp. 135–141. doi: 10.18653/v1/W19-5015.

A Hybrid Recommender System for MOOC Integrating Collaborative and Content-based Filtering

Samina Amin and Muhammad Ali Zeb

5.1 INTRODUCTION

A recommender system (RS) is an information system used to support user decision-making and recommend suitable products, information, or services in the environment of online stores; streaming services such as Amazon, YouTube, Facebook, and Netflix; and online learning (such as MOOCs). They help users make decisions according to their preferences and interests [1, 2]. Moreover, while browsing an online shopping platform, we encounter a multitude of products on the homepage. As the list of items increases, the task of choosing among them becomes increasingly challenging. Recognizing this need, and in tandem with the progress of various informational platforms such as YouTube, Amazon, Netflix, and MOOC websites, the field of RSs has been established and enhanced through the advancements in Artificial Intelligence (AI) and Machine Learning (ML).

RSs are currently extremely important for assisting users in managing the information overload they experience as a result of the vast amount of material on the web. They automatically propose the most suitable products that satisfy the users' desires. RSs have been frequently employed in consumer product trade platforms because of their ability to help users identify relevant products efficiently [3]. They have also garnered a lot of attention in MOOCs [4–7]. As the amount of data provided increases, users spend a lot of time searching for the information they need. RS is a solution in digital enterprises that carefully suggests products to customers on a needs-based assessment from among a vast number of available items.

RSs have undergone significant development over the years and have found applications in various domains, such as tourism [8–11], healthcare [12–15], advertising [16], news reporting [17, 18], e-commerce [19–22], music [23–25], movies [26–28], social networks [29–31], online learning and courses [32–36], and more. This chapter specifically emphasizes RSs personalized for designing suitable courses in e-learning/MOOCs, and we will explore this subject in the subsequent sections.

Systems that recommend educational information to students keep tabs on previous activities, are aware of preferences, support both teachers and students, help to find appropriate content, and improve learning results. A personalized RS will increase students' interest in a particular piece of information and lower the rate of course dropouts. The RS facilitates learners' decision-making toward selecting suitable content [37–39]. On MOOC platforms, understanding and identifying student interests has been attempted in a variety of ways, such as course recommendation, behavior prediction, understanding user intentions, and others [1]. One of these initiatives is for MOOC providers to employ an RS to promote courses to students [40–42].

There have been numerous empirical research studies conducted on MOOC RSs such as neighborhood-based methods [43] and latent interest models, which include user- and item-based collaborative filtering (CF) [44], content-based (CB) [45, 46], matrix factorization [47], and content-aware simulation methods [48], RSs based on sentiment analysis [49], and contextual recommendation [50]. A profile-based approach is offered for performing course RSs in a cold start scenario [35, 51, 52]. The suggested method collects user profiles from LinkedIn, evaluates how closely they resemble course profiles, and ranks the similarities.

In a MOOC RS, the main goal is to recommend relevant or similar courses that are interesting to the learners and have a high probability of being watched or read by the learner/student. Representatives of the largest online learning that implement recommendation systems are Coursera, Udemy, Udacity, etc. The main objective of this study is to design a hybrid RS for recommending suitable course content in online learning. The proposed RS combines a recommender module composed of a collaborative filtering (CF) system and a CB system. The proposed framework operates with the student's favorite course categories, viewed lectures, and reading/assignments history. A comprehensive list of recommended courses for the student is designed by applying the hybrid RS to evaluate the importance of the courses.

The proposed study aims to present an in-depth overview of the formulation and application of a state-of-the-art MOOC RS that makes use of CF, CB, and hybrid recommendation techniques. In the quickly evolving digital environment, the system is in line with the growing demand for adaptive, personalized, and effective learning solutions for smart e-learning education. The important topics that will be covered in this chapter are as follows: introduction to MOOCs, recommendation approaches, system design, and challenges and future trends.

5.1.1 Objectives

The proposed study has the following objectives:

- To propose an intelligent MOOC RS using a hybrid recommendation approach combined with CF and CB filtering.
- This approach to educational recommendation is expected to lead to improved learning outcomes and a more enjoyable learning experience for students.
- The proposed hybrid approach takes advantage of both learner interactions and course content to offer more accurate and diverse suggestions.
- Researchers, teachers, students, and experts in the domains of e-learning/academia, RSs, and artificial intelligence are the target audience for this study. It will be a helpful tool for learners who want to discover how intelligent RS might improve the MOOC learning experience for Internet of Thing (IoT)-enabled smart education.

The rest of the chapter is organized into four sections as follows: Section 5.2 provides preliminaries and background information. Section 5.3 discusses the evaluation metrics used for RS. Section 5.4 provides future research directions in the field of MOOC RSs and Section 5.5 concludes the proposed chapter.

5.2 PRELIMINARIES/BACKGROUND STUDY

5.2.1 Recommender System

RSs are ML models that are used to provide users with relevant or similar suggestions. They are employed in a variety of applications, including those that recommend movies (YouTube, Netflix), products to buy (Amazon), and text to read (such as books and news articles) [2, 53]. Figure 5.1 presents an example of an RS and its applications, inspired by a similar figure published in [54]. Personalized RSs [55] are capable of offering pertinent information that fits users' interests, addressing the issue of information overload. The majority of the time, recommendation technologies use a variety of sources of data to present customers with potential goods [56, 57]. In real-world circumstances, the RS makes suggestions for things based on the history of user–item interactions and then asks for user input to refine those suggestions.

In today's digital age, the amount of information and data is rising exponentially, and we may easily access an abundance of knowledge through applications available online. Online users may find it challenging to satisfy their interests or find the appropriate target information as a result of excessive information. Users in the online domain often face difficulties in fulfilling their specific interests or locating relevant information due to the overwhelming amount of data. To address this issue, RSs are used. These tools help users find their way through these vast information landscapes and point them in the direction of products or content that meet their needs. To ensure user satisfaction and maintain engagement within the system, the recommendation algorithm is crafted to display a curated list of relevant subjects that align with the user's potential interests. From a business perspective, an RS holds considerable significance as it contributes to enhancing commercial revenue. To illustrate, with the vast availability of millions of movies and television shows on internet streaming platforms, the implementation of a recommendation engine becomes essential for generating playlists that accurately anticipate user preferences. This, in turn, is expected to lead to an increase in subscription rates and an enhanced online streaming experience for users, as the suggested content aligns well with their interests.

Traditional RSs have been modeled using three paradigms, CF, content-based, and hybrid methods as described in the following subsection.

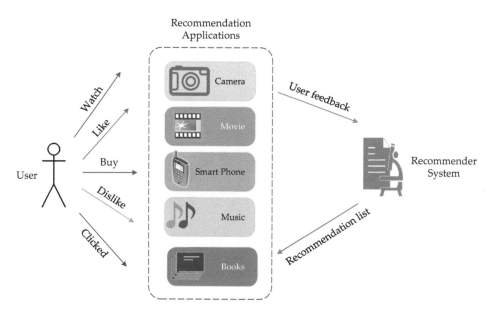

FIGURE 5.1 Example of an RS and its applications

5.2.2 Content-based Filtering

In CB RSs, apart from the user–item interaction user information and preferences, and other details related to content such as popularity, description, purchase history, etc., are also considered. The method, which functions as a conventional ML model with error optimization, is given the user features and content features. This method tends to have a high bias but the lowest variance when compared to other modeling techniques since it incorporates more descriptive information about the content [58, 59]. When making suggestions, CB filtering considers the features and qualities of the products (in our case, MOOCs) as well as the student's preferences or past behavior. For instance, it might suggest a course based on the course's subject matter, level of difficulty, or certain course material, and it considers what the student has already expressed interest in.

As a result, a MOOC RS using CB suggests courses that are probably going to match the user's interests and needs based on their choices and the content of MOOCs. By making it easier for students to find pertinent courses, this can enhance their learning experience. The CB recommendation algorithm is applied to match user profiles with MOOCs. To discover courses that are most like a student's profile, this algorithm frequently uses methods such as cosine similarity or other similarity measurements. The system ranks the suggested MOOCs according to how closely they resemble and are relevant to the student's profile. Courses are shown that are most similar to the student's preferences.

CB places greater emphasis on utilizing descriptions and dataset features rather than relying solely on historical interactions and students' preferences. Figure 5.2 shows the CB filtering structure. For instance, if a student shows an affinity for numerous courses within a specific category, they will likely also have an interest in other courses belonging to that same category. This characteristic makes CB less susceptible to both the "cold start problem" and fluctuations in student preferences.

One notable advantage of CB is its high level of explainability compared to CF. With CB, it is feasible to trace the rationale behind a particular recommendation

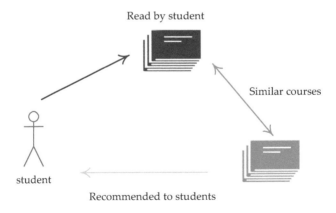

FIGURE 5.2 Content-based filtering in MOOC

because it leverages patterns found in item features without attempting to uncover hidden student preferences.

In CB, relevant features are extracted from course descriptions, titles, and tags. We can use techniques such as TF–IDF (term frequency–inverse document frequency) to weigh the importance of words in course descriptions. In addition, a profile can be designed for each student based on their historical interactions and the course attributes they have shown interest in.

5.2.3 Collaborative-based Filtering

In CF-based approaches, the recommendation system relies on the "user–item interaction matrix", which stores users' historical interactions with items [60, 61]. The fundamental idea behind CF methods is to identify similar users and their preferences based on their patterns of interaction. CF algorithms can be categorized into two main types: memory-based and model-based. Memory-based methods involve finding the most similar user to a new user and recommending items that the similar user has shown a preference for. In this approach, there is no consideration of variance or bias since it does not involve quantifying errors. On the other hand, model-based methods create a generative model based on the user–item interaction matrix, which is then utilized to make predictions for new users. This modeling approach considers both model bias and variance. In CF, the core idea is to leverage user interactions to provide personalized recommendations. This can be accomplished through either memory-based or model-based techniques as illustrated in Figures 5.3 and 5.4, which have been redesigned as proposed in [62].

When comparing CF to other recommendation systems, including CB and hybrid recommendation systems, its significance and usefulness have been shown in the domain of RS. However, there is still work being done in the field of CF to enhance the list of suggested things and produce precise suggestions while working with sparse datasets. A technique based on an econometric model can improve the predictability of the RS [63].

A popular method in RSs that leverages student behavior and preferences for making recommendations CF. This approach is particularly relevant in the context of MOOCs, as follows:

Student–student CF: This technique suggests courses to a student following the actions and preferences of other students who are comparable to them. The algorithm might suggest courses that Student B has enjoyed if, for instance, Student A and Student B have taken and liked courses that are comparable and Student A is looking for a new course.

Course–course CF: This technique suggests courses to a student following the courses that the student has previously taken and enjoyed. It identifies courses that are comparable to those in which the user has already expressed interest.

Calculation of similarity: The system determines how similar students or courses are. Based on their activity, it determines how similar students are to one another for student–student CF. It detects courses that are comparable based on CF behavior data for course–course CF.

For course–course CF, the system identifies courses like those the target student has already interacted with. In student-student CF, it recommends courses highly rated or liked by students similar to the target student.

Presentation and Ranking: The suggested courses are provided to the student for selection after being ranked according to their expected relevance to the student. CF is an effective technique for MOOC recommendations since it relies on the student community's collective knowledge rather than directly examining course content to provide individualized course choices.

Based on the fact that relationships exist between courses and student's interests. As shown in Figure 5.3, we can see that student-A and student-C are similar, hence, we recommend course-A and course-F to student-C since student-A likes both of them. In contrast, item-based CF uses similarity among items to determine whether a user would like them or not. For example, in Figure 5.4, since course-A (C++) and course-D (C#) are similar when student-C chooses course-A we will also recommend course-D to him.

- *Collaborative filtering techniques*

Uses techniques such as user–item matrix factorization, user-based or item-based CF, or more advanced methods such as matrix factorization with singular value decomposition (SVD), SVD++, or alternating least squares for matrix factorization. It implements techniques for handling sparsity and dealing with new users or items.

5.2.4 Hybrid Approach

A hybrid RS combines various recommendation techniques to generate its output. When comparing hybrid RSs with CF and CB systems hybrid systems typically exhibit

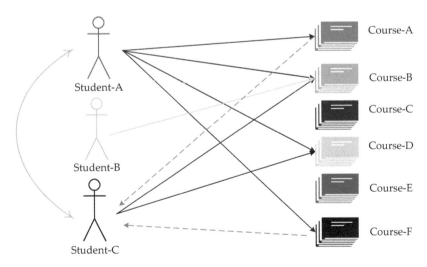

FIGURE 5.3 Student(user)-based filtering in MOOC

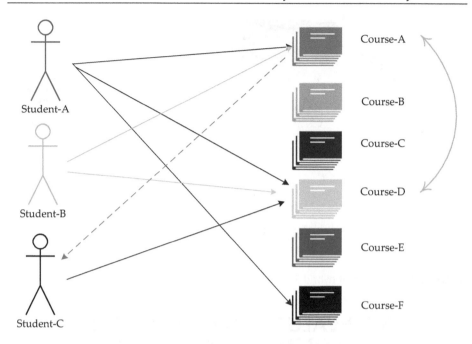

FIGURE 5.4 Course-based filtering in MOOC

higher recommendation accuracy. This is attributed to the absence of information concerning domain dependencies in CF and user preferences in CB systems. The fusion of both approaches results in an augmentation of shared knowledge, thereby enhancing the quality of recommendations. This knowledge enhancement makes it particularly promising to explore novel methods for combining underlying CF algorithms with content data and CB algorithms with user behavior data [2, 61]. Figure 5.5 shows an example of a hybrid recommendation approach for course recommendations in MOOC. This approach combines CF and CB based techniques to recommend courses to learners based on their interest.

5.2.5 Data Collection and Preprocessing

Gather data on user interactions with courses, such as ratings, reviews, and completion status. Collect information about course content, including metadata such as course descriptions, titles, and tags. Preprocess the data to ensure it is clean and organized for further analysis.

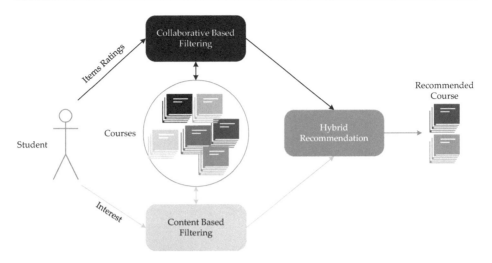

FIGURE 5.5 Example of hybrid RS in MOOC

5.3 EVALUATION METRICS FOR RECOMMENDER SYSTEMS

RS accuracy is popularly evaluated through three main measures [62].

5.3.1 Mean Absolute Error (MAE)

MAE is a widely used metric to calculate the recommender's prediction. MAE is calculated using the following expression (see Equation 5.1):

$$MAE = \frac{1}{|\hat{R}|} \sum_{r_{Sc} \in \hat{R}} |r_{Sc} - \hat{r}_{Sc}|$$

Consider the same RS as in the RMSE example. Calculate MAE@10 using the true and predicted ratings provided earlier.

Absolute_Differences = [|3.8–4.0| +|4.9–5.0| + |3.2–3.0| + |4.4–4.5| + |1.8–2.0| + |4.1–4.0|,|4.7–4.5| + |3.3–3.5| + |2.9–3.0| + |4.8–5.0|]

$$MAE@10 = \frac{(0.2 + 0.1 + 0.2 + 0.1 + 0.2 + 0.1 + 0.2 + 0.2 + 0.1 + 0.2)}{10}$$

$$MAE@10 = \frac{1.4}{10} = 0.14$$

A Hybrid Recommender System

In this case, MAE@10 of 0.14 means that, on average, the predicted ratings are off by 0.14 units from the true ratings for the top 10 recommendations.

A lower MAE indicates that the recommendations are, on average, closer to the true ratings, which suggests that the model's predictions are more accurate.

5.3.2 Mean Squared Error (MSE)

MSE measures the amount of error in statistical models. It assesses the average squared difference between the observed and predicted values. When a model has no error, the MSE equals zero. As model error increases, its value increases. The MSE is also known as the mean squared deviation (Equation 5.2).

$$MSE = \frac{1}{|\hat{R}|} \sum_{r_{Sc} \in \hat{R}} \left(r_{Sc} - \hat{r}_{Sc} \right)^2$$

Suppose we have a set of five true ratings and their corresponding predicted ratings for an RS. Table 5.1 lists the true ratings and predicted ratings.

Calculate the squared difference between each predicted rating and true rating:

- For the first rating: $(3.8-4.0)^2 = 0.04$
- For the second rating: $(4.9-5.0)^2 = 0.01$
- For the third rating: $(3.2-3.0)^2 = 0.04$
- For the fourth rating: $(4.4-4.5)^2 = 0.01$
- For the fifth rating: $(1.8-2.0)^2 = 0.04$

$$MSE@5 = \frac{0.04+0.01+0.04+0.01+0.04}{5} = \frac{0.14}{5} = 0.028$$

The MSE for this example is 0.028. This value represents the average of the squared differences between predicted ratings and true ratings, indicating how well the RS's predictions align with the actual user preferences. A lower MSE indicates better prediction accuracy.

TABLE 5.1 Example of True Ratings and Predicted Ratings for top@5

S.NO#	TRUE RATINGS	PREDICTED RATINGS
1.	4.0	3.8
2.	5.0	4.9
3.	3.0	3.2
4.	4.5	4.4
5.	2.0	1.8

5.3.3 Root Mean Squared Error (RMSE)

RMSE measures the average difference between a statistical model's predicted values and the actual values. Mathematically, it is the standard deviation of the residuals and can be seen in Equation 5.3.

$$RMSE = \sqrt{\frac{1}{|\hat{R}|} \sum_{r_{Sc} \in \hat{R}} \left(r_{Sc} - \hat{r}_{Sc}\right)^2} \qquad (5.3)$$

Where notation $\hat{R}$ shows the set of predicted ratings, r_{Sc} signifies the true ratings of the student S for course c, $\hat{r}_{Sc}$ and signifies the estimated ratings of the student S for course c.

Suppose we have a model that suggests 10 courses to a student, and we want to calculate RMSE@10. Here are the true and predicted ratings for the top 10 recommendations as outlined in Table 5.2:

$$RMSE@10 = \sqrt{\frac{1}{10} \sum_{i=1}^{10} \begin{array}{c} (3.8-4.0)^2, (4.9-5.0)^2, (3.2-3.0)^2, \\ (4.4-4.5)^2, (1.8-2.0)^2, (4.1-4.0)^2, \\ (4.7-4.5)^2, (3.3-3.5)^2, (2.9-3.0)^2, (4.8-5.0)^2 \end{array}}$$

$$RMSE@10 = \sqrt{\frac{1}{10}(0.04+0.01+0.04+0.01+0.04+0.01+0.04+0.04+0.01+0.04)}$$

$$RMSE@10 = \sqrt{\frac{0.28}{10}} = \sqrt{0.028} \approx 0.167$$

RMSE is a similar metric to MAE but considers the square of the differences, which penalizes larger errors more heavily.

TABLE 5.2 Example of True and Predicted Ratings for top@10

S.NO#	TRUE RATINGS	PREDICTED RATINGS
1.	4.0	3.8
2.	5.0	4.9
3.	3.0	3.2
4.	4.5	4.4
5.	2.0	1.8
6.	4.0	4.1
7.	4.5	4.7
8.	3.5	3.3
9.	3.0	2.9
10.	5.0	4.8

An RMSE of approximately 0.167 means that, on average, the squared differences between predicted ratings and true ratings for the top 10 recommendations are around 0.167 units.

Like MAE, a lower RMSE also indicates that the recommendations are, on average, closer to the true ratings, with smaller squared errors.

5.4 IMPLICATION AND FUTURE RESEARCH DIRECTION

The primary aim of RSs is to provide users with item recommendations, and tailoring these suggestions to individual learners presents a significant challenge. Traditional RSs are designed to make personalized course recommendations to individual learners. However, there has been a recent increase in the popularity of group activities, such as watching lectures with mates or doing assignments in a group. When predicting ratings, conventional methods often overlook the valuable metadata information associated with items. Therefore, the proposed approach takes advantage of metadata information to enhance recommendation accuracy and address the issue of data sparsity [64].

Building an intelligent MOOC RS using a hybrid approach is a complex task, but it can provide significant value by enhancing the learning experience for learners. It requires expertise in machine learning, data engineering, and software development, and it should be designed to evolve and improve continuously. One notable advantage of this proposed approach is its use of metadata to mitigate the cold start problem commonly encountered in group recommendation scenarios.

To conclude, the proposed chapter will contribute to the increasing amount of knowledge that is developing in the areas of MOOCs and RS. It will give readers an in-depth knowledge of how an intelligent MOOC RS is designed and put into action using CF, CB, and hybrid approaches. Additionally, by providing personalized and interesting learning experiences, it will also highlight how these technologies have the power to revolutionize smart e-learning education systems.

5.5 CONCLUSION

The rapid expansion of e-learning infrastructure has made it increasingly challenging for individuals to select the appropriate skill set for building a career in their area of interest. This can often be a bewildering process. Consequently, an RS proves invaluable in simplifying this decision-making, as it utilizes student data and preferences to narrow down the available information and choices. By automating the filtering process, an RS enables students to efficiently explore the vast expanse of online resources, offering a personalized experience. This research work aims to explore an RS that leverages CB and CF hybrid RS to sift through digitally available skills and courses, based on student-provided input information. To this end, the proposed chapter has explored a hybrid approach combined with CB, and CF to recommend the best courses to the learner. The suggested approach relies on MOOC filtering to regulate how the student should study best and to suggest learning content that complements their profile and e-learning understandings/involvements.

REFERENCES

1. J. Bobadilla, F. Ortega, A. Hernando, and A. Gutiérrez, "Recommender systems survey," *Knowledge-based Syst.*, vol. 46, pp. 109–132, 2013.
2. B. Walek and P. Fajmon, "A hybrid recommender system for an online store using a fuzzy expert system," *Expert Syst. Appl.*, vol. 212, p. 118565, 2023, doi: https://doi.org/10.1016/j.eswa.2022.118565.
3. M. Long et al., "A heterogeneous multi-relations-based method for knowledge-intensive service recommendation," *Comput. Ind. Eng.*, vol. 181, p. 109327, 2023, doi: https://doi.org/10.1016/j.cie.2023.109327.
4. G. R. Morales, A. P. Gallegos, P. V Torres-Carrión, and S. C. Carrión, "Comparative evaluation of the overall user experience of two MOOC platforms: Coursera and OpenCampus," in *Developments and Advances in Defense and Security: Proceedings of MICRADS 2022*, Springer, 2023, pp. 179–190.
5. Z. Liu, X. Kong, H. Chen, S. Liu, and Z. Yang, "MOOC-BERT: Automatically identifying learner cognitive presence from MOOC discussion data," *IEEE Trans. Learn. Technol.*, vol. 16, no. 4, pp. 528–542, 2023.
6. M. Jarnac de Freitas and M. Mira da Silva, "Systematic literature review about gamification in MOOCs," *Open Learn. J. Open, Distance e-Learning*, vol. 38, no. 1, pp. 73–95, 2023.
7. S. Amin, M. Irfan Uddin, M. Ali Zeb, A. A. Alarood, M. Mahmoud, and M. H. Alkinani, "Detecting dengue/flu infections based on tweets using LSTM and word embedding," *IEEE Access*, vol. 8, pp. 189054–189068, 2020, doi: 10.1109/access.2020.3031174.
8. R. K. Mishra, J. A. A. Jothi, S. Urolagin, and K. Irani, "Knowledge based topic retrieval for recommendations and tourism promotions," *Int. J. Inf. Manag. Data Insights*, vol. 3, no. 1, p. 100145, 2023.
9. Y. M. Arif, D. D. Putra, D. Wardani, S. M. S. Nugroho, and M. Hariadi, "Decentralized recommender system for ambient intelligence of tourism destinations serious game using known and unknown rating approach," *Heliyon*, vol. 9, no. 3, p. e14267, 2023.
10. L. Gamidullaeva, A. Finogeev, M. Kataev, and L. Bulysheva, "A Design Concept for a Tourism Recommender System for Regional Development," *Algorithms*, vol. 16, no. 1, p. 58, 2023.
11. A. Almomani et al., "Application of choice models in tourism recommender systems," *Expert Syst.*, vol. 40, no. 3, p. e13177, 2023.
12. M. Etemadi et al., "A systematic review of healthcare recommender systems: Open issues, challenges, and techniques," *Expert Syst. Appl.*, vol. 213, p. 118823, 2023, doi: https://doi.org/10.1016/j.eswa.2022.118823.
13. D. Sharma, G. Singh Aujla, and R. Bajaj, "Evolution from ancient medication to human-centered Healthcare 4.0: A review on health care recommender systems," *Int. J. Commun. Syst.*, vol. 36, no. 12, p. e4058, 2023.

14. M. Adnan, A. A. S. Alarood, M. I. Uddin, and I. Ur Rehman, "Utilizing grid search cross-validation with adaptive boosting for augmenting performance of machine learning models," *PeerJ Comput. Sci.*, vol. 8, p. e803, 2022.
15. R. Naseem et al., "Performance assessment of classification algorithms on early detection of liver syndrome," *J. Healthc. Eng.*, vol. 2020, p. 6680002, 2020, doi: 10.1155/2020/6680002.
16. F. García-Sánchez, R. Colomo-Palacios, and R. Valencia-García, "A social-semantic recommender system for advertisements," *Inf. Process. Manag.*, vol. 57, no. 2, p. 102153, 2020.
17. M. Karimi, D. Jannach, and M. Jugovac, "News recommender systems–survey and roads ahead," *Inf. Process. Manag.*, vol. 54, no. 6, pp. 1203–1227, 2018.
18. H. Abdollahpouri, E. C. Malthouse, J. A. Konstan, B. Mobasher, and J. Gilbert, "Toward the next generation of news recommender systems," in *Companion Proceedings of the Web Conference 2021*, 2021, pp. 402–406.
19. M. Loukili, F. Messaoudi, and M. El Ghazi, "Machine learning based recommender system for e-commerce," *IAES Int. J. Artif. Intell.*, vol. 12, no. 4, pp. 1803–1811, 2023.
20. D. T. Tran and J.-H. Huh, "New machine learning model based on the time factor for e-commerce recommendation systems," *J. Supercomput.*, vol. 79, no. 6, pp. 6756–6801, 2023.
21. A. L. Karn et al., "Customer centric hybrid recommendation system for E-Commerce applications by integrating hybrid sentiment analysis," *Electron. Commer. Res.*, vol. 23, no. 1, pp. 279–314, 2023.
22. S. G. K. Patro, B. K. Mishra, S. K. Panda, R. Kumar, H. V. Long, and D. Taniar, "Cold start aware hybrid recommender system approach for e-commerce users," *Soft Comput.*, vol. 27, no. 4, pp. 2071–2091, 2023.
23. T. Tofalvy and J. Koltai, ""Splendid Isolation": The reproduction of music industry inequalities in Spotify's recommendation system," *New Media Soc.*, vol. 25, no. 7, pp. 1580–1604, 2023.
24. M. Kleć, A. Wieczorkowska, K. Szklanny, and W. Strus, "Beyond the big five personality traits for music recommendation systems," *EURASIP J. Audio, Speech, Music Process.*, vol. 2023, no. 1, p. 4, 2023.
25. J. B. Smith, A. Vinay, and J. Freeman, "The impact of salient musical features in a hybrid recommendation system for a sound library," *In Joint Proceedings of the ACM IUI*, 2023.
26. S. Airen and J. Agrawal, "Movie recommender system using parameter tuning of user and movie neighbourhood via co-clustering," *Procedia Comput. Sci.*, vol. 218, pp. 1176–1183, 2023.
27. G. Behera and N. Nain, "Collaborative filtering with temporal features for movie recommendation system," *Procedia Comput. Sci.*, vol. 218, pp. 1366–1373, 2023.
28. Y. Mu and Y. Wu, "Multimodal movie recommendation system using deep learning," *Mathematics*, vol. 11, no. 4, p. 895, 2023.
29. S. Souabi, A. Retbi, M. K. Idrissi, and S. Bennani, "A recommendation approach based on correlation and co-occurrence within social learning network," *Concurr. Comput. Pract. Exp.*, vol. 35, no. 14, p. e6618, 2023.
30. S. Raza and C. Ding, "News recommender system: A review of recent progress, challenges, and opportunities," *Artif. Intell. Rev.*, vol. 55, pp. 749–800, 2022.
31. I. Ullah, N. U. Amin, A. Almogren, M. A. Khan, M. I. Uddin, and Q. Hua, "A lightweight and secured certificate-based proxy signcryption (CB-PS) scheme for e-prescription systems," *IEEE Access*, vol. 8, pp. 199197–199212, 2020, doi: 10.1109/ACCESS.2020.3033758.
32. H. Wan and S. Yu, "A recommendation system based on an adaptive learning cognitive map model and its effects," *Interact. Learn. Environ.*, vol. 31, no. 3, pp. 1821–1839, 2023.
33. H. K. Ahmad, C. Qi, Z. Wu, and B. A. Muhammad, "ABiNE-CRS: Course recommender system in online education using attributed bipartite network embedding," *Appl. Intell.*, vol. 53, no. 4, pp. 4665–4684, 2023.

34. L.-T. Zhao, D.-S. Wang, F.-Y. Liang, and J. Chen, "A recommendation system for effective learning strategies: An integrated approach using context-dependent DEA," *Expert Syst. Appl.*, vol. 211, p. 118535, 2023.
35. S. Amin, M. I. Uddin, A. A. Alarood, W. K. Mashwani, A. Alzahrani, and A. O. Alzahrani, "Smart e-learning framework for personalized adaptive learning and sequential path recommendations using reinforcement learning," *IEEE Access*, vol. 11, pp. 89769–89790, 2023, doi: 10.1109/ACCESS.2023.3305584.
36. S. Ali, Y. Hafeez, M. Humayun, N. S. M. Jamail, M. Aqib, and A. Nawaz, "Enabling recommendation system architecture in virtualized environment for e-learning," *Egypt. Informatics J.*, vol. 23, no. 1, pp. 33–45, 2022, doi: https://doi.org/10.1016/j.eij.2021.05.003.
37. N. Pal and O. Dahiya, "Analysis of educational recommender system techniques for enhancing student's learning outcomes," in *2023 3rd International Conference on Innovative Practices in Technology and Management (ICIPTM)*, 2023, pp. 1–5, doi: 10.1109/ICIPTM57143.2023.10118132.
38. M. Fayaz, A. Khan, J. U. Rahman, A. Alharbi, M. I. Uddin, and B. Alouffi, "Ensemble machine learning model for classification of spam product reviews," *Complexity*, vol. 2020, p. 8857570, 2020, doi: 10.1155/2020/8857570.
39. N. Mast et al., "Channel contention-based routing protocol for wireless ad hoc networks," *Complexity*, vol. 2021, p. 2051796, 2021, doi: 10.1155/2021/2051796.
40. A. Klasnja-Milicevic and D. Milicevic, "Top-N knowledge concept recommendations in MOOCs using a neural co-attention model," *IEEE Access*, vol. 11, pp. 51214–51228, 2023.
41. F. Aziz, H. Gul, I. Uddin, and G. V Gkoutos, "Path-based extensions of local link prediction methods for complex networks," *Sci. Rep.*, vol. 10, no. 1, p. 19848, 2020, doi: 10.1038/s41598-020-76860-2.
42. F. Aziz, T. Ahmad, A. H. Malik, M. I. Uddin, S. Ahmad, and M. Sharaf, "Reversible data hiding techniques with high message embedding capacity in images," *PLoS One*, vol. 15, no. 5, p. e0231602, 2020.
43. K. K. Jena et al., "E-Learning course recommender system using collaborative filtering models," *Electronics*, vol. 12, no. 1, p. 157, 2022.
44. X. Zhang, "Design and application of Japanese MOOC teaching resources system based on user collaborative filtering recommendation algorithm," in *Innovative Computing Vol 1-Emerging Topics in Artificial Intelligence: Proceedings of IC 2023*, Springer, 2023, pp. 431–438.
45. H. Ezaldeen, S. K. Bisoy, R. Misra, and R. Alatrash, "Semantics aware intelligent framework for content-based e-learning recommendation," *Nat. Lang. Process. J.*, vol. 3, p. 100008, 2023, doi: https://doi.org/10.1016/j.nlp.2023.100008.
46. S. Bhaskaran and R. Marappan, "Enhanced personalized recommendation system for machine learning public datasets: Generalized modeling, simulation, significant results and analysis," *Int. J. Inf. Technol.*, vol. 15, no. 3, pp. 1583–1595, 2023, doi: 10.1007/s41870-023-01165-2.
47. X. Sun, B. Li, R. Sutcliffe, Z. Gao, W. Kang, and J. Feng, "Wse-MF: A weighting-based student exercise matrix factorization model," *Pattern Recognit.*, vol. 1, no. 138, p. 109285, 2023.
48. P. Mishra and V. Jain, "Course recommendation system using content-based filtering," in *2023 7th International Conference on Trends in Electronics and Informatics (ICOEI)*, 2023, pp. 1431–1436, doi: 10.1109/ICOEI56765.2023.10126063.
49. V. N. and A. K. K. M., "E-learning course recommendation based on sentiment analysis using hybrid Elman similarity," *Knowledge-Based Syst.*, vol. 259, p. 110086, 2023, doi: https://doi.org/10.1016/j.knosys.2022.110086.
50. S. Tahir, Y. Hafeez, M. A. Abbas, A. Nawaz, and B. Hamid, "Smart learning objects retrieval for e-learning with contextual recommendation based on collaborative filtering," *Educ. Inf. Technol.*, vol. 27, no. 6, pp. 8631–8668, 2022, doi: 10.1007/s10639-022-10966-0.

51. S. Amin et al., "Recurrent neural networks with TF-IDF embedding technique for detection and classification in tweets of dengue disease," *IEEE Access*, vol. 8, no. July, pp. 131522–131533, 2020, doi: 10.1109/access.2020.3009058.
52. Z. Ullah et al., "Certificateless proxy reencryption scheme (CPRES) based on hyperelliptic curve for access control in content-centric network (CCN)," *Mob. Inf. Syst.*, vol. 2020, p. 4138516, 2020, doi: 10.1155/2020/4138516.
53. C. Channarong, C. Paosirikul, S. Maneeroj, and A. Takasu, "HybridBERT4Rec: A hybrid (Content-Based Filtering and Collaborative Filtering) recommender system based on BERT," *IEEE Access*, vol. 10, pp. 56193–56206, 2022, doi: 10.1109/ACCESS.2022.3177610.
54. D. Ferreira, S. Silva, and A. Abelha, "Recommendation system using autoencoders," *Appl. Sci.*, vol. 10, no. 5510, pp. 1–17, 2020, doi: 10.3390/app10165510.
55. J. Shin and O. Bulut, "Building an intelligent recommendation system for personalized test scheduling in computerized assessments: A reinforcement learning approach," *Behav. Res. Methods*, vol. 54, no. 1, pp. 216–232, 2022, doi: 10.3758/s13428-021-01602-9.
56. A. M. Mehdi, C. F. Trafford, and Behrouz, "Reinforcement learning based recommender systems: A survey," *arXive:2101.06286v1*, pp. 1–37, 2021.
57. A. Khan et al., "Summarizing online movie reviews: A machine learning approach to big data analytics," *Sci. Program.*, vol. 2020, p. 5812715, 2020, doi: 10.1155/2020/5812715.
58. J. Son and S. B. Kim, "Content-based filtering for recommendation systems using multiattribute networks," *Expert Syst. Appl.*, vol. 89, pp. 404–412, 2017, doi: https://doi.org/10.1016/j.eswa.2017.08.008.
59. U. Javed, K. Shaukat, I. A. Hameed, F. Iqbal, T. M. Alam, and S. Luo, "A review of content-based and context-based recommendation systems," *Int. J. Emerg. Technol. Learn.*, vol. 16, no. 3, pp. 274–306, 2021.
60. L. Vuong Nguyen, T. Nguyen, J. J. Jung, and D. Camacho, "Extending collaborative filtering recommendation using word embedding: A hybrid approach," *Concurr. Comput. Pract. Exp.*, vol. 35, no. 16, p. e6232, 2023.
61. G. Geetha, M. Safa, C. Fancy, and D. Saranya, "A hybrid approach using collaborative filtering and content based filtering for recommender system," in *Journal of Physics: Conference Series*, vol. 1000, no. 1, 2018, p. 12101.
62. Y. C. Chen, L. Hui, and T. Thaipisutikul, "A collaborative filtering recommendation system with dynamic time decay," *J. Supercomput.*, vol. 77, no. 1, pp. 244–262, 2021, doi: 10.1007/s11227-020-03266-2.
63. P. Yadav, S. Tyagi, and H. Kaur, "Evolutionary extreme learning machine based collaborative filtering," *Int. J. Adv. Technol. Eng. Explor.*, vol. 10, no. 104, p. 858, 2023.
64. V. R. Yannam, J. Kumar, K. S. Babu, and B. Sahoo, "Improving group recommendation using deep collaborative filtering approach," *Int. J. Inf. Technol.*, vol. 15, no. 3, pp. 1489–1497, 2023, doi: 10.1007/s41870-023-01205-x.

Federated Learning in Healthcare

Muhammad Hamza

6.1 INTRODUCTION

Advances in artificial intelligence (AI) and machine learning (ML) [1] are leading us to a very promising future. Especially when we investigate the developments that we have made so far in the very specific domain of deep learning and where we stand now from where we were before. But this is only the beginning of a future where we will be able to provide clinical-grade decision-making and rare disease predictions to patients. To achieve this level of accuracy and precision we need access to many medical data records. The current approaches that we follow prevent us from doing this and achieving the progress that we need. There are reasons that we do not get access to the healthcare data that is sitting in the data silos of different organizations. Currently, it is not being utilized to the point that it just sits there and is of no use. Federated learning (FL) is a framework that includes different privacy preservation techniques that we apply to overcome the problems with classical ML models. Let's take an AI-based tumor detector as an example, it will require us to provide our model with a large dataset of healthcare records related to tumors with different data types, anatomies, and pathologies. We will then be able to train a detector that is able to detect tumors given records of different patients. This is not easy to do because obtaining this type of data is nearly impossible. The nature of this type of data is highly sensitive and organizations govern this data very strongly making sure not a single person's data is leaked due to legal and ethical implications. It is possible that we can regenerate patients' faces using computed mammography or magnetic resonance imaging data [2–6].

Organizations do not have a systemic way of data collaboration with each other or with different types of services that might need access to data, not that it needs security and governance or its due to privacy issues. Organizations do not have a systemic way of data collaboration with each other or with different types of services that might need access to data, along with additional concerns of data security and privacy. It is also costly to maintain this data, clean it up, and make sure the data has some meaningful information to it so that once it is shared or collaborated the party that needs to study this data can easily make use of it. Such data also always has some business value to it [7].

FL is a solution to these problems that we have with the classical way of doing ML. This was developed for various use cases but got a lot of attention in healthcare. It provides us with a solution that can allow us to train ML models on various medical records that are sitting in the data silos of different organizations, with FL we can securely access data and preserve the privacy of the patients. Data does not have to leave the data center of the participating party rather we send our model to these parties then train our model there and send back model updates to our centralized server, which then takes an average of these models and creates a global model that is trained with the collaboration of all these participating parties that allowed access to their data for training model. This does not send any sensitive information or reveal any patient's identity, in fact, data does not leave the participating party so they retain complete control while making sure it is secure and private. Successful implementation of FL on a global scale could enable healthcare providers with solutions such as precision medicine, and better treatment and decision-making. Training AI models on the lifestyles, behaviors, and choices that patients make allow us to predict rare diseases that could lead to mild consequences and avoid further damage. This could also help provide better decisions to help diagnose the patients by using the information given by those who have been treated with similar symptoms and diseases all while making sure patient data is private, secure, and anonymous.

While the future of FL seems promising there are some challenges that we must consider and address. We need to make sure the performance of these models is highly efficient and that the predictions and recommendations given by these models are to the clinical grade level. All of this without compromising the privacy or security of the patients. We will discuss the pivotal role of FL in healthcare. How we can make the most out of FL in the very specific domain of healthcare. We will go through various privacy preservation techniques that we can use to guarantee the privacy of patients and the security of the data so that all the participating parties that collaborate with their patient's data retain full access and control over it while the researchers and trainers have no direct access to data and they only get what they need to the point both of the parties are satisfied with output that is derived from the implementation of FL. This does not come without new challenges we face in FL and some considerations that must be taken during this process [2, 6, 8].

6.1.1 Background

ML models are large datasets that help us train these models to the point where these models can provide better predictions and suggestions that can be utilized in

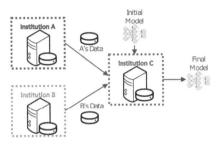

(a) Collaborative Learning through Centralized Data Sharing

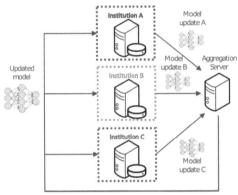

(b) Data-private Collaborative Learning using Federated Learning

(c) Data-private Collaborative Learning using Institutional Incremental Learning

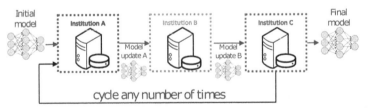

(d) Data-private Collaborative Learning using Cyclic Institutional Incremental Learning

FIGURE 6.1 System architectures for multi-institutional collaboration

real-world scenarios. Services such as spam filters and recommendation systems are common examples of these ML models. You might wonder how these models are trained and perform so well and where these mountains of data come from that help to train these models. Free services such as email, music streaming services, and various other services we enjoy are an exchange for our data that is then gathered and used to train models. In 2016 Google introduced the term FL. Meanwhile, we saw the rising concerns about the use and misuse of personal data when the Cambridge Analytica scandal happened. When Facebook's data was breached it got global attention and the world realized that free services in exchange for user's data could lead to real-world consequences. FL is a way to train models on decentralized data instead of collecting data in one place and then training models. FL provides users with a foundational model that is trained on the user's device and then model updates are sent back to the server averaged and with several iterations until we have a very optimized model. Once we have an optimized model, we can go to the next step which is deployment [9, 10].

FL is a genius way of training models and performing ML tasks. However, we measure its efficiency through its impact on healthcare. Personal data such as healthcare data is highly sensitive and confidential due to its nature. However, it is not easy to share this data with a third party. Doing so could lead to potential risks such as lack of security, data breaches, and less control over the data. FL solves this problem once and for all by sending foundational models to participants then training models there and sending updates iterating over it until we get an average model that we can deploy and use in production. These models can contribute to better medical analysis and improved predictions which leads to better disease diagnoses and thus a better quality of life overall.

6.1.2 Objectives

This chapter aims to discuss the core objectives of FL in healthcare. We discuss how FL is used to preserve privacy while enabling data analysis and medical research in a distributive and collaborative approach. ML is widely used in day-to-day tasks but very limited in healthcare where FL solves this problem unlocking the full potential of ML. However, this sounds fascinating, but it takes a lot of techniques combined to achieve this purpose and we'll be discussing these various techniques in detail such as data anonymization, differential privacy, secure multi-party computation, and homomorphic encryption.

Combining these techniques with ML is the core of FL, which helps us to build robust models for better predictions and disease diagnosis. While it seems very promising there are challenges and considerations, we must take with this approach such as do we trust certain participants, do we go trustless and aim for a direction of FL that does not require trust between participants and different entities, or how do we make sure data isn't biased and is fair and overcome a lack of standardization. We'll study all of these in detail in the chapter later.

6.2 PRIVACY-PRESERVING MEDICAL RESEARCH AND ANALYSIS

Privacy-preserving learning techniques are merging techniques that help preserve the user's privacy. ML algorithms were designed at the very beginning to process and analyze data, which is called training. In all hospitals medical records are being generated and records of the patients along with their diagnostic history are stored on computers and data is being generated in large amounts. Analyzing this data manually and making some sense of this data could be expensive, time-consuming, and prone to human errors. If we train ML models on this data and make data available to ML models this could lead to better accuracy, it can help healthcare providers with better decision making.

Studying these meaningful insights from the models or the given results can help pave the way for further medical research and analysis. It has always been a very important subject for researchers to study medical data and produce better results which could help healthcare providers; however, due to a lack of data availability and interoperability, it's not easy to do so on these records and make use of the data that is available at every hospital in every healthcare department.

Major concerns are that the healthcare providers have violated patients' identity, dignity, and trust. At the same time, we know how important it can be to make data available to ML for training better models that would produce better results and help healthcare providers. We cannot overlook the need to keep all this private and these concerns are the main reasons why to this day not many organizations share their data with researchers for medical analysis or scholarly studies, these concerns are true and impose legal implications with legal consequences. FL is a solution to all these problems.

The main concept of FL is to solve this issue, especially in healthcare. This can be a life-changing implementation. Healthcare departments will not have to share their data with any third party that they don't trust and don't want to have any legal consequences faced by the authorities or the patients. Certain techniques can allow us to train models on their data without having any knowledge about the individuals or any specific details about them. Data never leaves the storage centers of these healthcare departments, and we will study these techniques in detail that allow us to preserve patients' privacy and let us train on data and help both researchers and healthcare providers.

6.2.1 Privacy-Preserving Techniques

Privacy preservation techniques are the building blocks of FL. We assume that the number of participating parties is large, and we can assume that it might be in the millions, and all of these are collaborating on different scales with various types of medical records. It is not possible to make sure that all these participating parties are completely legitimate and do not have intentions to either corrupt or produce errors in the training process.

The model is being trained locally in FL, so we also need to make sure that for those who are participating in the training process, their data is not being revealed or there is no information leakage from the model's parameters as the model is being trained. To prevent these types of issues we have privacy-preserving techniques which act as a major building block in FL. They guarantee the privacy of the data and make sure no information is revealed, that the identity of those who collaborate remains completely anonymous, and that there is no relation between the data that is being used for training and the individual's identity. These techniques are data anonymization, differential privacy, secure multi-party computation, and data homomorphic encryption. These techniques act as a building block and we can see that these are four major pillars of privacy preservation in FL [8, 11].

6.2.2 Data Anonymization

Medical health records include detailed information about the patients such as their social security number, address, and name, or any other related information that is part of the identity of a patient. This type of information is always attached to healthcare records and misuse of this information can risk the privacy of the patient and have legal consequences for the organization that might collaborate this data with others for the sake of training ML algorithms.

Data anonymization is a privacy-preserving technique in which we either add noise or pseudo-anonymize the data and change any information that is related to the identity of a patient. This information can vary for different datasets but primarily for the healthcare records this includes names, addresses, and different types of personal records which identify the patients or help identify the healthcare providers their patients and keep their patients organized based on their identity.

Data anonymization converts all this information to pseudonyms or to some meaningless information that is basically of no use or cannot be used to identify a patient. This protocol is used in FL and allows us to perform computation and train models on data that is needed for the sake of training and removes the information that is not needed, and we can still train the model without the need for that information. We can train our model without knowing the name or home address of a patient when we need to train our model for a specific use case such as precise medicine, so it's easier to anonymize patients' identity and it opens the doors to training models on data easily without risking privacy.

6.2.3 Differential Privacy (DP)

When we have access to the dataset, we need to analyze it and we need to do this without compromising the privacy of the patients. This can only be done via DP because it allows us to analyze the dataset without revealing the information of the individuals. This is combined with other privacy preservation techniques in FL so that once data is anonymized and there is no information to be revealed about an individual then we analyze data without access to the individual private information.

This allows training models without having any specific information about the user and this is used to protect the outputs of the algorithm. It involves replacing statistical queries with comparable algorithms that add random noise. This random noise is added to the algorithms that do the analysis to make all the analysis private. However, as the dataset increases and becomes larger or if we must analyze a large dataset then it can become a drain on the performance, to avoid this we can combine it with secure multi-party computation to overcome this problem. This will allow both privacy and performance at the same time and work efficiently together [12].

6.2.4 Secure Multi-party Computation (SMC)

SMC is completely suited for the use case of FL scenarios, where every party holds onto the information that they have and performs the computation on the data without revealing any private information or any information that is related to the data. There are two major aims for the SMC which are to basically go for accuracy and privacy. SMC makes sure that the information stays private and there is no leakage of the information when we implement the computation and follow the protocols of the SMC. When parties collaborate with their data this will prevent them from sharing incorrect information and it makes sure that all the parties are sharing honest information and the results that are provided from this protocol are completely correct.

When there is a large number of collaborating parties and it is hard to determine the number of parties, hypothetically we can assume this can be in the millions, then it is not possible to just guarantee that all the parties are completely legitimate and have good intentions while it is also not possible to take all that data and put this together in a single dataset. Combining these datasets into a single dataset will also give rise to certain problems as well which again causes privacy issues.

SMC allows us to share only the computed insights from the data and hides any sensitive information and this protocol takes care of information security.

Due to the nature of SMC, it can be utilized to get insights on the datasets and send weight updates to the central server without ever knowing the private information or any information that the parties do not want to reveal or send to the central server. This way central server gets weights from the collaborating parties but cannot derive input from this output that is given and then combining all these weights it gets an average of these weight to have a global result output which can be used by the model [13].

6.2.5 Homomorphic Encryption

All the organizations store data and data collaboration is needed but organizations do not want to give access to plain text records. There is a need for converting these records into a form that is only readable by that organization. Anyone else trying to access these records should not be able to read it or if they can read it then it's entirely meaningless to third parties. Converting plain text records or different types of records into cyphertexts is called encryption. Now you wonder if this can be a solution to securing data, we can have data on servers and then encrypt this data using the normal encryption techniques. Proper encryption means data can be encrypted with a public key, contain no relation to the original data, and can only be decrypted with the private key only available to the authority that originally encrypted the data.

This can give birth to issues related to privacy. We know that with encryption it is close to impossible to expose any information but when an organization itself decrypts data this can expose information thus having the risk of leaking information from the users because when we have to train a model and send our model to the participating party that model needs some access to data and if that data is not readable or meaningless for anyone it makes sense that it will be useless for the model as well. The model won't be able to learn anything from fully encrypted data if the participating party tries to give access to data, then it must use its private key which could compromise its private key. Once that is compromised this could lead to a privacy risk and illegal access to the data. If someone gets a hand on that key organization could end up losing access to their data and exposing all the information that is held for millions of patients.

A better solution to this problem is homomorphic encryption which allows encrypting data to cipher texts and computation can be performed on this data. This takes out the risk of compromising privacy because you can still perform computation and get meaningful insights from the data. Once a dataset is encrypted and we want to train our model on that data the participating parties do not have to worry about leaking any information at all. Our model will be able to learn and perform computation and this information will not be meaningless for the model rather it will hold some useful meaning to it. If there is no need to decrypt data that means there is no need to share the private key and that guarantees top-level security and privacy. However, this does not come without its limitations and there is always a performance overhead with large and complex computations. Which means this can become computationally intensive and slow [13–16].

6.3 FEDERATED LEARNING

A sophisticated framework that is built on top of several privacy preservation techniques that not only allow us to do ML and computing but also maintain data privacy and confidentiality. Data always remains decentralized and model updates are sent back while iterating this process until a model is completely trained and ready to be deployed.

This is how the step-by-step mechanism of FL works to ensure privacy and perform ML. ML is becoming normal in our day-to-day routine and researchers are always working to optimize these models and provide better performance. Voice assistants and chatbots are all trained on huge chunks of data. This requires data to be present on the central server and then trained on that data. A common example would be electronic vehicles as those vehicles generate millions of gigabytes of data every day. This data is then stored on the central servers and then ML is implemented using this data to provide better service by the electronic vehicle manufacturers [11].

This all seems like a very normal way of doing this but if we take a moment to think about this way of ML, we can categorize it as the classical way of ML. Large amounts

102 Federated Learning

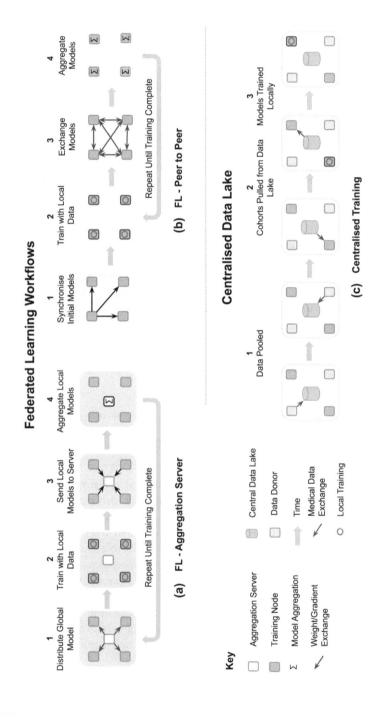

FIGURE 6.2 Example of federated learning (FL) workflows and the difference with learning on a centralized data lake [11].

of data are generated daily and uploading all the data is expensive and time-consuming. On the other hand, there is always a privacy risk involved in it as well. Data does not only include information about the vehicle but also about the users that are driving those vehicles, and that type of information can be very confidential as well [17].

If someone can get access to the central server they will not only have access to the model that is trained on this data but also to the complete dataset. With that data, they can use it to identify the vehicle and hack into it or track the movement of it causing damage to the vehicle or the owner of that vehicle. However, classical ML in some very basic scenarios can work such as Google Photos which stores your data in the cloud and continues to train the models on that data and allows you to perform certain actions such as organizing your photos or detecting faces and allowing you to find photos of different people. Now we might think that in this use we have potential dangers as well but now we understand there is a risk involved in classical ML however the factor of that risk of privacy can depend on the use cases involved.

This is where FL makes a huge difference, and we can take examples of both electronic vehicles and cloud apps such as Google Photos. Let's investigate the example of the electronic vehicle first, which we discussed how it works in the classical model; however, if we apply FL in this use case we won't upload millions of gigabytes of data every day to the third-party server it removes the problem of risking privacy for a better experience.

We simply send a global model to these vehicles and let that train on the data that is generated by the vehicles and make sure that model updates are sent back and an updated model once ready is deployed and vehicle owners continue to have the same benefits as they did before while risking their privacy and potentially always being at the risk of getting hacked and incurring some sort of damage. This also saves the manufacturers the bandwidth and the storage space and does not need so much computational power which they can utilize their vehicles to train the models.

Now in cloud applications such as Google Photos if FL is applied it removes any privacy issues such as no third-party access to your data and in case a third-party server is compromised then your data won't be affected and the ML that is done to organize your photos or detect places will be present and allow you to use those features without any privacy concerns.

TABLE 6.1 Some Terminologies and Their Abbreviation

TERMINOLOGY	ABBREVIATION
Federated Learning	FL
Artificial Intelligence	AI
Secure Multi-party Computation	SMC
Differential Privacy	DP
Machine Learning	ML

6.3.1 Applications in Disease Diagnosis and Prediction

FL is a general learning paradigm, but it has several use cases in healthcare and removes the need to pool data for model training and development. It spans across the whole domain of healthcare and provides efficiency in every possible way. For example, predicting or detecting a tumor is not easy due to the unavailability of datasets out there. There is a solid reason for that, as it is possible to reconstruct the face of the patient with computed tomography (CT) or magnetic resonance imaging (MRI) data. This type of detection requires different parameters such as anatomies, pathologies, and different data types which are not easy to obtain from the authorities that govern this data. However, if this type of data is provided and shared easily and different organizations can simply participate either in the training or testing phases they can contribute to this global scaling of FL and provide benefits to all the patients with high-quality disease diagnoses and prediction. This provides equality for all even if someone is in a remote location or at a big city hospital, they enjoy the same quality of treatment, and this all happens with FL.

Because FL makes it possible to train models using decentralized and dispersed health data, it has the potential to be very significant in the field of healthcare. If patient privacy is upheld, this can facilitate the development of more precise and customized models as well as the analysis of larger amounts of data. Additionally, FL can facilitate the training of models using hard-to-get and hard-to-aggregate data, such as data from rural or underserved areas. Furthermore, by facilitating data sharing and analysis throughout many businesses, ML can aid in the elimination of healthcare data islands. Also, FL is now more effective at learning from data that is dispersed over several sites and cannot be merged into a single dataset. Diagnosis is the identification of an illness by examining its symptoms. This technique is used in various domains to study the cause and effects. Some real-world use cases include drug recovery, COVID-19 prediction, and the wide usage of EHRs to predict the mortality rate [7, 8, 11, 16].

6.3.1.1 COVID-19 Diagnosis

COVID-19 was the primary focus of research in 2020. This became a priority for the research when the World Health Organization (WHO) declared it a pandemic. Various activities such as diagnoses, prevention, or prediction of someone getting this disease were being studied and the development of a possible vaccine was underway. During this time healthcare systems were underutilized and were not used to their full potential. The major reason for the underutilization of these systems was that they did not have access to this information while the institutes governing the data had access to data but did not use this access properly. There are privacy policies that prevent access to data and legal implications as well. Some patients might not give consent to the use of their data or provide for their identity to be released. This problem, or problems such as this, can easily be solved using FL.

The development of a global-scale FL system would have allowed better prediction and prevention of COVID-19. Due to not being able to predict this disease very efficiently or analyze what was available, the pandemic almost got out of hand and did massive damage in terms of both financial and human lives. This would have been not the case with FL where people's data would be secure and in their control, and global awareness of the disease with better prediction and control and better and more efficient treatments would be available. This is how, not only in COVID-19, but in diseases such as this we can utilize FL and provide benefits at a global scale, and this can have huge impacts on the lives of both patients and healthcare providers.

6.3.1.2 Estimation of Blood Pressure

The prevalence of chronic heart disease, identified as the leading cause of global mortality by the World Health Organization (WHO) from 2000 to 2019, underscores its profound impact on both individuals and public healthcare systems. The imperative to understand the dynamics between a healthy and compromised cardiovascular system has prompted clinicians to rely on electrocardiogram (ECG) and blood pressure (BP) readings.

However, the invasive nature of obtaining continuous arterial blood pressure (ABP) readings, coupled with the associated costs, has prompted a quest for more efficient and privacy-preserving methodologies. FL can be utilized to analyze data and findings based on the patient's data. This can be used to predict chronic heart diseases and allow healthcare providers to be much more efficient in their work and help them cure patients, so they enjoy longevity and a healthy life by making better lifestyle choices before they even have the disease, this is very much possible with the use of FL.

6.3.1.3 Clinicians

Clinics are at different locations to provide healthcare services to patients in every town, city, or village. They operate on their own and they have a lot of data that is being generated but there is no use for this data. They all have their methods of treatment, and some might differ from others; they all have various experiences which can cause biases in the diagnoses and yield very different outcomes as well. This can be solved with FL having it as an intermediate party which can help remove bias from decision-making and allow clinicians to make better decisions and diagnose patients in a much more effective way.

6.3.1.4 Patients

Using FL patients can all have equal treatment. This can happen if we are to implement FL for the patients who are being treated either in remote locations or in big city hospitals. For example, all the patients are treated locally and if we are to implement FL on a large scale then we can form a system where it's easier and consistent to make accurate and similar decisions for the treatment of all patients regardless of their locations. A large-scale global FL system will ensure that all the clinics where patients are treated have access to this system which then will provide them with better decision-making and allow them to take reasonable actions. However, there could be some diseases that are not very common, and this could be a way to prevent those diseases in their early stages and make sure a proper diagnosis is given so mild consequences are there to face.

6.3.1.5 Healthcare Providers

Precision medicine is a way that healthcare providers provide better treatment to patients using their health data and personal life, such as the environment they live in or the kind of life choices they may be making. This is done to provide better treatment and prevent further harm or predict which treatment would work best for which group of people. This could help healthcare providers to be highly accurate in their decisions and allow patients to be treated in a way that actually works for them and not go through the rigorous process of experimentation and then find out what could work, which can have major impacts on patients' lives and the lives of those around them.

6.3.1.6 Cancer Research

FL is useful in cancer research and prediction because it addresses privacy problems connected with sensitive medical data. It allows for scanning and analysis of mammography, computed tomography, magnetic resonance imaging, and X-rays which help to derive information and provide knowledge that is needed to train models to the point that these models can be deployed and utilized in an efficient treatment process and disease predictions.

This allows for both patients and doctors to treat and make better decisions. By training cancer prediction models on a variety of datasets, this decentralized method improves generalization and robustness. FL also lessens the need to transfer substantial amounts of medical data, lowering privacy concerns and guaranteeing legal compliance. The system supports customized models for various institutions, and the real-time updates feature allows for constant adaptability to new trends. FL is a promising approach since it allows for adaptive learning to happen in a decentralized manner.

6.4 CHALLENGES AND CONSIDERATIONS IN HEALTH DATA COLLABORATION

Despite all these advantages of FL, there are certain challenges and considerations we must take while working with FL. Even if it's FL or NON-FL-based learning these challenges are faced in both ways. We must consider these challenges such as Data Quality, Standardization, and Biasness. We must take measures to solve these problems such as careful study design, common protocols for data acquisition, structured reporting, and sophisticated methodologies for discovering bias and hidden stratification. In the below, we discuss these challenges and considerations [3].

6.4.1 Data heterogeneity

Data heterogeneity means diversity in data, encompassing types of data that are very diverse and come from various sources such as databases, different medical records, electronic health record systems, and different types of logs. Data heterogeneity makes it difficult to train decision-making algorithms due to data quality, modalities, distribution, and labeling. It can have a bias in the decision-making or provide low-quality predictions that are not very useful, or these predictions are faulty to the point they become useless due to data heterogeneity.

Addressing and solving this issue could lead to better algorithm training and development. Acquisition of data that is not affected by data heterogeneity and successfully mitigating the impact of data heterogeneity can be a pivotal step in the advancement of FL scaling on a global scale. This progress can enhance the utility and effectiveness of the framework and its techniques for every user.

6.4.2 Data Traceability

FL involves multi-party computation with a diverse range of hardware, software, and networks, which is needed for safety-critical applications. Key challenges that we face in this regard include the diverse range of environments in which FL operates, making system reproducibility difficult. Mandatory traceability of assets, especially in non-trusted federations, poses execution integrity challenges. Finding the exact number of contributions from participants and establishing a fair compensation model is not an easy task to do or achieve. Privacy concerns arise as researchers lack direct access to training data, impacting their ability to understand unexpected results. The distributed nature of FL also hinders the explanation and interpretability of global models, necessitating secure viewing facilities. Addressing these challenges is important for the successful deployment of FL in healthcare.

6.4.3 Data Security and Privacy

Healthcare data is highly sensitive. Therefore, it must be protected with high security and the privacy of the data should be tightened with well-structured protocols that guarantee the privacy of data. Some of the key considerations are the trade-offs, strategies, and remaining risks regarding the privacy-preserving potential of FL. FL is not one solution for all. It is much more efficient than traditional ML, but it still has its own risk and privacy issues. These models provide better privacy but there is a trade-off in achieving this level of privacy and the trade-off for this is performance and these techniques affect the performance of the models. For example, this could affect the accuracy of the model greatly.

We also come across the issue of trust or no trust at all. If we are to trust, then we must consider all the parties that are participating in the collaboration as trusted parties. This can be achieved by agreeing on a mutual agreement and making sure all the parties are trustworthy and those who may want to corrupt the model or misuse the information are eliminated by this method. This reduces the need to go the extra mile for privacy but again this becomes a matter of trust which has nothing to do with either methods or technology and is purely based on human interaction.

This has its benefits as well as its drawbacks. If we implement a no-trust process where we don't need to establish trust, we can include all the parties that may want to participate and contribute to the training of the model. We might eliminate the problem we had before, but this introduces many new problems to deal with such as intentional data leakage, corruption of data, or the intentional performance degradation of the model. To overcome this, we must follow strict policies and then advance encryption techniques, and follow strategies that help us authenticate all the parties and their identity.

6.4.4 Ethical Considerations

When working with FL we need to make sure it's fair, free from bias, transparent, and that you are in complete ownership of your data. Let's say you, and anyone like you, are using the same model despite having the same model both of you don't get the same results for your same problem that means there's no fairness in this and this is ethically wrong. No matter what, everyone should be getting the same service regardless of their location, ethnicity, or gender. It's equally important that the trained model is free from any bias. The results that are provided are not in favor or against a specific topic or one very specific discussion. All the participating parties have a right to know how their data is being used and utilized. How models are being used to train on the data that they provided, and all the details of the complete work FL is called transparency [2, 3, 11, 18].

6.5 CONCLUSION AND FUTURE DIRECTIONS

ML has a lot of potential to solve many of the problems that we face, especially in healthcare. ML is limited due to a lack of data, so we are not able to achieve its full potential. This can be solved using FL, which tries to solve the ML problem of lack of access to data. However, direct access to data is not possible due to privacy concerns and issues related to collaboration. FL uses combinations of techniques that preserve privacy and allow training models on the devices of participating parties and send updates to the central server until a global model is trained and ready to deploy. This also comes with its risks and challenges that we must consider and address those challenges accordingly so that we can scale this to a global scale.

Despite all the advances made in FL by researchers and contributors, it still has a lot of challenges and it needs further improvements for the future which we can think of as the future direction of FL. This includes working on better privacy preservation techniques that are not only good at preserving the privacy of users but also have highly efficient performance as well. Data acquisition is still a challenge that needs improvement in terms of healthcare. Organizations ranging from large scale to small scale still have a lot of data that they are either holding onto and don't want to contribute or don't have a method to acquire the data efficiently.

A solution is much needed, especially in the healthcare domain, for the acquisition of the data so any participating party does not have to worry about the system architecture or FL that would just allow them to contribute or communicate [3, 7, 19]. Security, besides privacy, poses a risk as well so we not only need systems and frameworks that are privacy preserving but also secure in the communication back and forth. Ethical considerations on top of all these things add another layer of complexity to this as well and we also need to investigate this as well. Having a governance framework that makes sure there is trust, fairness, and accountability will ensure the global scaling of FL in healthcare.

REFERENCES

1. Y. LeCun, Y. Bengio, and G. Hinton, "Deep learning," *Nature*, vol. 521, no. 7553, pp. 436–444, 2015, doi: 10.1038/nature14539.
2. J. De Fauw *et al.*, "Clinically applicable deep learning for diagnosis and referral in retinal disease," *Nat Med*, vol. 24, no. 9, pp. 1342–1350, 2018, doi: 10.1038/s41591-018-0107-6.
3. F. Wang, L. P. Casalino, and D. Khullar, "Deep learning in medicine—promise, progress, and challenges," *JAMA Intern Med*, vol. 179, no. 3, pp. 293–294, 2019, doi: 10.1001/jamainternmed.2018.7117.
4. A. Khan *et al.*, "Summarizing online movie reviews: A machine learning approach to big data analytics," *Sci Program*, vol. 2020, p. 5812715, 2020, doi: 10.1155/2020/5812715.
5. Z. Ullah *et al.*, "Certificateless proxy reencryption scheme (CPRES) based on hyperelliptic curve for access control in content-centric network (CCN)," *Mob Inf Syst*, vol. 2020, p. 4138516, 2020, doi: 10.1155/2020/4138516.
6. M. Fayaz, A. Khan, J. U. Rahman, A. Alharbi, M. I. Uddin, and B. Alouffi, "Ensemble machine learning model for classification of spam product reviews," *Complexity*, vol. 2020, p. 8857570, 2020, doi: 10.1155/2020/8857570.
7. M. J. Sheller *et al.*, "Federated learning in medicine: facilitating multi-institutional collaborations without sharing patient data," *Sci Rep*, vol. 10, no. 1, p. 12598, 2020, doi: 10.1038/s41598-020-69250-1.
8. N. Truong, K. Sun, S. Wang, F. Guitton, and Y. Guo, "Privacy preservation in federated learning: An insightful survey from the GDPR perspective," *Comput Secur*, vol. 110, p. 102402, 2021, doi: 10.1016/j.cose.2021.102402.
9. R. Naseem *et al.*, "Performance assessment of classification algorithms on early detection of liver syndrome," *J Healthc Eng*, vol. 2020, p. 6680002, 2020, doi: 10.1155/2020/6680002.
10. S. Amin, M. I. Uddin, M. A. Zeb, A. A. Alarood, M. Mahmoud, and M. H. Alkinani, "Detecting dengue/flu infections based on tweets using LSTM and word embedding," *IEEE Access*, vol. 8, pp. 189054–189068, 2020, doi: 10.1109/ACCESS.2020.3031174.
11. N. Rieke *et al.*, "The future of digital health with federated learning," *NPJ Digit Med*, vol. 3, no. 1, p. 119, 2020, doi: 10.1038/s41746-020-00323-1.
12. M. Pettai and P. Laud, "Combining differential privacy and secure multiparty computation," in *Proceedings of the 31st Annual Computer Security Applications Conference*, in ACSAC '15. New York: Association for Computing Machinery, 2015, pp. 421–430. doi: 10.1145/2818000.2818027.
13. E. Hosseini and A. Khisti, "Secure aggregation in federated learning via multiparty homomorphic encryption," in *2021 IEEE Globecom Workshops (GC Wkshps)*, 2021, pp. 1–6. doi: 10.1109/GCWkshps52748.2021.9682053.

14. F. Wibawa, F. O. Catak, M. Kuzlu, S. Sarp, and U. Cali, "Homomorphic encryption and federated learning based privacy-preserving CNN training: COVID-19 detection usecase," in *Proceedings of the 2022 European Interdisciplinary Cybersecurity Conference*, in EICC '22. New York: Association for Computing Machinery, 2022, pp. 85–90. doi: 10.1145/3528580.3532845.
15. A. Girka, V. Terziyan, M. Gavriushenko, and A. Gontarenko, "Anonymization as homeomorphic data space transformation for privacy-preserving deep learning," *Procedia Comput Sci*, vol. 180, pp. 867–876, 2021, doi: 10.1016/j.procs.2021.01.337.
16. Z. Shi, Z. Yang, A. Hassan, F. Li, and X. Ding, "A privacy preserving federated learning scheme using homomorphic encryption and secret sharing," *Telecommun Syst*, vol. 82, no. 3, pp. 419–433, 2023, doi: 10.1007/s11235-022-00982-3.
17. F. Aziz, H. Gul, I. Uddin, and G. V Gkoutos, "Path-based extensions of local link prediction methods for complex networks," *Sci Rep*, vol. 10, no. 1, p. 19848, 2020, doi: 10.1038/s41598-020-76860-2.
18. G. Kaissis *et al.*, "End-to-end privacy preserving deep learning on multi-institutional medical imaging," *Nat Mach Intell*, vol. 3, no. 6, pp. 473–484, 2021, doi: 10.1038/s42256-021-00337-8.
19. M. Joshi, A. Pal, and M. Sankarasubbu, "Federated learning for healthcare domain – pipeline, applications and challenges," *ACM Trans Comput Healthcare*, vol. 3, no. 4, 2022, doi: 10.1145/3533708.

Scalability and Efficiency in Federated Learning

7

Alyan Zaib

7.1 INTRODUCTION

To handle or safeguard the maximum amount of demands while managing the optimal outcome and performance, federated learning systems must be scalable and efficient. The federated system's scalability and success are attributed to several factors, including distributed architecture, exchange efficiency, model bending, flexible learning techniques, self-protection, selective collection, tolerance of failure mechanisms, service-aware cooperation, and constant monitoring and optimization. All of those suggestions help to build an integrated learning environment that evaluates consistency and addresses some of the issues of shared learning across many devices. Section 7.1 looks at how to evaluate government projects and highlights how essential it is to manage the sharing of resources while developing trust and authority

We will look at ways to make federated learning systems more effective when dealing with huge amounts of data. By utilizing the efficiency and scalability of federated learning, we want to take advantage of what are creative and efficient techniques. Think of it as similar to a gathering of people exchanging their knowledge or ideas while developing their knowledge together. Even though there is a lot to learn, we have come across innovative approaches for making sure that this process goes without problem. Our research will concentrate on developing these learning systems so they can manage huge quantities of data in a logical and successful method. We have designed a few smart ways to get these systems to connect, combine their knowledge, and make effective utilization of all of their assets. This will allow them to develop into highly intelligent learners, just as we communicate with one another and share ideas. This is preparing you for the quickest and most effective approach to learning together. If federated learning is implemented among a large variety of edge devices, such as smartphones, IoT equipment, or edge-computing nodes, scalability becomes very complicated. It is a challenge to balance the variations between all of these devices depending on computational capability, energy boundaries, and communication conditions.

Key concepts for efficiently scaling federated learning systems are revealed through the discussion of techniques for adjusting to a wide range of different devices and users. Section 7.2 focuses on using research technologies and collaborative modeling to enhance training model performance across the distribution chain. This section includes novel approaches to effective joint modeling that make use of the latest developments in federated learning algorithms to lower demand and stress on computers. The objective is to meet strict performance requirements while maintaining accuracy in contexts with limited resources. Section 7.3 examines bandwidth optimization and communication techniques, highlighting the critical role that communication protocols play in federated learning systems. Modern methods for lowering bandwidth requirements are included, along with a thorough examination of communication overhead. This section emphasizes how critical it is to maximize record transfers among devices and the server to minimize the pressure on network sources and assure the easy operation of federated learning structures. This will vary from industrial and banking information to scientific data. The large number of statistics accumulated daily requires thorough evaluation and a good way to infer new understanding or make predictions, which has led to many advances in systems getting to know and deeply mastering strategies. Federated learning has a high stage and springs in reachable, while we're interested in making sure that information does not leave the servers, even for training; or due to privacy issues concerning particular information. It is not viable to accumulate all neighborhood statistics inside the server records center and offer centralized education. The main concept behind FL is to test the statistics in distribution to ensure that the facts are not sent to the important server.

In FL for scalability and efficiency configuration, the communication link between the server and the corresponding device is repeated until the desired result is achieved. However, in the deep learning model of convolutional neural networks (CNNs) and multilayer perceptron (MLP) training has millions of parameters, which provides a lot of communication between the server and device. Additionally, the above restrictions cause delays in informing and updating the stakeholders.

$$f(x_1,...,x_K) = \frac{1}{K}\sum_{i=1}^{K} f_i(X_i)$$

.... (7.1)

Where
    K represents the number of nodes
    X_i is the actual view by node and it is the weight of the given model
    f is the local object function and it also explains the weight of the function.

7.1.1 Scaling Up a Federated Learning System

Expanding the performance and capacity to manage numerous devices and their interactions or data origin with the same security, efficacy, and performance can be done through the process of scaling up a federated system. To achieve this, the federated learning system needs to be completely solved, including the enhancement of technical operations as well as the company facts. Likewise, the needs and content have to be handled and looked at, and for long-term effectiveness, the federated learning system structure must be scaled up in both managerial and physical parameters.

For scaling up the federated learning system we can use a single approach where every model is trained along with multiple devices and different servers without any transfer and exchange of the row data.

Real-world federated learning software requires booming, flexible, and scalable decentralized systems that can handle scaling to large numbers of end users and large-scale models [1]. This framework ensures that these solutions are highly robust and scalable. First, use a decentralized architecture with load balancing to ensure that computing and communication loads are equal to the servers and secure blockage. It gives correct information through efficient protocols and not using other synchronous methods to ensure seamless communication between the devices and main servers. Standard compression techniques such as judging and cutting help control the size of the update and solve the problem of increasing data volume. Improving privacy protection by using different technologies to protect participants' personal information during combined learning. The scalable aggregation method helps solve the optimization problem along with decentralized and parallel methods. The cost varies depending on the difference in technology used to better the learning process (Figure 7.1).

7.1.1.1 Resources for Scaling

Resource aware clients.
Client heterogeneity.
Using 10×–1000× more clients per round.
Maximize resource utilization.
Simulate network issue.

7.1.2 Steps for Scaling Federated Learning Systems

7.1.2.1 Service-Oriented Architecture

Service-oriented architecture refers to a design in which management, actions, and decisions are distributed across multiple components, often without a single source of control or authority. It is also called distributed architecture. This approach contrasts with the centralized model, where one site or server has control over the entire system. Efficient verbal exchange protocols are paramount in this dispensed structure,

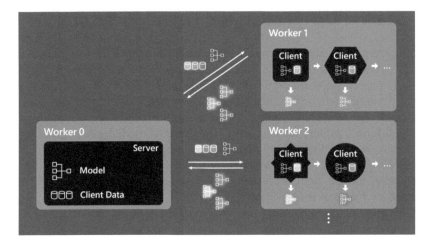

FIGURE 7.1 A scalable federated learning simulation (From 1) [1]https://www.microsoft.com/en-us/research/blog/flute-a-scalable-federated-learning-simulation-platform/

facilitating the seamless change of version updates between devices and the server. Asynchronous techniques enhance the responsiveness of interactions, allowing devices to function independently without expecting synchronous coordination. The adaptability of federated learning, an indicator of its scalability, is in addition fuelled with the aid of adaptive learning of costs that dynamically adjust to the diverse characteristics of collaborating devices.

7.1.2.2 Dynamic Node Selection

Dynamic node selection is the process in federated learning which is used to select the better and good device which are too much intelligent use to train the model. The main goal is to improve the overall efficiency, speed of integration, and functioning of the federated learning system by choosing the right equipment. Due to the increasing demand for instant responses from cloud computing services on mobile devices, federated edge learning (FEL) has emerged as a new computing model that uses edge devices to achieve effective machine learning while protecting personal data. Realization of FEL faces the problem of limited equipment and communications and uneven information distribution; this encourages some existing research to focus on the selection of tools to optimize the time spent and different types of datasets.

7.1.2.3 Batch Processing and Incremental Processing

The gradual procedure, commonly referred to as the mini-batching process, forms an essential element of batching in a federated learning system. During this procedure, the dataset is fragmented into smaller subparts, with each subpart signifying a segment of the whole data. These subparts, also known as batches, are subsequently dealt with in a sequential fashion. It is noteworthy that throughout this procedure, modifications occur to the model parameters following each mini-batch. The batch process is also called batching, the process is where multiple bits of data are combined and the grouping of the data can be used in a large group for testing. When the parts or parameters are updated then the new one is updated all batches are not updated simultaneously. To address the previous limitation, we propose a federated single mini-batch, where the user introduces the model of a single mini-batch of their data at each iteration. The main idea in batch and incremental, or mini-batch, processing is to process multiple data points simultaneously to improve the performance of training or inference operations in machine learning models. The selection of components depends on factors such as computing resources, memory limitations, and the need to compromise performance and model changes.

7.1.2.4 Parallelization Techniques

Parallelization is a technique in federated learning similar to that of a group of people working together on a project, each doing their own job without reporting directly to the other. A smart way to make your designs better, faster, and more versatile. Many small devices work together, like a team, to train smart models. Every device can provide services without sharing personal information. They divide tasks, learn faster, and keep secrets. It's like a team effort, everyone takes responsibility to build a better model. Parallelization strategies play a pivotal position in the formidable project of scaling up federated learning, in which the collaboration of several gadgets necessitates green and simultaneous processing. As the wide variety of collaborating gadgets grows, parallelization becomes vital to distribute the computational workload correctly. This technique entails dividing the training system into smaller responsibilities that can be completed concurrently on a couple of devices or servers.

7.1.2.4.1 Techniques Used Are

Device-centric parallel learning.
Non-synchronous learning.
Combined-model learning.
Simultaneous data learning.
Staged processing.

7.1.2.5 Deployment Management

Deployment management, also called resource management, is an essential technique used for scaling up federated learning. It confirms the ideal performance and is easy to use and manage the resources among the different devices. Using these resources improves the scalability and efficiency of a federated learning system. Federated learning has been explored as a promising way to train machine learning models without sharing private data. Due to limited resources, current solutions do not pay attention to the management of network resources, so new solutions need to be designed to take full advantage of software and hardware resources. From a resource management perspective, we describe recent work on a coastal management system and explore challenges and future directions that will ensure FL is successful. Resource management can combine all the scalability and efficiency records to improve the scaling up of federated learning. As federated learning scales up, effective deployment control includes strategic planning and coordination to install fashions and updates across allotted nodes. This encompasses the careful orchestration of model distribution, model control, and updates to house a wide variety of members. Efficient deployment management systems enable the continuous tracking of system performance, ensuring that the federated learning surroundings operate optimally. There are few computational resources to improve and scale up federated learning such as flexible contribution, end-user assets, information transmission, computing power, etc.

7.1.2.6 Refined Communication Protocol

In refined communication protocol communication can control the exchange of information between different clients or servers [2]. It certainly decreases the data transfer and also minimizes the data size and cleans the communication results and the reliability of the communication process.

Federated learning is a decentralized learning model that grants multiple devices or nodes to learn from local data without the need for centralized sharing. This can increase the privacy, efficiency, and effectiveness of machine learning, especially in fields such as healthcare, finance, or the universe. However, critical learning also introduces some communication problems such as network communication, latency, heterogeneity, and security. Refining communication protocols is an important thing for scaling up federated learning, especially as the range of devices taking part increases. A state-of-the-art conversation protocol guarantees positive and stable fact-trade between devices and the central server, minimizing latency and optimizing bandwidth usage. As federated learning scales, the communication protocol ought to be adaptive to varying network situations, numerous tool talents, and potential privacy issues. By refining the protocol, the system can enhance the reliability of version updates, streamline the aggregation process, and reduce communication overhead, as a result contributing to the overall performance of the federated learning atmosphere.

7.1.2.7 Personal Information Security and Network Security

Personal information security and network security are also called privacy and security. The privacy and security demanding selection due to broadcast the quality of training process. Federated learning is a new type of artificial intelligence built with distributed data and training, bringing learning to the edge or directly from the device. FL, often referred to as the new dawn of intelligence, is a new science that is currently in its infancy and does not receive much trust from the community, mainly due to security and privacy implications. In order to improve the current state of research in this field and ensure the widespread use of FL in many aspects, security and privacy issues must first be identified, observed, and recorded. FL is preferred in applications where security and privacy are important and transparency is important.

7.2 OPTIMIZATION TECHNIQUES FOR EFFICIENT COLLABORATION MODELS

This new technology solves the problems of data privacy, scalability, and communication efficiency, making it suitable for the era where big data and security are about privacy. As the field of public education continues to evolve, it should explore and identify current challenges, and suggest future directions for improvement and additional use. We also cover issues related to public education, such as effective communication, security, and organizational structure. Finally, we offer recommendations for research and technological studies that can improve public education and practices in real situations

Efficient collaboration in federated learning means optimizing various methods of the model training process to get good results while preserving the distributed and privacy-preserving nature of the framework [3]. Here are some optimization techniques for efficient collaborative models in federated learning. Optimization techniques are instrumental in ensuring the efficiency and effectiveness of collaborative models in a federated learning system. These techniques intend to display various components of the collaborative learning method, including verbal exchange performance, version update compression, and privacy maintenance. One key optimization strategy entails version compression, in which techniques including quantization and pruning are employed to reduce the scale of version updates exchanged between devices and the server. This is not the best for minimizing the bandwidth needs, however, it does speed up the overall learning system.

Another important optimization lies within the adaptive adjustment of gaining knowledge of rates. Adaptive mastering costs dynamically tailor the tempo of version updates to the unique characteristics and contributions of each participating device, making sure a green convergence of the collaborative model. Privacy-keeping techniques are integrated to protect privacy throughout the collaborative learning procedure.

Selective aggregation techniques constitute another optimization approach. These techniques prioritize high-quality updates from devices, streamlining the aggregation method and focusing on the most applicable facts.

7.2.1 Collaborative Model Averaging

Model collaboration, also known as model fusion, plays an important role in FL. It involves integrating the local design of the user interface into a global model while preserving the user's private profile [4]. However, since the accuracy and reliability of the international design depends on the selection method, it is very important to choose the appropriate method. In federated learning to collaborate the model's average, the model created by the client transfers the user's data not to the server, but to the main server, which aggregates all the models into the global model as labels. The global model is then sent back to the client and the same process continues to improve the model's performance. In this chapter, we propose three central server model aggregations, which are the average of all models (AMA), the single choice model (OMS), and the best model environment (BMA). This chapter uses a neural network model to obtain a summation by averaging the neural network coefficients model.

It is an ML technique where the learning rate is used to find the step size in the gradient descent (GD) to train on the progress of the optimization. In this method, we explore how to develop a system that combines these changes with learning in an adaptive gradient in federated learning. We proposed two algorithms to illustrate the idea behind the design of the FL switching method and how to use changing learning. We use examples to show how a simple combination of local reforms can make a difference and then show how federated learning can quickly change the adaptive system. We propose an algorithm that replaces the stochastic gradient descent (SGD) learning method to avoid the use of verification methods. The concept of adaptability from extrapolation process: to estimate the error of gradient flow based on SGD, we compare the results with one full step and two half steps.

7.2.2 Multi-device Regularization

One of the main challenges in federated learning is the different information and conflicts between users, leading to conflicts between local networks and instability of international standards. To overcome these limitations, we introduce a new architecture method created by grafting local and global subnetworks of many different networks into each local model. A model consistent with the group's hybrid approach to online knowledge distillation. The arrangement using various collaborative organizations plays a vital role in ensuring that the blocks of the local network are well aligned with the shared sub networks of the global model. Therefore, local updates at each customer make local models less differentiated from international competitors, and this change also reduces variations in the samples collected by various customers. We will then explain the details of the proposed algorithm. In federated learning, the purpose is to analyze a version over facts that are ongoing and has been generated by way of m distributed nodes. As a going for walks example, recall getting to know the sports of cell phone customers in a cell community primarily based on their man or woman sensor, text, or photograph statistics

7.2.3 Parallel Learning or MTL

Multi-task learning (MTL) is a machine learning method in which a model is trained to carry out multiple tasks at the same time. Improving overall performance by developing a better model for sharing and using cross-functional information, rather than training a separate model for each job.

Federated learning poses new challenges and physical problems when training learning models on shared devices. Our method and theory take into account, for the first time, the high cost of communication, delays, and the offense tolerance of learning many tasks. As we show through simulations of real-world data integration, the result achieves a high speed compared to other methods in the integration process.

The increase in the amount of data generated by smartphones and IoT devices has spurred the development of federated learning (FL), which is the basis for the collaboration of devices in technical standards. Initial work in FL focused on developing a global model with consistent performance for the user, but due to the variability of the local distribution, the model edge could hurt the client. Multi-task learning (MTL) networks can learn individual patterns by generating appropriate penalty problems. Penalty scores can capture the relationship between individual patterns but avoid the assumption of local distributional information. In this chapter, we propose to examine the MTL in the regime under the flexible assumption that each local distribution is a mixture of unknown distributions. This theory covers most of the existing FL algorithms and makes federated EM-like algorithms suitable for both client-server and full-scale configurations.

The formula for general multi-task learning or parallel learning is:

$$\min_{W,\Omega} \left\{ \sum_{t=1}^{m} \sum_{i=1}^{n_t} l_t(W_t^T X_i^i, y_t^i) + R(W,\Omega) \right\}$$

(7.2)

7.2.4 Modeling Compression

Model distillation, also called knowledge distillation, is the process of training small, simple examples (students) to make behavior predictions of larger, more complex examples (the teacher). The aim is to transfer the knowledge brought by the teacher to small samples and to make it more effective while continuing similar studies.

Large samples may need to transfer invalid data between server and client for training. To solve these problems, we are investigating new and innovative hybrid methods to create different models from dense networks with reduced storage and bandwidth requirements.

To solve privacy and communication issues, this point presents the FL framework as a compression model. First, the design compression framework provides an immutable, well-supported, and secure model in FL while preserving the identity of each client.

7.2.5 Adaptive Model Updating

It is the process in machine learning which is used to update or change the specific module in the data during the training of data or model [5]. Modeling updates in federated learning involves modifying model updates based on the performance, characteristics, or conditions of an individual customer in an integrated system. This approach's goal is to improve the efficiency, coordination, and overall effectiveness of the FL. The revised model is a tool for collaborative modeling. In the context of collaboration and learning in government, this approach involves updating the model. Model modification is an optimization process that can increase the flexibility, functionality, and performance of the collaboration model, especially in FL or different federated-related activities.

7.2.6 Federated Transfer Learning (FTL)

Information is often dispersed indifferent environments and they cannot be simply combined due to various legal and strategic pressures. To solve this important problem in machine learning, we launched a new technology and framework called federated transfer learning to get better statistical models based on shared data [6]. FTL enables the sharing of information without accommodating user security and enables the exchange of data connections in supervised databases, thus creating a flexible and efficient model by using rich text in the party domain.

7.2.7 Asynchronous Federated Learning

We present a new asynchronous joint optimization algorithm to improve flexibility and scalability. We show that for strongly convex and finite non-convex problem families the scheme can converge almost linearly to the global optimum [7]. The results show that the proposed algorithm converges quickly and can avoid errors in many applications.

7.2.8 Decentralized Computing and Model Saving

Edge computing means processing data close to where it is created rather than conditionally on federated cloud servers. It involves computing, storing, and processing data on local devices or edge servers, thus reducing latency and bandwidth usage.

Model deployment is the process of making a machine learning model available, typically in a production environment. Modeling in the context of edge computing refers to using machine learning models directly on edge products or edge servers for local inference.

Federated learning is used in a dispersed deep learning system where user trains their personal restricted neural network models using personal data and then combines them into a universal model of the root server. Mobile border computing aims to use mobile applications at the border of wireless fidelity. Federated learning in portable computing is a promising decentralized structure for deploying deep learning algorithms in various application cases.

7.3 COMMUNICATION AND BANDWIDTH OPTIMIZATION STRATEGIES

Communication and bandwidth optimization strategies are essential elements of the federated learning system that protect efficiency and can reduce the vestige of resources. The communication and bandwidth optimization strategies are grouped on the basis of terms and conditions related to the system or clients under the pressure of the federated learning system.

It's good to be aware of and balance communication efficiency to manage the model's accuracy and data privacy. The bandwidth optimization can decrease the data amount that can be exchanged between the different servers and the clients or devices which can be linked or work with the servers. The equipment included in this FL organization can reach millions of devices, and the bandwidth of all the equipment related to the environment may become time-consuming or ambiguous. So for this, it is continuous network and transmit during message. Due to the bandwidth and power of the equipment, the connection may be slow. Collaboration in contact between the equipment and the key server is actually an important step in the FL environment. Communication models from various communication sources download, load, and train ML models. However, this situation also brings problems. Network and transmit during message is required with customers participating in the joint venture. Communicating with customers who rely on network bandwidth and power can help make the international learning model better. Using customer-optimized systems can help reduce the overall communication costs required to implement reliable global systems. It is very important to optimize communication and save bandwidth. We can do this by making the messages sent between the device and the central server smaller and more efficient. One way is to use a compressed version of the model; this means fewer things are used to represent the model's data. We can also use methods such as differential compression to introduce significant changes to the model rather than the entire model. Another trick is to reduce the precision of the numbers in your model so that the numbers are simpler but still useful. Think of it ascending a message in a more compact form, such as using shorthand, so that the devices can share information without using too much bandwidth. There are some important strategies to optimize communication and bandwidth in federated learning.

$$s_d(i) = \sum_{i=1}^{n} \gamma_i * N_{in} \tag{7.3}$$

where

RI denotes the range of confirmed records.

s_d denotes the proportion of statistics segments.

TABLE 7.1 Evaluate Scalability and Efficiency in FL

FL ALGORITHMS	UPSTREAM AND DOWNSTREAM COMPRESSION	SCALABILITY AND PARTIAL PARTICIPATION	FEASIBILITY FOR NON-IID ENVIRONMENT
DGC, Gradient Dropping, Storm, Variance based	Upstream	Weak	Yes
TrendGrad, ATOMO, QSGD	Upstream	Weak	No
SignSGD	Both	Strong	No
Federated Averaging	**Both**	**Strong**	**No**

7.3.1 Model Size Reduction

Model size reduction is also called model compression and is used to scale down the size of the ML model without affecting its performance, usually by reducing the number of frameworks or using a more efficient representation. The aim is to make the model lighter and need less memory and computing resources. The model size reduction is particularly important in situations where limited resources (such as limited storage or bandwidth) are an issue. Although FL reduces the amount of data that needs to be sent, changing the format does not remain an issue of privacy and poor communication, especially in wireless networks. To solve privacy and communication issues, this method presents the FL framework as a compression model. First, the design compression framework provides an immutable, well-supported, and secure model in FL while preserving the identity of each client. Model size reduction is a crucial side of optimization strategies for green collaboration models in federated learning. In this context, the purpose is to reduce the size of the model being transmitted between the gadgets and the valuable server for the duration of the collaborative schooling procedure. This discount in model size addresses challenges related to bandwidth constraints, verbal exchange overhead, and the efficient usage of network sources

7.3.2 Communication Privacy

Also called differential privacy, the main goal of communication privacy is to secure when we can train the model. In federated learning and communication optimization, communication privacy can be used to reduce leaked information during model updates. This clamor guarantees that updates won't uncover subtle elements of any single device's information. By consolidating differential security, combined learning frameworks can improve the security and protection of the collaborative learning network. In communication privacy, we need to safely exchange model updates and maintain the security of individual data.

7.3.3 Storing and Predictive Loading

Also called caching and perfecting [8], in storing and predictive loading it is a part of communication and bandwidth optimization. It is used to reduce unnecessary data exchange, minimize response time, and can also increase system efficiency. The proposed caching plans in this proposal can significantly improve cache performance, effectively ensure users' security, and essentially diminish communication costs. Re-enactment tests are conducted to assess the execution of these caching plans and the exactness of the planned forecast models utilizing real-world datasets. Effective cache administration plays an imperative part in improving information speed and general productivity. This challenge has been broadly considered and connected within the setting of combined learning designing, where compelling cache administration procedures are pivotal for optimizing the execution of dispersed machine learning models.

7.3.4 Independent Updates

Also called asynchronous update, in unified learning this is an approach where devices or servers taking part in a federated learning system don't synchronize their updates at set intervals. Instead, devices freely perform neighborhood upgrades and communicate with the central server independently, submitting their updates whenever they are prepared to. In asynchronous federated learning, the server does not wait for each device to complete training on the data. In synchronous federated learning, the server waits for the end device to finish updating the model each time and then aggregates the updates into half an instance in a shared system. Most previous FL methods used a synchronous process where, with each change, the global server distributes the centralized model to the selected client and collects all updates from the clients using a weighted average strategy. For synchronization reasons, the server must wait for all local updates before being collected, so this process is expensive. The existence of lagging is inevitable due to the heterogeneity of the device and the unreliability of the network.

7.3.5 Model Subdivision

In model subdivision, we can divide the model into different workable pieces. Each piece or part contains a subset of the model specification. Dissimilar portions or parts are assigned to different devices during the federated learning process. Subdivision helps make the learning process more efficient. It's like having groups of specialized brains, each better at their own tasks, and then working together to make the whole brain smarter without adding too much pressure. It is used in federated learning processes when all the devices are disparate, have dissimilar processor performance, and the entities can change their privacy discussion. It helps to divide the learning process along with separate objects while correcting the system's scalability, efficiency, reliability, performance, etc.

Some of the models used on the FL model are autonomous updates, distribution of end points, segmentation of the model, etc.

7.3.6 Local Learning and Centralized Synthesis

Local learning and centralized synthesis are also called local training and global aggregation. It is used to allow all devices to train on their own local data which is not related to their collecting regional restoration. Federated learning is a method of training models of custom data distributed across multiple devices. To protect data privacy, global models can only be trained through communication and updating, which poses a scalability problem for large models. To this end, we present a new federated learning system that combines the study of local updates on behalf of each device and a global model for all devices. The global model can therefore be smaller as it only works on local devices, thus reducing the communication gap. Accordingly, we present a comprehensive analysis showing that the combination of local and global models can reduce differences in profiles as well as differences in product distributions. Model integration, also known as model fusion, plays an important role in FL. It involves integrating the local design of the user interface into a global model while preserving the user's privacy. However, the accuracy and reliability of the international design depend on the installation method chosen, so it is important to choose the appropriate method. Initially, simple averaging of weighted samples is the most commonly used method. However, due to limitations in processing negative samples, other methods have been investigated. Because FL is used in many areas, it is important to have a good understanding of its mounting methods, advantages, and limitations.

7.4 SUMMARY

This chapter informs of the challenges and various strategies associated with scaling up federated learning, strategies to improve the efficiency of collaboration models, and the implementation of connectivity and bandwidth optimization strategies. Federated learning's strength lies in its capacity to harness insights from numerous devices at the same time as keeping information private. Scaling up this paradigm necessitates a sophisticated infrastructure capable of accommodating an expanding array of participating gadgets. Achieving this entails the implementation of an allocated structure that lets in horizontal scaling, shelling out computational and verbal exchange masses across servers. The incorporation of green communication protocols, coupled with asynchronous strategies, guarantees seamless interactions between devices and servers. Additionally, fault-tolerant mechanisms and adaptive studying charges make a contribution to the robust scaling up of federated learning systems, making an allowance for the dynamic inclusion of an increasing number of devices. Collaborative modeling demands a nuanced set of optimization strategies to make certain of performance and effectiveness. Model compression techniques, together with quantization and pruning, play a pivotal function in decreasing the dimensions of version updates exchanged between devices and the primary server, thereby optimizing bandwidth usage. The implementation of adaptive learning costs introduces dynamism to the learning manner, making sure it adapts to the various characteristics of participating devices. Privacy-preserving techniques are vital in keeping data confidential while concurrently optimizing the collaborative learning procedure. Further, selective aggregation techniques prioritize updates, streamlining the aggregation procedure and enhancing the overall efficiency of the collaborative version. Efficient conversation and bandwidth control stand as critical additives in the fulfillment of federated learning. Lightweight communication protocols limit delays and decrease the extent of facts exchanged at some stage in the mastering process, contributing to common performance. The concept of decentralized processing allows for parallelization, efficiently dispensing the computational load and optimizing the device's overall performance. Bandwidth-saving techniques, which include version compression and selective aggregation, similarly benefit the green usage of network resources. The integration of monitoring and analytic tools presents insights into machine performance, facilitating informed selection-making to address ability bottlenecks. Continuous optimization of federated learning algorithms ensures ongoing performance in collaborative knowledge aggregation, ensuring a responsive and adaptive device.

In conclusion, the holistic success of federated learning hinges on a meticulous balance between scalability and efficiency. The elaborate interaction of scalable architectures, optimized collaborative fashions, and streamlined conversation strategies propels federated studying right into a realm wherein collaborative intelligence is harnessed seamlessly across a diverse and allotted panorama of devices.

REFERENCES

1. Liu, Y., et al., A secure federated transfer learning framework. *IEEE Intell. Syst.*, 2020. **35**(4): pp. 70–82.
2. Pouriyeh, S., et al., Secure smart communication efficiency in federated learning: Achievements and challenges. *Appl. Sci.*, 2022. **12**(18): p. 8980.
3. Chen, M., et al., Communication-efficient federated learning. *National Acad Science*, 2021. **118**(17): p. e2024789118.
4. Lyu, L., et al., Collaborative fairness in federated learning. *Privacy and Incentive*, 2020. **2020**: pp. 189–204.
5. Wang, S., et al., Adaptive federated learning in resource constrained edge computing systems. *IEEE Journal on Selected Areas in Communications*, 2019. **37**(6): pp. 1205–1221.
6. Saha, S. and T.J.I.A.Ahmad, Federated transfer learning: Concept and applications. *Intelligenza Artificiale*, 2021. **15**(1): pp. 35–44.

7. Chen, T., et al., Vafl: A method of vertical asynchronous federated learning. arXiv preprint, 2020. arXiv: 2007.06081,arziv.org, 2020
8. Djekidel, M.S., et al. Toward an efficient in-network caching using federated learning. In *2023 5th International Conference on Pattern Analysis and Intelligent Systems (PAIS)*. 2023. IEEE.

Privacy Preservation in Federated Learning

8

P. Keerthana, M. Kavitha, and Jayasudha Subburaj

8.1 INTRODUCTION

In recent years, artificial intelligence (AI) has gradually impacted every aspect of people's lives. Contemporary deep learning (DL) algorithms integrated with vast amounts of data provide deep learning (DL) technology, a potentially valuable tool for addressing real-world problems. But as added and extra deep learning applications start to appear, protecting information confidentiality is becoming a significant concern [1]. Large datasets are being gathered more frequently, which is a rising trend in both industry and academia, as artificial intelligence relies heavily on data. For the purpose of training a model, older deep learning (DL) techniques always need a sizable quantity of information, much of which contains complex data. The drill procedure is classically approved on a federal server. These elements make it more probable that concerns about security and privacy will surface throughout the learning process.

Numerous researchers have put up solutions to address privacy and security concerns, including homomorphic encryption [2], differential privacy [3], and federated learning. Google initially presented the federated learning prototype in 2016 [4]. Federated learning was originally implemented, according to Google, on the Google Keyboard, primarily for two reasons: to safeguard handlers' private information and to enhance the quality of the verbal model [5].

In today's data-driven world, most apps and services, such as those related to healthcare and medicine, autonomous cars, and finance, are powered by artificial intelligence (AI) technology and complex machine learning (ML) algorithms. According to predictions, artificial intelligence will "change the world more than anything in the history of mankind" and has already made strides in all facets of human existence. Centralized storage and computing are among the major reasons why AI technology has not yet realized its complete possibility and why the realization of such applications has met with persistent difficulties.

The overwhelming majority of real-world situations include the generation and storage of data, especially personal data, in data silos that are either the data centers of service providers or the devices of end users. Training data must be combined on a data server as the majority of old-style machine learning is tracked in a central manner. In essence, it takes work to gather, aggregate, and integrate heterogeneous data scattered across several information foundations, by way of steadily managing and then handling the information. Conveying high speeds, veracity, and volumes of heterogenous data between organizations presents a number of challenges, not the least of which are the industry competition, the intricate administrative processes, and, most importantly, information security rules and guidelines such as the EU's General Data Protection Regulation (GDPR). Important information collecting and dispensation at a potent cloud server in classical machine learning algorithms carries the danger of a single point of failure and serious data breaches. First and foremost, the system's poor transparency and provenance resulting from centralized data processing and administration may cause end users to lose faith in the system and make GDPR compliance more challenging.

Federated learning (FL) has garnered interest from academia and industry as a potential means of addressing these issues. Generally speaking, FL is a method for implementing machine learning algorithms in decentralized collaborative learning environments. Instead of gathering and processing training data at a central data server, the algorithm is run on several local datasets kept at separate data sources, or local nodes, such as PCs, wearables, tablets, and smartphones. FL keeps the training dataset and computation at internal sites while enabling local nodes to cooperatively train a shared ML model. A central server is needed to coordinate the training process (centralized FL) or use a peer-to-peer underlying network infrastructure (decentralized FL) to aggregate the training results and compute the global model since only the training results (i.e., parameters) are exchanged at a specific frequency [6].

Due to the difficulties in adhering to stringent data protection laws governing the extensive collection and processing of personal data, the conventional cloud-centric machine learning algorithms are no longer appropriate in many situations. The majority of individual information is created at the periphery via end-user devices (such as wearables, smartphones, and tablets), which are outfitted with progressively more potent computational power and Internet access. Owing to the extensive use of these individual devices and the increasing privacy concerns, decentralized artificial intelligence (AI) has become popular.

FL is another cloud-centered machine learning technique which allows collaborative training of ML models while maintaining unique individual information on devices, potentially mitigating issues connected to data privacy. Normal distributed learning assumes that local training datasets on compute nodes are equally distributed and have about equal sizes. This is where FL differs from normal distributed learning.

8.1.1 Background of Distributed Machine Learning

In the context of big data, distributed ML systems and methods have been the subject of much research recently. To shorten the total model training time, previous research has either focused on the actual system features or the theoretical convergence speed of suggested techniques. Among the earliest distributed machine learning algorithms are bulk synchronous parallel (BSP) algorithms. These techniques have a meeting rapidity which is comparable to conventional synchronic and central gradient algorithms because of hash limits on the computation and communication processes.

A more workable option is the stale synchronous parallel (SSP) algorithm, which does away with rigorous iteration boundaries and permits workers to be out of synchronization for a predetermined amount of time. Actually, SSP is now at the core of many kinds of distributed parameter server designs that are in use today. Four tiers can be distinguished in distributed machine learning systems, contingent upon the division of the task.

Data sharing – level 0: Each user will upload its private or anonymized data to a central server after gathering and preparing it locally. The server determines the combined data to finish the knowledge assignment.

Sharing model – level 1: Each user equipments (UE) has the ability to create a local machine learning model using its own data, as opposed to uploading data directly, and then the trained model is shared to the server.

information exchange – Level 2: The knowledge that is extracted after exercise resident information, such as the relationships among various qualities, is shared further, in contrast to sharing machine learning models.

Sharing results – Level 3: Each model merely transmits results or outputs to the main server, the task training is entirely locally processed.

Different types of information, such as data or models, are generated and locally processed on devices on the local plane before being sent to a central server for combination. A detailed description is given of the four tiers of the planned circulated learning outline, which are represented by representative machine learning approaches and include distribution data, allocation models, distribution knowledge, and allotment results.

8.1.2 Existing Distributed Learning Frameworks

There are several existing distributed learning frameworks that facilitate the training of machine learning models across multiple devices or servers. Keep in mind that the landscape of distributed learning frameworks is dynamic, and new frameworks may have emerged since writing. Here are some prominent distributed learning frameworks.

TABLE 8.1 Distributed Learning Frameworks in the Market

FRAMEWORK	PURPOSE
TensorFlow Federated (TFF)	Established by Google, TensorFlow is an exposed source framework specifically designed for federated learning. It permits the working out of machine learning models across dispersed devices while addressing confidentiality concerns.
Apache Spark MLlib	Apache Spark MLlib is a portion of the Apache Spark project and offers dispersed machine learning capabilities. It allows for scalable machine learning on a cluster, supporting a variety of algorithms for classification, regression, and clustering.
PySyft	PySyft is a Python library for encrypted, privacy-preserving machine learning. It offers capabilities for safe multi-party computation and federated learning and is constructed on top of well-known deep learning frameworks such as PyTorch and TensorFlow.
Leaf	Leaf is an open-source federated learning framework that provides a simple interface for researchers and developers to experiment with and deploy federated learning systems.
PaddleFL	PaddleFL is a federated learning framework developed by PaddlePaddle, an open-source deep learning platform. It supports collaborative model training while preserving data privacy.
SyferText	An extension of PySyft, SyferText is a privacy-preserving natural language processing (NLP) library. It enables the training of NLP models across decentralized data sources using federated learning.
FLAME	Federated learning framework (FLAME) is an open-source federated learning framework that supports various machine learning models and is designed for use in edge computing environments.
PyTorch/Federated	PyTorch/Federated is an extension of PyTorch that enables federated learning. It allows users to define models and training procedures for decentralized training across multiple devices.
Microsoft Federated Learning (MS FL)	Developed by Microsoft, this framework focuses on enabling federated learning scenarios. It integrates with the Microsoft machine learning framework and provides tools for privacy-preserving machine learning.
Horovod	Horovod is an open-source distributed deep learning framework developed by Uber. It's intended to scale the training of deep neural networks across multiple GPUs and servers, using techniques such as ring-all for efficient communication.

8.2 LITERATURE REVIEW

Weaknesses in privacy are among the most common concerns with traditional machine learning. Businesses in the industrial sector make investments to safeguard their intellectual property. Nevertheless, conventional machine learning (ML) and deep learning model optimization frequently violate those privacy criteria. In order to train, validate, and test models, it is necessary to keep potentially massive quantities of data close to the large processing power. In order to avoid data leaks or assaults, critical data sets like these need to be coordinated and consolidated at a high-security level [7]. But there are still threats. Thus, security hazards exist in the typical ML technique, necessitating the search for alternatives. Federated learning suggests a novel architecture as a solution to these problems in order to restrict data transfers and, as a result, the data footprint. Even though federated learning is applied in the majority of circumstances, investigators showed that numerous issues still need to be resolved. For instance, a great deal of research has shown that, in many real-world circumstances, federated learning, which was initially designed to safeguard privacy, is more susceptible to attacks by malevolent nodes than traditional deep learning frameworks. Since the parameters are the only information collected by a federated learning server—the client's identity is kept private—the anonymous clients can be comprised by attackers who upload malicious data to the server [8].

It is possible to provide machine learning that protects privacy by employing encryption based on ring learning with errors (RLWE). However, there are a number of difficulties in putting this strategy into practice in real-world applications. One such difficulty is that RLWE-based encryption has significant computational and communication overhead, which can lead to long training durations. Moreover, there has not yet been a thorough analysis of the security guarantees of RLWE-based encryption in the particular setting of machine learning applications [9]. For Internet of Drones (IoD) contexts, Pu et al. [10] introduce PMAP, a lightweight, privacy-preserving mutual authentication and key agreement system. In order to provide mutual authentication and secure session keys between communication entities in Internet of devices (IoD) systems, PMAP uses physical unclonable functions (PUF) and chaotic systems. Comparing PMAP to the current authentication and key algorithm (AKA) and IBE-Lite (a standard policy or scheme) schemes, their evaluation demonstrates PMAP's superior performance in terms of computing cost, energy consumption, and communication overhead as well as its resilience to security assaults [11].

Using the delay differential cell (DD-Cell) as an entropy source, Sala et al. [12] present a re-configurable architecture that combines a physical unclonable function (PUF) with a true random number generator (TRNG) on an Field Programmable Gate Arrays (FPGAs) platform. In comparison to previous PUF+TRNG architectures, their work provides a favorable trade-off between PUF and TRNG performance, demonstrating competitive results in compactness and TRNG throughput. On the other hand, our study addresses a distinct facet of Internet of Things security by putting forth a multi-key cryptography that is both lightweight and privacy-preserving. This ensures that data remains secret during transmission and aggregation procedures in untrusted environments [13].

8.3 PRIVACY CHALLENGES IN DISTRIBUTED LEARNING

8.3.1 Privacy Preservation in Federated Learning

Privacy preservation is a crucial aspect of federated learning, a machine learning approach that enables model training across decentralized devices or servers holding local data samples without exchanging them. The following are some key techniques and considerations for privacy preservation in federated learning.

- Homomorphic encryption (HE)
  HE protects user privacy by swapping parameters within the encryption mechanism. In HE, the processes required to handle the original data are employed to encrypt it into ciphertext. This procedure manipulates the plaintext without requiring decryption; it is comparable to linear algebraic operations. The model or data are not shared and cannot be deduced from the opposing model's data.

- Secure multi-party computation (SMC)
  SMC works with several parties or clients that provide private inputs to collaboratively compute individual data or inputs while upholding total confidentiality. By using secure two-party computing (2PC), SecureML allows data owners to encrypt, process, and secretly distribute their data over two non-colluding servers. It is included in the two server-model category and allows each client to train different models on their combined data without sharing anything except the results. However, doing so comes with a significant processing and communication burden, which can discourage participants from working together. This approach is a fast, safe, fault-tolerant protocol for secure aggregation that was proposed by [3].

- Secret sharing
  Secret sharing is a cryptography technique that guarantees that a secret consists of N shares and that it can only be rebuilt if a sufficient number of shares are linked. These methods have been used in traditional methods. The method shows how to divide a data (or secret) S into n pieces so that S can be easily reconstructed from any m pieces; yet, even knowing every detail about any $m - 1$ piece doesn't reveal anything about S. Strong key management schemes for cryptographic systems that can continue to function safely and dependably can be built using this technology. The SMC protocol's offline phase is rather complex, and the system was initially intended to secure aggregate gradients.

8.3.2 Privacy Attack

While distributed learning offers several advantages, it also poses unique privacy challenges. In distributed learning, "privacy attacks" refer to methods or strategies that can be used to get unwanted access to private data from a machine learning model or the training set of data. Malicious actors attempting to access sensitive or confidential data for illicit purposes or lawful users who could unintentionally jeopardize the data's privacy can both carry out these assaults. We will look at a few of the prevalent privacy threats that have been found in relation to distributed learning in the sections that follow. The following are some key privacy attacks associated with distributed learning.

8.3.2.1 Model Inversion Attack

This technique involves training an inversion model—a different kind of machine learning model—on the target model's (your model's) output first. Predicting the input data, or the original dataset, for the target model is the responsibility of the inversion model. Through the analysis of the predictions made by the inversion model, the attacker might uncover details about the data subject that you had not intended for the target model to disclose.

Differential privacy, federated learning, and safe multi-party computing are a few security mechanisms that can stop these attacks:

- **Differential privacy:** It is a method of safeguarding individual privacy by inflating data with noise. This method makes sure that no personally identifiable data points are disclosed in the model's result. Differential privacy offers a statistical assurance that data privacy is safeguarded by introducing noise into the data.
- **Federated learning:** By using this security method, several devices may work together to train a machine learning model without disclosing their personal information to a single server. Federated learning involves the devices updating their local models encrypted and sending them to a central server, which combines the modifications and transmits a new global model. This method protects the privacy of the data by making sure that it stays on the devices and is not accessible by the central server.
- **Safe multi-party computing:** Through the use of this approach, several parties can collaboratively compute a function on their private data without disclosing any information about it to one another. Every participant encrypts their data before sharing it with the others in a safe multi-party computation. To get the intended outcome, the parties then compute the encrypted data without disclosing any personal information.

8.3.2.2 Model Stealing Attack

The model-stealing attack technique is used in ML-as-a-service to compromise confidential machine learning models. Orekondy et al., (2019) proposed the knockoff attack framework in which the attacker attacks the model's architecture, sampling approach, and data distribution, which may differ from the victim's selections. The authors demonstrated that when the attacker utilized training data that was comparable to the victim's model, and models with a higher learning capacity than the victim's model, the attack model's prediction performance increased. Recent research by [14] demonstrated that the prediction performance of the attack model could be enhanced by a novel kind of model stealing assault in which the attacker could utilize both the victim's prediction output and its interpretation.

It is expensive to train a model because it requires gathering a large number of pertinent samples, preparing data to address a particular issue, identifying an efficient machine learning model, and giving it the processing power it needs. What if, with no work on your part, a rival could just take this model that you have just designed? This kind of assault is referred to as a model extraction or model theft attack. Similar to several adversarial assaults in practice, it operates by utilizing samples to query the target model and use the model's replies to create a duplicate model. When used in a black-box setup, it can:

- Duplicate a functional, efficient model at a reasonable cost.
- Duplicate the model to make it easier to develop alternative assaults (adversarial reprogramming, membership inference, adversarial sampling, etc.).

8.3.2.3 Membership Inference Attacks

One method for identifying the data used to train a machine learning model is "membership inference". By just viewing the output of the machine learning model, an attacker may frequently launch membership inference attacks without gaining access to the model's parameters. Where the target model has been trained on sensitive data, membership inference may give rise to security and privacy issues.

8.3.2.4 Data Exfiltration

Data exfiltration usually entails a cybercriminal using several cyberattack techniques to take data from business or personal devices, such as computers and mobile phones. The theft or unlawful removal or transport of any data from a device is a typical definition of data exfiltration. Organizations should be able to stop data exfiltration in addition to identifying possible threats and shielding people, systems, and data from security breaches without compromising efficiency or performance. With the rise of remote and mobile working in the modern workforce, this has gotten harder and harder. As a result, organizations need to make sure that private information doesn't end up on anonymous servers in areas where cyberattacks are common. They should also stop data from being transferred illegally to third-party servers, which are increasingly being used as the source of modern cyberattacks.

8.3.2.5 Data Poisoning Attacks

Data poisoning is a kind of assault that is growing increasingly common as malicious actors have access to new tools and more processing power. Even though data poisoning was originally encountered more than 15 years ago, it has subsequently evolved into the most significant weakness in AI and machine learning. For instance, there have been several compromises of Google's anti-spam systems. Malevolent individuals manipulated the spam definition and tainted the algorithm, allowing malicious emails to get past the filter.

Companies should anticipate a rise in data poisoning assaults by 2024 given the growing popularity and use of new machine learning and artificial intelligence techniques. Keeping that in mind, let us examine this issue in more detail and discuss how businesses may be ready for it.

8.3.3 Privacy Risk in Distributed Machine Learning

8.3.3.1 Threat Modeling

Threat modeling is crucial in federated learning to identify and address potential risks to the privacy and security of the distributed learning system. Distributed machine learning participants may be hostile or inquisitive [15]. An auto insurance provider with few user attributes, for instance, might aim to enhance its risk assessment model by adding more characteristics of other companies, such as banks, tax offices, etc. The other participants' only responsibility is to contribute more feature details without giving out their personal information to other players in order to earn prizes in the form of money or goodwill. On the other hand, rivals might pose as allies before harming the training model or stealing the machine learning model. Here are some key components of threat models in federated learning:

1. **Attackers:**
    - **Outsider attack:** Malevolent parties or hackers that operate outside of the federated learning system and try to get illegal access, jeopardize the privacy of models, or interfere with the learning process.
    - **Insider attack:** Users of the federated learning system who have the malevolent intent to exploit weaknesses or divulge private information, such as device owners or organizations.
2. **Sybil Attacks:**
    - A Sybil attack operates many active false identities (also known as Sybil identities) concurrently on a single node in a peer-to-peer network. By obtaining the majority of influence within the network, this kind of assault seeks to weaken the authority or power in a reliable system. This impact is provided by false identities. Threat actors can access the system and carry out unlawful acts if a Sybil assault is successful. For instance, it makes it possible for a single entity, such as a computer, to establish and

manage several identities, including user accounts and accounts based on IP addresses. These phony identities deceive users and systems into thinking they are real. Sybil attacks can be prevented by identity validation (direct validation and indirect validation), social trust graphs, etc.

3. **Collusion Risks:**
   - **Collusion among participants:** Coordinated actions taken by participants to pool data and obtain more insights than planned, possibly at the expense of privacy.

8.3.3.2 Adversarial Models

A machine learning approach called adversarial machine learning seeks to trick models by providing them with erroneous data. As such, it addresses both the generation and identification of hostile samples, i.e., inputs designed specifically to deceive classifiers. These attacks are referred to as adversarial machine learning, and a number of domains, including spam detection and picture classification, have seen a substantial amount of studies on them. The most extensive study on adversarial machine learning has been conducted in the field of image recognition, where modifications are applied to images that cause a classifier to provide erroneous predictions. Businesses are discovering that as machine learning swiftly becomes an essential part of their value offering, safeguarding it is becoming more and more crucial. As a result, adversarial machine learning is becoming a more significant issue in the software industry.

Google, Microsoft, and IBM have started to invest in the security of machine learning systems. Businesses such as Google, Amazon, Microsoft, Tesla, and others who have lately made large investments in machine intelligence have also seen aggressive assaults. There is a vast array of variants in adversarial attacks against machine learning systems. Traditional machine learning techniques include linear regression and support vector machines (SVMs), both of which are often utilized in deep learning systems. This section of contentious machine learning looks at a class of attacks intended to make classifiers less effective on particular tasks. Most adversarial attacks may be divided into three groups:

1. Poisoning attacks
2. Evasion attacks model
3. Extraction attacks

8.3.3.2.1 Poisoning Attacks

The attacker manipulates the labels or training data to make the model perform poorly when it is deployed. Therefore, poisoning is just the act of an adversary contaminating training data. Since operational data can be used to retrain machine learning (ML) systems, an attacker could taint the data by adding malicious samples, which would disrupt or impair retraining.

8.3.3.2.2 Evasion Attacks

Evasion assaults are the most prevalent and extensively researched type of attack. The attacker manipulates the data during deployment in order to deceive classifiers that have previously undergone training. Since they occur during the deployment phase, these are the most effective attack types and the ones that are used most commonly in malware and intrusion scenarios. Attackers usually obscure the content of spam emails or malware in an attempt to evade detection. Since samples are classified as legitimate while having no impact on the training set, they are therefore modified to evade detection. Evasion is exemplified by attempts to spoof biometric verification systems.

8.3.3.2.3 Extraction Attacks

An attacker can probe a black box machine learning system to retrieve the data it was trained on or reconstruct the model. This technique is recognized as model extraction or model stealing. This is particularly significant if the model itself or the training data is sensitive. An attacker may utilize model extraction attacks, for example, to take advantage of a stock market prediction model and utilize it for their own financial gain.

8.4 DIFFERENTIAL PRIVACY TECHNIQUES

Differential privacy is a notion used in data analysis and machine learning to preserve privacy while enabling the extraction of valuable information from the data. The main goal is to give firm assurances that the inclusion or exclusion of any particular person's data will not materially affect a model's or statistical analysis's result. The following is an outline of differential privacy's operation.

The core idea of differential privacy is to add controlled noise to the output of a function or analysis, ensuring that the impact of any individual's data is indistinguishable within a certain privacy parameter. The mechanism is defined as follows:

$$Pr[M(D) \in S] \leq e\epsilon \times Pr[M(D') \in S] \quad (8.1)$$

Where

- M is the function or analysis applied to the data.
- D and D' differ in at most one individual's data.
- S is the set of possible outputs.
- ϵ is the privacy parameter, representing the near privacy guard (lower ϵ provides stronger privacy).

8.4.1 Steps in Achieving Differential Privacy

Step 1 – Determine sensitivity: Analyze the sensitivity of the function or analysis being done on the data in order to determine its sensitivity.

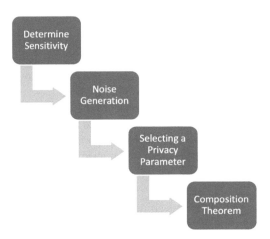

FIGURE 8.1 Steps in achieving differential privacy

Step 2 – Noise generation: To reduce the impact of any one person's data, add randomly chosen noise that has been precisely tuned to the computation.

Step 3 – Selecting a privacy parameter: Select the suitable privacy parameter (ϵ) according to the required degree of privacy. Stronger privacy is offered by smaller values of ϵ, but noisier outputs are possible.

Step 4 – Composition theorem: To make sure that the total privacy stays within the intended constraints, apply the composition theorem to a series of computations.

Federated learning is a machine learning approach where a model is trained across decentralized edge devices (such as smartphones or IoT devices) without exchanging raw data samples. Differential privacy plays a crucial role in federated learning to ensure the privacy of individual user's data.

Here are some differential privacy techniques applied in federated learning:

1. **Federated averaging with differential privacy (DP-FedAvg)**
   - The idea of differential privacy is utilized in machine learning and data analysis to protect privacy while making it possible to extract useful information from the data. The primary objective is to provide definite guarantees that the inclusion or omission of any specific individual's data will not significantly impact the outcome of a computation or statistical analysis.

2. **Differentially private stochastic gradient descent (DP-SGD) in federated learning**
   - Differential privacy can be incorporated into the optimization algorithm used in federated learning, such as stochastic gradient descent (SGD). DP-SGD adds noise to the inclines calculated on each local device before updating the global model. This helps in achieving differential privacy during the training process.

3. **Privacy-preserving aggregation techniques**
   - Techniques such as secure aggregation are employed to protect the privacy of local updates during the aggregation phase. This involves encrypting the local model updates before they are sent to the central server for aggregation, preventing the server from learning individual updates.

4. **DP-federated learning with shuffling**
   - Shuffling the order of model updates before aggregation helps in providing additional privacy guarantees. This prevents the central server from linking specific updates to individual devices, making it more challenging to infer information about individual data points.

5. **Homomorphic encryption in federated learning**
   - Homomorphic encryption allows the aggregation of encrypted model updates without decrypting them. This ensures that the central server never sees the raw model updates or individual user data during the federated learning process.

6. **Local differential privacy in federated learning**
   - Local differential privacy techniques can be applied at the local level on each device before any data is shared with the central server. This ensures that individual contributions are protected before they are used to update the global model.

7. **Noise injection in model updates**
   - Similar to DP-SGD, the addition of noise directly to the model before updating helps to achieve differential privacy in federated learning. This can be done by adding Laplace or Gaussian noise to the model parameters.

8. **Dynamic privacy budget allocation**
   - In federated learning scenarios, the dynamic allocation of privacy budgets ensures that each participating device's contribution is appropriately protected. This involves adjusting the amount of noise added before the local updates and maintaining privacy.

9. **Asynchronous federated learning algorithm**
   - When creating a new asynchronous federated learning algorithm, a number of criteria need to be taken into account, including robustness to asynchrony, communication efficiency, and convergence speed.

10. **Secure multi-party computation (SMPC)**
    - SMPC allows multiple participants to jointly compute a function over the inputs, thus protecting their privacy. The parties collaborate to finish computations without sharing any personal information.

The choice of differential privacy techniques in federated learning depends on the specific necessities of the application, the level of privacy desired, and the characteristics of the data involved. Balancing privacy with model accuracy is an ongoing challenge, and researchers continue to explore new methods and improvements in this domain.

8.5 SECURE-AGGREGATION FOR PRIVACY-PRESERVING MODELS

In federated learning (FL), when participants contribute their local models to a central server, secure aggregation is an essential technique to guarantee the privacy of model updates. Allowing the aggregate of model updates while keeping the raw contributions from each individual member hidden is the aim. Clients engage in federated learning by training local models on their personal data and sending updates to a central server. In conventional aggregation, the global model is updated by averaging these updates.

8.5.1 Challenges

Sensitive information about the local data of specific users may be deduced by an attacker with access to the communication channel or the central server if model changes are sent in clear text.

- **Computational overhead:** Using completely homomorphic encryption might result in a considerable increase in computational overhead. Effective optimizations and implementations are essential.
- **Communication overhead:** There may be an increase in communication overhead when sending and processing encrypted data. Effective procedures are required to lessen this effect.
- **Key management**: Ensuring the security of the encryption and decryption procedures requires proper key management.

8.5.2 Secure Aggregation Steps in Federated Learning

Secure aggregation in federated learning involves ensuring that the model updates contributed by individual devices are aggregated in a way that the central server cannot learn the specifics of any individual update. Techniques such as secure multi-party computation (SMPC) or homomorphic encryption can be employed for secure aggregation as shown in Figure 5.1.

Privacy Preservation in FL

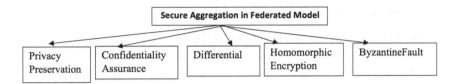

FIGURE 8.2 Secure aggregation

8.5.2.1 Training Model on Local Devices

Using its own data, each participating device, such as an IoT device or smartphone trains a local model.

8.5.2.2 Local Model Update

All devices create a model update using its local data following local training. The model's parameter adjustments from the training phase are usually included in this update.

8.5.2.3 Encryption

Using cryptographic methods, each participant encrypts its model update. For this kind of application, homomorphic encryption is frequently employed. The privacy of each update is preserved by homomorphic encryption, which allows calculations to be completed on encrypted information without having to first decode it.

8.5.2.4 Aggregation on Encrypted Data

Aggregation (such as averaging) is carried out directly on the encrypted data by the central server, which also gathers the encrypted model updates. The aggregate result can be computed by the server without requiring it to be decoded with each individual update.

8.5.2.5 Decryption of the Aggregated Data

- The decryption key is stored securely to prevent the central server from discovering the specifics of individual updates. The aggregated result is decrypted to acquire the final global model update after the aggregation is finished.
- Thanks to homomorphic encryption, mathematical operations can be carried out on encrypted data while maintaining the encryption of the resulting information.
- Since fully homomorphic encryption allows addition and multiplication to be performed on encrypted data, it is especially strong.

8.5.2.6 Homomorphic Encryption

- **Partially homomorphic encryption (PHE):** Confirms that only one kind of operation (multiplication or addition) can be performed on encrypted data.
- **Somewhat homomorphic encryption (SHE):** Permits a restricted set of addition and multiplication operations to be evaluated on encrypted data.
- **Full homomorphic encryption (FHE):** Encrypted data can be subjected to an infinite number of addition and multiplication operations. Although FHE requires more computing, it is also more potent.

8.5.2.7 Blockchain Technology

- Blockchain technology's decentralization, security, credibility, and tamper-proof ability allow it to monitor the harmful behavior of servers or devices in federated learning and guarantee the transparency of the training process, offering a novel approach to privacy protection
- Deep-chain architecture was suggested in the literature. It integrates blockchain with secure aggregation protocols to track and audit the whole federated learning process as well as guarantee the secrecy and accuracy of local parameters throughout the communication.
- The value-driven system encourages everyone to participate fairly in cooperative training. However, blockchain technology itself continues to have issues with low scalability and low throughput, making it challenging for these approaches to serve large-scale applications in real-world settings and raising doubts about their efficacy.

8.6 CONCLUSION

The increasing amount of data in distributed systems may be efficiently utilized by the rapidly developing field of distributed learning technology. However, the development of this technology has increased worries about user security and privacy when participating in the learning process. As a result, we first concentrated on looking at the security and privacy issues that come with distributed machine learning in our study. We then carried out a thorough analysis of all the protective strategies that have been proposed in the literature to counter these kinds of attacks. In addition, this assessment delineated the distinct attributes of attackers throughout several tiers of distributed learning systems, delineating multiple research obstacles and plausible avenues for further inquiries into this domain. Continuous innovation and research are essential to improving privacy-preserving methods as distributed learning progresses, guaranteeing the responsible and moral use of machine learning models in decentralized settings. We discovered via theoretical analysis that our approach accomplishes the ciphertext operable function, solves the fundamental system security problem, and realizes two revocation functions. Compared to previous systems, the computational complexity is better while achieving user privacy. Furthermore, by offloading some of the decryption work to the cloud server, our technique may effectively minimize the number of requests sent to users. As a result, our plan may increase productivity while simultaneously guaranteeing privacy. Next, we want to preserve huge data in the Internet of Things in a distributed storage environment by combining the benefits of blockchain's anonymity and decentralization. Differential privacy is a key concept that ensures that aggregated model modifications do not inadvertently expose individual contributions. Safe aggregation methods, such as homomorphic encryption and safe multi-party computing, enable collaborative learning without revealing raw data. Devices may calculate and exchange just the necessary model updates thanks to federated averaging algorithms and local model updates, which minimizes the exposure of sensitive data. In summary, the privacy issues associated with distributed learning are a careful balancing act between the security of individual data inputs and cooperative model training. To tackle these issues, differential privacy, secure aggregation methods, and local model updating techniques are essential elements. In future the privacy protection algorithms can be used such as central protection, local protection, and combined central and local protection techniques.

REFERENCES

1. McMahan B, Moore E, Ramage D, Hampson S, Arcas y B A. Communication-efficient learning of deep networks from decentralized data. In *Proceedings of Artificial Intelligence and Statistics*, 1273–1282, 2017.
2. Leroy D, Coucke A, Lavril T, et al. Federated learning for keyword spotting. In *Proceedings of IEEE International Conference on Acoustics, Speech and Signal Processing*. 6341–6345, 2019.
3. Shokri R, Shmatikov V. Privacy-preserving deep learning. In *Proceedings of the 22nd ACM SIGSAC Conference on Computer and Communications Security*, 1310–1321, 2015.
4. Fallah A, Mokhtari A, Ozdaglar A. Personalized federated learning with theoretical guarantees: a modelagnostic meta-learning approach. *Advances in Neural Information Processing Systems*, 33, 1–122020.
5. Li Z, He S, Chaturvedi P, et al. APPFLx: Providing privacy-preserving cross-silo federated learning as a service. In *2023 IEEE 19th International Conference on e-Science (e-Science)*, Limassol, Cyprus, 1–4, 2023.
6. Kavitha M, Sujaritha M. A sensitive wavebands identification system for smart farming, *Computer Systems Science and Engineering*, 43(1), 245–257, 2022.
7. Mistry D, Mridha M F, Safran M, et al. Privacy-preserving on-screen activity tracking and classification in e-learning using federated learning. *IEEE Access*, 11, 79315–79329, 2023.
8. Ghimire B, Rawat D B. Recent advances on federated learning for cybersecurity and cybersecurity for federated learning for internet of things. *IEEE Internet of Things Journal*, 9(11), 8229–8249, 2022.
9. Lyubashevsky V, Peikert C, Regev O. On ideal lattices and learning with errors over rings. In *Proceedings of the Advances in Cryptology—EUROCRYPT 2010*, Berlin/Heidelberg, Germany: Springer, 1–23, 2010.

10. Pu C, Wall A, Choo K-K R, et al. A lightweight and privacy-preserving mutual authentication and key agreement protocol for internet of drones environment. *IEEE Internet Things Journal*, 9, 9918–9933, 2022.
11. Li T, Sahu A K, Talwalkar A, Smith, V. Federated learning: challenges, methods, and future directions. *IEEE Signal Processing Magazine*, 37(3), 50–60, 2020.
12. Sala R D, Scotti G. Exploiting the DD-Cell as an ultra-compact entropy source for an FPGA-based re-configurable PUF-TRNG architecture. *IEEE Access*, 11, 86178–86195, 2023.
13. Tribhuvanesh O, Bernt S, Mario F. Knockoff nets: Stealing functionality of blackbox models. In *CVPR*, 2019.
14. Milli S, Schmidt L, Dragan A, Hardt M. Model reconstruction from model explanations. In *Proceedings of the Conference on Fairness, Accountability, and Transparency*, 2019.
15. Reddy G P, Pavan Kumar Y V. A beginner's guide to federated learning. In *2023 Intelligent Methods, Systems, and Applications (IMSA)*, Giza, Egypt, 557–562, 2023.

Federated Learning

Trust, Fairness, and Accountability

9

Sana Daud

9.1 INTRODUCTION

Over the course of the last decade, artificial intelligence (AI) has seen substantial development and advancement [1]. Notable AI systems that gained prominence upon their first introduction include Big Blue, ImageNet, and Alpha Go. They facilitated the creation of newer software applications such as ChatGPT, DALL·E 2, and Tesla Autopilot. Deep learning models and computers have the ability to do several jobs that are within the capabilities of humans. They possess the ability to perceive visual and auditory stimuli, create visual art, operate a vehicle, participate in interactive electronic entertainment, and do more activities. The most captivating aspect of AI once resided in enhancing its speed and intelligence. However, now, intelligence alone is inadequate. In recent years, there has been a notable increase in accidents, as well as other occurrences where artificial intelligence (AI) has made errors resulting in harm to individuals. Machine learning/deep learning (ML/DL) algorithms used to predict recidivism rates before trial are facing issues. Similarly, AI-driven applications may provide inaccurate responses to fundamental inquiries and encounter challenges [2], while self-driving vehicle prototypes may lack the necessary training or readiness to handle infrequent but fatal scenarios [3]. The reliability of responsible AI (RAI) [4] has been diminished because of the aforementioned occurrences, causing people to express concerns. Terms such as "strong AI", "fair AI", "ethical AI", "explainable AI" (XAI), and others are already in existence [5]. Reliable artificial intelligence is an innovative idea introduced by RAI. The European Union formulated the AI Act in 2021 [6]. The purpose of this is to provide guidance to developers of AI systems on objectives and the methods they should use in order to gain trust [7]. The rules outline three essential activities that an AI system must consistently do. First, the artificial intelligence (AI) must undergo government approval and adhere to specified rules. The second objective should be to ensure that individuals adhere to values. Finally, it is essential for AI to perform well in both real-world scenarios and digital interfaces. Expanding upon these three fundamental concepts, reliable AI systems should abide by four ethical guidelines: safeguarding people's privacy, honoring their entitlement to privacy, ensuring equitable treatment, and offering an explanation. The European Commission formulated the following seven criteria with the aim of fostering confidence in AI among people [5, 8].

- Human decision-making and supervision;
- Enhanced durability and protection against potential risks;
- Data governance and confidentiality;
- Transparency;
- Principles of fairness, impartiality, and inclusivity;
- The health of the planet and its inhabitants;
- Assuming responsibility.

Specialists have formulated detailed recommendations, in addition to those provided by the European Commission, to ensure the reliable functioning of AI systems and establish their legitimacy. Extensive investigation on reliable AI [8, 5] has identified the fundamental attributes of trustworthy AI as explanatory capability, robustness, prudence, and accountability. While faith in AI is not the only determinant in today's context, it remains crucial. Individuals also want to maintain the confidentiality and safety of their personal data. Consequent to this condition, new rules and regulations have been developed. Two notable examples of recent data protection legislation are the General Data Protection Regulation (GDPR) in the European Union and the California Consumer Privacy Act (CCPA) in the state of California in the United States [9]. Several ML/DL models are trained by utilizing data that is distributed across different groups and updated independently in isolated silos by those organizations. As a result, AI systems are affected by these legislative developments. Federated learning (FL) was introduced by Google in 2016 as a means to safeguard AI data. FL is an independent model designed for machine learning. Although members of a federation have the ability to cooperate with FL, each member has authority over their own confidential information, which stays inside the federation. Presently, the act of publicly disseminating data is prohibited by law, and it is mandatory for every individual to own a personal copy of the information [10]. These principles may exacerbate the issues of data silos and fragmentation. Florida provides a viable answer to these issues. Reliability is of utmost importance in Florida when it comes to dealing with privacy issues, protecting the aggregation process, promoting cooperation, maintaining responsibility and supervision, and building user confidence. By adhering to these standards, individuals may engage in collaborative machine learning projects that effectively protect privacy via various means. Utmost standards of confidentiality and dependability will be maintained. It is important to evaluate the dependability of deep learning, federated learning

(FL), and centralized machine learning. The merging of machine learning (ML) and deep learning (DL) poses risks such as adversarial attacks, algorithmic bias, data breaches, and operational challenges. Nevertheless, the extensive user base, multitude of users, information dissemination, communication networks, and vulnerable areas in FL contribute to increased complexity. This necessitates the investigation of someone's trustworthiness. Furthermore, Florida has difficulties in formulating development strategies, ensuring compliance with privacy regulations, upholding fairness, and disseminating information that machine learning and deep learning algorithms are incapable of doing [11]. So far, nothing is known regarding the presence of reliability pillars, FL-specific metrics, or methods for analyzing the reliability of FL models. Moreover, it is crucial to possess the capacity to authenticate the dependability of federated learning models and use the latest federated learning technologies. This chapter contributes to the current literature by addressing the gaps in knowledge.

9.2 RELATED WORK

This section analyzes current methodologies focused on reliable federated learning (FL) and defines crucial attributes of trustworthy artificial intelligence (AI), such as explanatory capability, reliability, privacy, fairness, and responsibility [8]. I recommend familiarizing yourself with the abundant literature that has been produced on the subject of combined machine learning and deep learning in recent years. On the other hand, there is further evidence to uncover about fair FL. The methodology that closely mirrors the one used in this chapter is FedEval [12]. It thoroughly analyzes several factors that are essential for the reliability of AI. The stability of FL models is assessed by their efficacy in intercommunication, time efficiency, and resource conservation.

A tool used for evaluating federated learning systems is known as FedEval, and it is open-source. An evaluation of the effectiveness of FL and unified training in attaining intended results. A privacy measure investigates the effects of novel logic hacks on users. Finally, stability measurements evaluate the performance of different data collecting techniques when non-IID data is used. An innovative method for validating the precision of AL models is presented in [13, 14]. Evaluating the dependability of supervised machine learning and deep learning models using tabular data may be a straightforward, versatile, and adaptable procedure. This entails assessing the models' capacity to assume responsibility, uphold fairness, and manage mistakes. The most detrimental aspect of this work is the incapacity to use FL models. FL places a high priority on privacy since it is their duty to safeguard the data of their entire user base. If you endorse the findings of the FL model, it is essential to meticulously and discreetly collect data. Encrypted works include a notable subset of works and procedures. There are two further classifications: perturbation users and anonymization users. To protect privacy against an attacker that only tells partial truths, [15] used techniques such as homomorphic encryption, secret sharing, and ternary gradients. Modifications to the model parameters performed by different individuals on different computers may be implemented by [16] and remain compatible for integration. As stated by [17], the use of global differential privacy successfully safeguarded private health information in an FL setting, despite encountering an interruption. This scenario provided enough isolation. In addition, they deliberated on strategies for obfuscating the origin of a client's trained model by using differential privacy techniques. Anonymization-based methods differ from perturbation-based approaches in that they maintain privacy without compromising the usefulness of the data. proposed an innovative method to estimate the information exchanged between variances in batch input data and local gradients throughout each training session.

This chapter is the first to our knowledge that identifies, illustrates, and discusses the fundamental ideas, principles, and measurements for implementing effective FL. Additionally, it presents a groundbreaking notion that has not been before contemplated: federation. This pillar analyzes the complex patterns and elements of FL systems in order to assess their degree of reliability.

9.3 PRIVACY

FL is seeing growth due to its commitment to safeguarding information. In order to gain the confidence of the public, FL models must consistently safeguard user information. Florida currently has existing privacy standards, but, there are still apprehensions surrounding the dependability of the firms and persons involved. It is important for everyone to get accurate information, not just the service provider. Therefore, modifying the parameters of the model should not disclose any data. Ensure complete isolation inside the group, preventing any kind of communication between its members. Presently, this methodology is the most efficient method for preserving secrecy. Even in instances when external assaults are initiated, there is still a possibility for information to be disclosed. The primary idea in this point is to use privacy-preserving methods to mitigate the vulnerability of systems to privacy risks. Considering the potential for information breaches throughout the FL process, what is the extent of information acquisition or loss?

Currently, the possibility of acquiring information from client modifications. Guidance on safeguarding your data. This notion explores the fundamental methods of safeguarding data in Florida.

9.4 STABILITY AND STRENGTH

For the European Commission, the challenge of cracking AI is one of the three attributes that contribute to its reliability. The remaining two attributes are adhering to established standards and principles of behavior. In order to mitigate the risk of hacking or malicious exploitation, it is necessary for devices to possess exceptional speed and intelligence. In the past, three different methods have been used to investigate this topic.

In order to evaluate the stability of FL models, this study introduces an additional fourth model. As stated in [5], FL models need to have the capability to handle threats that extend or modify current information. Furthermore, it is essential for FL model trainers and users to possess resilient hardware and software to safeguard against unauthorized access. Furthermore, it is essential that FL algorithms possess the qualities of being easily modifiable and fast in execution, as stated in [50]. The ultimate consideration for this endeavor is the establishment of consumer and data trust. As a result, FL models that have strong data and customers are more likely to be reliable and dependable. Below, you can find further information and data pertaining to each idea. possessing the capacity to manage and navigate through uncertain or potentially dangerous situations. Florida permits anyone to introduce contaminants into FL models, potentially modifying their educational value and diminishing their reliability. There are two categories of pernicious hazards: those that do harm to data and those that cause harm to models. Frequently, labels are inverted, so exposing concealed patterns or modifying the training data in ways that make it hazardous to use after it has been "poisoned". In order to expand the impact of model poisoning, we want to train in another manner. If this is an FL hack, it has the capability to alter the gradient or result in an inaccurate model update. This may be achieved by managing the alterations made by a participant, either at their initial construction or via a model substitution. Before evaluating this strategy, ascertain if the FL model has any defensive mechanisms. Assess the effectiveness of these protections by subjecting them to real-world attacks.

- Detoxification
  The major goal is to educate people on how to safeguard themselves against potentially life-threatening conditions. People often use Byzantine-resilient defense as a defensive strategy. Diverse resilient data gathering methods have shown their capacity to detect malevolent alterations made by clients and reduce their impact. Outlier detection, in contrast, identifies and eliminates explicit impacts, making it a more effective safeguard against poisoning risks. Previously, updates with excessively high error rates were not accepted, and parameter modifications were distributed to identify neurons that exhibit infrequent activity.

- Possessing tangible physical power
  Adverse impacts may be used to induce undesirable outcomes. These arise when small modifications are made to the input data that have a substantial influence on the outcome. To determine this, one may use gradient-based methods, a conventional poisoning attack that alters specific local data (data poisoning), or a model poisoning assault. This calculation demonstrates the functioning of a model replacement attack, which exists inside a system. The covert encryption may empower at least one compromised client to initiate a novel model offensive.

- Confirming the existence of a cover
  The system chooses clients, transmits messages to scattered clients, and acquires models to guarantee that clients comply with federation requirements.

- This is the Federation Scale
  The level of confidence in the process diminishes as the number of users increases. In order to train your FL models, you need a precise amount of gear, network connections, and model parameters. This is seen in the number of users. The network's computing capacity and security are enhanced with an increased number of users. Utilizing the federated learning (FL) technique becomes more secure as the number of clients increases.

The company's degree of recognition served as a novel criterion for assessing reputation. The reputation score was calculated using a subjective logic model for each communication received from a customer. The server may authenticate the client's local update and ascertain the duration of time that has passed.

A user's reputation is bolstered by favorable engagements with others, such as delivering dependable updates. This also holds true for unfavorable encounters. Collaborating with a user who has a poor reputation value is ill-advised.

- File size in bytes
  Each time, it subjects them to training against the existing global model to assess whether the new local modifications are superior or inferior. Each user has a specific number that represents the extent to which training at that client enhances the performance of the global model after a cycle.

9.5 FAIRNESS

Data is the underlying cause for the lack of fairness in AI. Florida users may provide diverse quantities and types of information. Insufficient representation of the full population in the data might result in biased selection of research participants. If selection bias is present, it might lead to an uneven distribution of names or attributes [11]. Florida has significant challenges in dealing with each of these issues. The primary factor to be taken into account in this part is the judicious choice of customers. There are two sorts of fairness in fair AI: fairness at the user level and fairness at the network level. It seems logical that users belonging to a certain network should not be subjected to unjust treatment. It is important to provide equitable treatment for all users, irrespective of their network, by treating them on par with others who have comparable characteristics. If you move to Florida, you are not subject to these rules. When analyzing performance fairness and class distribution, we may see phenomena at the user level. However, this theory takes into account the network's viewpoint Performance fairness guarantees that a user's remuneration is directly proportional to the quantity of information they offer. In addition, class distribution thoroughly examines all participant data to identify any inconsistencies in labeling.

- Degenerative mistakes

The success of the exam may be ascertained based on this numerical value. The data from each user's global model is tested and aggregated to ascertain the accuracy of the test. For optimal efficiency, it is essential that all users be given identical scores on the examinations.

- Score disparity
  This program calculates the disparity in F1 score between a certain group of users (π) and the entire network. The value of this integer is within the range of 1 and –1. As close to 0 as practical should be the discrimination number. If this index were extrapolated to a global scale, it would provide factual data and confidential details pertaining to the client's demographic. The F1 rating for each sample from the dataset will be:

The term F1 (Xv–) represents the F1 score specifically for the safe group. The value of "π" is calculated as F1 (w(X+) – F1 (w (X–)).

- Changes in the allocation of labor
  The value represents the extent to which the data points differ from a certain set. The term used to refer to this is the coefficient of variation (CV).

- Getting ready for a lesson
  The training set of an ML/DL model is partitioned into distinct categories known as classes. This determines if the data sets were suitably chosen to provide a precise depiction of the complete population.

- The classification is unjust
  There are two distinct perspectives to consider while observing the gap between classes. A more comprehensive approach to identifying class mismatches in federated learning involves requesting each user to provide the server with their own class distribution. By using an extra well-balanced sample and the gradients of a neural network model, this approach allows for achieving a high level of proximity to a given target.

9.6 EXPLAINABILITY

AI must strictly comply with transparent and veracious norms in its functioning. When it comes to what it can do and why, AI should be clear. It is essential that decisions be comprehensible to all those affected by them. Using "interpretability" as a replacement for "explainability" is erroneous. The notion of interpretability is at the top of this hierarchy. This term refers to the effortless comprehension of a model in a passive manner. However, "interpretability" pertains to the ability to understand the internal mechanisms of an AI system. Examine a basic model to comprehend it. Post-hoc methods may enhance the interpretability of complex models that are initially difficult to comprehend.

As FL is trained using an ML/DL model, it is necessary for the computational model to be capable of offering an explanation. Nevertheless, assessing unprocessed data or secured model characteristics directly poses difficulties because of the need to maintain privacy.

- Precise algorithms
  If a concept is easily comprehensible without any further explanation, it might be seen as lucid. The interpretation of this term may vary among individuals based on their IQ. Prior to becoming perceivable by computers, several mathematical examinations and methodologies need to function on models. Afterward, the test assesses the model's simplicity by considering the number of components and links, as well as the ease of comprehension for each component. One may comprehend decision trees, decision rules, logistic regression, k-nearest neighbors (KNN), and Bayesian models. What is the apparent cost? There are many approaches to ascertaining the dimensions of a model.

Simplifying a model involves first reducing the number of components or elements it contains. This enhances comprehension. An effective approach to streamlining models is to eliminate the need for superfluous information.

Given that all participants share the same comprehensive feature space, there exist several approaches to effectively describe a model that may be readily used for horizontal federated learning. Nevertheless, it is essential that you refrain from sending the server any feature-related data in order to enable the calculation of the feature value score. The party does not have complete overlap in the feature space, hence vertical feature learning cannot be instantly applied with Shapley Additive explanations (SHAP). Another variant of SHAP is used by a different user to assess the significance of different sections in vertical FL.

- Generating visual representations
  Some individuals proposed the implementation of a real-time server-based dashboard that presents data during the whole lifespan, from client generation to training and release. The system presents the list of users who took part in each training cycle, together with the status of the model.

9.7 ACCOUNTABILITY

The EU guidelines [7] enumerate seven prerequisites for AI to be deemed trustworthy. Accountability is one among them. It is essential to prioritize the completion of activities while taking into account your responsibilities. IBM's research pioneered the first iteration of the "factsheet" idea. This would be used to document comprehensive information throughout the whole of the ML/DL procedure. Vigilance is another essential principle in the realm of labor. Despite the abundance of documentation, it requires substantial effort from all those involved to guarantee that FL models are generated in strict adherence to the design, development, and deployment plans.

IBM bolstered this strategy by augmenting FL with more power. To generate thorough documentation including the project, the personnel involved, the data, the model configuration, and the outcomes, you may use the FL factsheet template. The factsheet should only provide details pertaining to the additional layer of settings while refraining from including any sensitive information about the concerned users since FL's design is notably sophisticated and prioritizes privacy. Keep reading to discover the content that factsheets scrutinize.

- Project plans
  The factsheet provides details on the project's historical context, primary goal, and comprehensive timetable. Further information on the project may be obtained here. The project's aims are explicitly outlined in the primary goal, while the historical context provides details on the existing knowledge and the circumstances that precipitated the initiative.

The FL employee list is included. In order to authenticate the individual completing the form, both their identity and the name of their employer are confirmed.

It captures data pertaining to the use of the FL technique. It consists of two parts: the methods performed to prepare the data for processing and the source of the data.

Simply provide a detailed description of the FL model's setup. The first step involves the selection of the ML/DL model and the optimization strategy. Subsequently, the aggregator presents the global hyper-parameters, encompassing the upper limit for the number of rounds, the maximum duration for waiting, and the precision of the shutdown. Last but certainly not least,

- What is the method or process?
  This portion of the factsheet provides comprehensive information about the specific approach that you are required to acquire. The dimensions of the model, the rate at which data is uploaded in bytes, the average duration of training, and the rate at which data is downloaded in bytes are all shown.

- Automated auditing processes
  This statistic has several uses. Possible approaches include functional testing, user feedback testing, speed testing, or other methods. It might also be vigilant for a mistake or an attack. Some corporations go as far as hiring or compensating experienced hackers to actively search for security vulnerabilities in order to maintain vigilant surveillance.

9.8 FEDERATION

Refers to the establishment of a political system in which power is divided between a central authority and various states or regions.

FL managers encounter challenging obstacles such as safety concerns, resource limitations, communication difficulties, and the need for efficiency. Ensuring the model's security and monitoring the simultaneous study of hundreds of users is a formidable undertaking. Global models may need more time to reach a consensus due to their use of heterogeneous consumer data. Customers may terminate their use if there is any instability in the network, users, or tools. If models are trained improperly, they may potentially deteriorate in performance. Moreover, additional investigation into the building of FL systems is essential. There is presently a deficiency in research and understanding of FL algorithms. The main topics covered in this part are client and model management, along with optimization techniques. The analysis focuses on the system's management of client and model data. Optimization techniques may modify the frequency and efficiency of model execution.

The system has the ability to handle client connections and monitor the health of each individual. If your design follows a client–server architecture, it is essential that the client registration remains on the primary server. When a user first registers, they are provided with the initial local model and are asked to fill out an information request. A user is inquiring about the device's identification number, the duration of the link's interruption, or the device's power capacity. Choose a client. It prevents user attrition, optimizes resource allocation, and establishes faster connections with users. This design approach ensures that the client selection is also retained on the primary server. This is the crux of decision-making. The client picker chooses selected users to train in each round based on pre-established parameters.

- Analyze the process of co-versioning
  It ensures that the global models are consistent with the ones used locally. In this case, it might refer to a repository where local versions of models are kept and connected to global versions of models. Model changes and aggregations may be performed independently when using this register. The mapping enables the server to carry out asynchronous aggregations, making it feasible. Another advantage is the capability to terminate the process prematurely if a model reaches convergence before the set number of iterations.

- Altering the approach
  It has the capability to identify when the global model is not functioning at its highest level of efficiency. To this end, it checks the overall performance of global mode across all clients in order to ascertain whether the decline is happening on a worldwide scale. If the deterioration is universally pervasive and remains consistent, a new job for training a global model is launched.

- A programming language designed specifically for gathering data
  The name "aggregation algorithm" often evokes the concept of the average, while other optimization algorithms have been suggested as potential expansions that may be beneficial in different settings. The meeting may be conducted either in a single venue or across many machines. While decentralization mitigates the risk of bottlenecks, single points of failure, and trust issues, it may sometimes increase the complexity of networks. This metric utilizes these two parameters to assess the dependability of the aggregation job.

9.9 DESIGN OF A FEDERATED TRUST ALGORITHM

This section provides further details on the establishment of Federated Trust. The purpose of this algorithm is to assess the dependability of FL models by evaluating the principles, pillars, and measurements outlined. This study is the first endeavor to ascertain the precision of FL models.

The algorithm must include all five reliable federated learning elements. In other words, the final score must be calculated by including at least one metric from each element.

FR-2: The collective trustworthiness score of all the concepts and planks should be equal to the sum of their individual trustworthiness ratings.

NF-1: The technique should be optimized for improved speed and ease of use for the FL model, users, and server. The method should have autonomous components that may be configured in various ways. **PC-1:** The program does not allow storage of confidential FL model files on PC-1.

PC-2: Must ensure that the algorithm does not disclose or provide other parties access to any confidential information on customers, the computer, or the FL model.

PC-3: The parameters may be calculated concurrently on both the central computer and the client's local devices.

If the measurements provided by each client include sensitive information, it is essential that the cooperation between the clients and the server in determining these metrics be conducted securely and confidentially.

The users educated each other on the proper use of the FL model while respecting confidentiality. This section provides instructions on how to alter and set up the model.

- Creating the foundation for FL's framework
  The necessary parameters for training and evaluating the federated learning model for the protocol-setting tool. It offers details on the quantity, model parameters, data collection method, and client selection.

- A concise summary of the facts
  it offers very valuable information for ensuring the responsibility of the organization, the participants, and the training itself. The text contains information on the main issue that requires resolution, the source of the data, the procedures utilized for preprocessing, and whether or not differential privacy measures were used.

The average scores of each user within the test group were used, along with the performance of their model. There is no personal information included. This input encompasses several factors such as the user's engagement level, the extent of social stratification, the duration of typical training sessions, the dimensions of the average model, the number of bytes uploaded and downloaded, and other pertinent particulars.

Furthermore, it includes the user's test accuracy coefficient, class imbalance coefficient, feature value coefficient, intelligence score, and participation rate.

9.10 AN EARLY FEDERATED TRUST ALGORITHM VERSION

- How can I choose and implement a FL framework?
  The most efficacious and advantageous technologies for training diverse federated learning models were found to be Federated Tensor Flow, Flower, FLUTE, LEAF, Federated Scope, FedEval, and FedML. After doing a thorough analysis and comparison, Federated Scope was selected as the benchmark instrument.

9.11 STATISTICS CHOOSING AND ESTABLISHING A SHARED TRUST

Not all measures can be determined using traditional means, such as equations or other practical methods. The goal here is to provide a basic illustration that may be used in any Federated Scope framework-oriented federated learning project. The underlying ideas, principles, and metrics should remain consistent. It is likely that the prototype version excluded some ideas and techniques. If that is the case, here are a few reasons.

Data anonymization and encryption techniques are used to ensure privacy and protect sensitive information. The configuration file for the Federated Scope structure lacks instructions on how to use these two techniques. Furthermore, the privacy of the sample data was protected by using differential privacy.

Risk of information disclosure (Privacy). To compute this metric, it is essential to execute several neural networks throughout each training iteration. This would significantly increase the complexity of the mathematical calculations.

What is the level of resilience of the protection against poisoning? Without written evidence, it is difficult to ascertain the frequency at which the poisoning argument is used. The operation of Federated Scope does not conform to this approach. The software also validates the efficiency of this approach by assessing its resistance to poisoning assaults.

9.12 EXPERIMENTS

This section illustrates the integration of Federated Scope and the Federated Trust architecture to guarantee the dependability of FL applications during the model-building procedure. Each demonstration event has two groups. Illustrate how variations in the number of users and their configurations might impact the reliability of the dataset, as shown with the FEMNIST dataset. Subsequently, we performed two further experiments to scrutinize the security of the Internet of Things (IoT) network, using the N-BaIoT dataset. These studies illustrate how training may modify a practical application.

9.12.1 Trustworthiness Scores for Experiments with FEMNIST

The objective of these challenges is to train machine-learning models to accurately interpret handwritten numerical digits by using the FEMNIST dataset.

Experiment 1 involves the examination of 50 users, with a random selection of 60% of users each time. The exam consists of 25 training cycles. This test is equipped with differential privacy, which is a very desirable feature, with a value of 20.

Experiment 2 has a sample size of 100 users, each with a 40% individual probability of being selected. There are a total of 50 training sessions. All of them had the same configuration for the project specifications, data, and participants. The model failed to clearly indicate the purpose or location of the FL project.

9.12.2 Limitations

The Federated Trust version is not perfect for assessing the overall dependability of FL models. In order to fully comprehend a concept, it is necessary to take into account other aspects besides the union scale, which represents the robustness pillar. To provide an example, let's examine the customer image measure discussed It is an essential element of the idea of customer reliability. Nevertheless, assessing the client's visual representation in the performed tests posed a significant challenge. The notion of equitable selection of clients is another idea. The customer involvement variation number may be easily determined by analyzing the dispersion of selection rates among the customers. However, this variance measure may not be the most effective in displaying the level of fairness in customer selection in FL.

9.13 CONCLUSIONS AND FUTURE WORK

This chapter offers a comprehensive summary including the most vital aspects of FL that you can depend on. A novel taxonomy incorporates the addition of a recently identified structure called "federation" with the already recognized ones from prior research. The following principles include accountability, fairness, privacy, explainability, and reliability. Users and FL models are invited to assess the trustworthiness of FL models in this new pillar. The fundamental principles and methodologies outlined in the literature on FL models have been enhanced by additional ones. Federated Trust was created to assess the authenticity of FL models that are extendable, adaptable, and extremely flexible, according to the suggested categorization. The feasibility and efficacy of the Federated Trust prototype were assessed by testing utilizing Federated Scope.

REFERENCES

1. Britta Daffier. Why Artificial Intelligence (AI) will be the technology of 2023, 2023. .
2. Garling. Wu. 5 Big Problems With OpenAI's ChatGPT, 2022
3. Uzair Muhammad. Who is liable when a driverless car crashes? 2021.
4. Virginia Dignum. Dignum. *Responsible artificial intelligence: how to develop and use AI in a responsible way.* Springer Nature, 2019.
5. Bo Li, Peng Qi, et al. Trustworthy AI: From Principles to Practices. *ACM Comput. Surv.*, aug 2022. Just Accepted .
6. Madiega Tambiama. Artificial intelligence act. *European Parliament: European Parliamentary Research Service*, 2021
7. AIHLEG of the European Commission. Ethics guidelines for trustworthy ai, 2019.
8. Hanchan Liu, Yiqi Wang, et al. Trustworthy AI: A Computational Perspective, 2021. .
9. José M. Alcaraz Calero, Felix J., Izidor Mlakar, Manuel Gil Pérez, Alberto Huertas Celdran, Jose M. Zakirul, A. Bhuiyan, Gregorio Martínez Pérez, and Garćña Clemente. Protector: Working to secure private information in the US and Europe. *Networks of Computers*, 181: 107448, 2020.
10. Qiang Yang, Yang Liu, Han Yu, Tianjian Chen, Yan Kang, and Yong Cheng. Federated education. *Synthesis Lectures on Artificial Intelligence and Machine Learning*, 13(3): 1–207, 2019.
11. Peter Kairouz, H Brendan McMahan, et al. Advances and open problems in federated learning. *Foundations and Trends® in Machine Learning*, 14(1–2):1–210, 2021.
12. Di Chai, Leye Wang, Kai Chen, and Qiang Yang. Fedeval: A benchmark system with a thorough evaluation methodology for federated learning. *arXiv preprint arXiv:2011.09725*, 2020.
13. Alberto Huertas Celdran, Jan Kreischer, Melike Demirci, Joel Leupp, Pedro M. Sanchez, Muriel Figueredo Franco, Gérôme Bovet, Gregorio Martinez Perez, and Burkhard Stiller. A framework assessing trustworthiness of supervised machine and deep learning models. In *SafeAI2023: The AAAI's Workshop on Artificial Intelligence Safety*, 2938–2948, 2023.

14. Alberto Huertas Celdrán, Jan Bauer, Melike Demirci, Joel Leupp, Muriel Figueredo Franco, Pedro M. Sánchez Sánchez, Gérôme Bovet, Gregorio Martínez Pérez, and Burkhard Stiller. Ritual: A platform quantifying the trustworthiness of supervised machine learning. In *2022 18th International Conference on Network and Service Management (CNSM)*, 364–366, 2022.
15. Ye Dong, Xiaojun Chen, Liyan Shen, and Dakui Wang. EaSTFLy: Efficient and secure ternary federated learning. *Computers & Security*, 94:101824, 2020.
16. Keith Bonawitz, Vladimir Ivanov, Ben Kreuter, Antonio Marcedone, H Brendan McMahan, Sarvar Patel, Daniel Ramage, Aaron Segal, and Karn Seth. Practical secure aggregation for privacy-preserving machine learning. In *Proceedings of the 2017 ACM SIGSAC Conference on Computer and Communications Security*, 1175–1191, 2017.
17. Pedro Miguel Sánchez Sánchez, Alberto Huertas Celdrán, Ning Xie, Gérôme Bovet, Gregorio Martínez Pérez, and Burkhard Stiller. Federated trust: A solution for trustworthy federated learning. *ArXiv*, 2023, abs/2302.09844.

Federated Optimization Algorithms

10

S. Biruntha, S. Rajalakshimi, and M. Kavitha

10.1 INTRODUCTION

A training paradigm called federated learning (FL) allows several clients to collaboratively train a global model without exchanging their individual data. Distributed learning (DL), which was initially presented to optimize a given model in star-shaped networks made up of a server interacting with computer machines, is the foundation of federated learning. The dataset in DL is owned by the server, which also distributes it across computers. The disparity in processing capability between servers and clients in the federated learning system is a significant phenomenon that is overlooked by the aforementioned approaches. We are aware that clients' computer power is comparatively low in the real-world environment. The client's computational burden is further increased by the strategy of altering the client loss function. Servers only take on the role of aggregating local models and producing global models; they frequently have significant processing power and network conditions. The machines provide the predicted gradients at each optimization round, and the server aggregates them to complete an stochastic gradient descent (SGD) step. Later, DL was expanded to take into account SGD, and FL expanded DL to allow optimization without requiring clients to share data. Federated learning, which is widely used, efficiently safeguards the confidentiality and privacy of data by transferring model parameters between the client and the server (data never leaves the client). Naturally, clients in the federated learning system have inadequate network conditions and processing capability, yet they nonetheless bear the brunt of the model training workload. The server's robust network infrastructure and processing capacity enable it to handle light tasks that are beyond its capabilities. The most common example is Google's keyboard input technique, which trains a recurrent neural network (RNN) for next word prediction using a federated learning platform. Federated learning is also frequently utilized in the security business for voice print recognition and portrait identification, and in the medical field for precision medicine, novel medication discovery, and clinical auxiliary diagnosis. In order to sample, the server removes local models that are more likely to support the convergence of the global model during aggregate. The significance technique is frequently employed in sampling algorithms. By comparing client gradient data, this approach aggregates the local gradients of the "important" clients. These days, the most common approach is to change the client's loss function. Its goal is to alter the client's loss function by, for example, normalizing it using the last round of the global model or including a near term in it.

10.2 LITERATURE REVIEW

Currently, the majority of researchers sample their clients and alter their loss functions in an attempt to lessen the detrimental effects of heterogeneity. These are clearly useful uses, but the neural network model needs to be trained before utilizing them. In order to accomplish this, a wireless network must be used to gather sample data from all clients or sensors. This approach is accompanied by worries about privacy and transmission costs [1–3].

Luckily, to address the security and efficiency requirements of next-generation wireless systems, a distributed learning framework known as federated learning has been developed. In federated learning, a collective prediction model was developed that allows several data owners (clients) to collaborate on model training and usage while preserving the privacy of all local training data [4]. FL's distinctive foundation has made it attractive in many applications, including in digital health, automotive networks, and Internet of things (IoT) devices. Federated learning is thus ideally suited for the upcoming generation of wireless systems because of its wide range of application potential and communication characteristics.

This chapter combines the privacy protection and transmission volume reduction features of FL with a range of study topics. It minimizes the expense of gradient or model transmission. Even if the gradients or model are the only things sent in the FL framework, their size is still too large to meet the real-time requirement. This portends well for the upcoming wave of wireless technology. For example, the size of the convolutional neural network (CNN) VGG-16 model is 552 MB, whereas the AlexNet 1 CNN is 240 MB. The use of the neural network (NN) model still carries a high cost for clients, especially when there is inadequate communication [5].

Consequently, there is a broad concern regarding how to decrease the broadcast cost of the model while satisfying the requirements of FL's next-generation wireless systems. To solve this issue, a model compression—also referred to as gradient-compression—technique has been presented in federated learning. There are three main categories for this method [6, 7].

Often referred to as gradient parameter pruning, this neural network is the original kind of compression method. Parameter pruning-based model compression strategy in [8] can greatly decrease the size of the neural network model by lowering the number of neural network model parameters by configuring some less crucial filters in the neural network. Guo et al. [9] introduced a multi-dimensional pruning strategy that compresses the CNN model on spatial–temporal, spatial, and channel redundancy. After the compression of the spatial–temporal model, the channels with low relevance scores were removed. The position of the yield tensor in each channel was evaluated using an artificially learned score.

By setting the irrelevant parameters in the neural network model to zero, the first kind of model compression technique focuses only on the vital ones [10]. The benefit of this strategy is that it operates simply. That being said, it ignores the importance of trivial features.

Second, compression can be carried out via quantization. A realistic hierarchical architecture in [11] for decomposing the stochastic gradient into normalized block gradients, which were quantal with a low-dimensional Grassmannian codebook and a uniform quantizer, respectively. A bit-allocation technique was introduced in this situation to reduce distortion. Quantized-SGD (QSGD) is a family of gradient update compression methods with convergence guarantees, first presented by Alistarh et al. in [12]. With QSGD, the user may effortlessly trade off communication bandwidth and convergence time.

Models for storage, deployment, and transmission are less burdened when neural network parameters are reduced by this kind of approach. However, using this tactic will result in a far lower accuracy rate. Furthermore, similar to the prior method, attackers can access the model right away and initiate a series of attacks since, when a masterful quantization technique is executed, the model exhibits no structural alterations and no discernible loss in accuracy. The last type of compression technique is weight sharing, which reduces the size of the model by increasing the degree of reuse of the model parameters.

Knowledge distillation [13] is a relatively recent technique in the field of model compression that reduces the complexity of a big, trained model by extracting its information. However, it is incompatible with FL because its objective is to reduce the cost of constructing complex models.

Many studies have currently shown that most model parameters for gradient or neural networks are redundant or superfluous. Therefore, there has been a great deal of interest in figuring out how to reduce and compress the amount of extraneous characteristics that are transmitted. In convex optimization formulation, a number of quick and simple techniques are proposed for an approximate solution, with theoretical guarantees for sparseness, to reduce the coding length of stochastic gradients and solve the optimal sparsification effectively [14].

10.3 FEDERATED AVERAGING AND MODEL AGGREGATION IN MACHINE LEARNING

10.3.1 Architecture of Federated Learning and Model Aggregation

Model training occurs on client devices rather than a central server thanks to federated learning's (FL) decentralized machine learning architecture. Usually, the architecture consists of the following elements:

1. Centralized database:
   The federated learning process is coordinated and the global model is initialized by the centralized server. It transmits the first model to the client devices that are taking part.

2. Client devices:
   Model training takes place locally on each client device, which has its own local dataset.

3. Communication protocol:
   A systematic collection of guidelines that specify how to send or receive data, particularly across a network, is called a communications protocol.

4. Aggregator:
   A key component of FL is model fusion also known as model aggregation. It entails protecting user data privacy by merging locally created models from client devices into a single global model.

10.3.2 Methods of Aggregating Models

10.3.3 Key Components and Considerations

- Communication protocol:
  Monitoring techniques can be used to determine when to stop the federated learning process and evaluate convergence.

- Federated averaging:
  In each round, a new global model is created by averaging the models from all devices. This aids in distributing the effect of every device's contribution.

- Privacy preservation:
  Throughout the federated learning process, user data may be protected using strategies, such as secure aggregation or differential privacy.

- Heterogeneous devices:
  To enable efficient cooperation, the architecture should take into consideration variances in device capabilities, such as processor speed or memory.

- Convergence monitoring:
  Guarantees safe and private model update communication between client devices and the centralized server.

10.3.4 Federated Averaging Algorithm

1. Initialization:
   A global model is initialized on a central server. The initial global model is then sent to all participating client devices.

2. Local model training:
   All client device trains the global model on its local dataset. The training process is typically performed for a static number of local epochs.

3. Model update transmission:
   After local training, each client device calculates the difference between its locally trained model and the initial global model. The model update, often represented as the difference in model parameters or gradients, is then transmitted to the central server.

4. Aggregation
   The centralized server collects all the model updates from the client devices and the updates are aggregated, typically using simple averaging, to create a new global model for better usage.

5. Model distribution:
   The updated global model is then directed to all client devices for the next round of training.

6. Iterative Process
   Steps 2 to 5 are repeated for multiple rounds to iteratively improve the global model.

10.3.5 Advantages of Federated Averaging

- Privacy preservation:
  Since only model changes are exchanged with the central server, individual client data stays on the client device.

- Decentralized training:
  Less centralized data processing and storage is required because training takes place locally on devices.

- Global model improvement:
  By working together, the global model gains knowledge from a variety of datasets, which could enhance the model performance as a whole.

10.3.6 Considerations and Variations

- Non-IID data:
  Non-identically distributed data (IDD) among client strategies can provide difficulties for federated averaging. Adjustments such as weighted averaging can help with this problem.

- Communication efficiency:
  It's critical to reduce communication overhead. One can use techniques such as compression or quantization to minimize the size of model updates that are communicated.

- Convergence monitoring:
  Monitoring systems are frequently used to evaluate convergence and determine whether to terminate the federated learning process.

- Hyperparameter tuning:
  For best results, parameters such as the learning rate and the quantity of local training epochs may need to be carefully adjusted.

A key approach in federated learning is federated averaging, which shows how cooperative model training may be accomplished while honoring the privacy restrictions present in distant datasets.

10.3.7 Federated Learning Principles

As shown previously, federated learning promotes local model computation on edge devices and combines these models on a server to make a new universal model that is sent to every consumer. Clients start learning again with this new approach, and eventually, they send it to the server for a new aggregate. This cycle of specialization and generalization continues until an appropriate model is generated. A communication circle often refers to a cycle of specialization and generalization. More rounds may be needed if new information is obtained or clients join in after the first model converges.

Federated learning relies heavily on the way specialized models are brought together at the server. In the context of deep learning, two families of algorithms with different techniques implemented might be considered. The first tactic places a strong emphasis on generalization. By considering local models as a whole (all layers and neurons), the aggregation approach creates a new model that may potentially challenge all of the layers and weights associated with neurons. We shall discuss the FedAvg and FedMA algorithms in more detail as illustrations of this methodology. We should also talk about the FedProx algorithm, which in order to prevent outliers, penalizes clients that stray too much from the norm.

10.3.8 Federated Model Aggregation

This chapter's main contribution is the model aggregation based on NN. By creating a model for n clients using the model aggregation technique, the global model for handwritten script identification is produced. A gradient-based optimization algorithm is used to optimize the learning process and converge on both local and global model updates. The federated stochastic variance algorithm and the federated averaging approach are equated to reduce the gradient. It is discovered that the averaging method outperforms the other traditional strategy. Reinforcement learning demonstrates customized federated learning contexts and positive outcomes. The results, however, only marginally beat the federated average approach, indicating a potential research topic. The identically distributed and independent dataset 24 used the same averaging technique. The impact of the divergence of the model weights is lessened when non-IID and imbalanced data are aggregated using the FedAvg model. Motivated by these noteworthy successes, we decided to persist with model aggregation approaches and the federated learning framework. Here, we propose the general structure for federated learning experiments. Furthermore, utilizing a modified model aggregation technique, our research partially investigates three customized federated learning frameworks. Also discussed are three primary model aggregation techniques that use the average of neural network model coefficients (Figure 10.1).

10.3.9 Federated Learning Framework

The main workings of federated learning are:

1. **Clients:** For our experiment, we take four clients into account. This thesis selects datasets related to breast cancer, handwritten scripts, and fingerprints. The training, testing, and validation data are distributed individually to each client.
2. **Centralized server:** The central server is where this model mostly works. In federated learning situations, the centralized server plays a crucial role in combining the models to create an updated or global model.
3. **Fetching the global model:** Every client is seen as active in this model, meaning that each client takes part in the federated learning framework. The central server sends a global model to the clients. Accordingly, the global model $M \equiv G(M)$ is sent to all the clients from the central server.
4. **Local model training:** Each client begins training the data model after obtaining the global model $M \equiv G(M)$. During local model training, each client computes $M \leftarrow M - \sigma\, 5f\, n\, (M; b)$, which determines the average gradient on its local data.

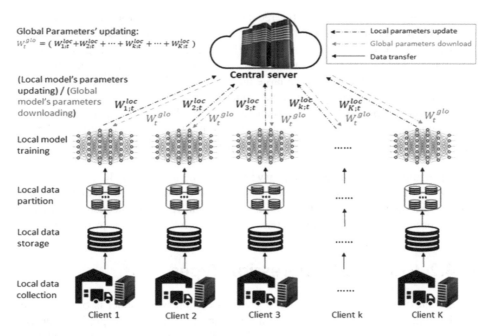

FIGURE 10.1 An outline of federated learning

10.4 GRADIENT COMPRESSION AND QUANTIZATION IN MACHINE LEARNING

10.4.1 Gradient Compression

Gradient compression is the term for methods used in deep learning (DL) and machine learning (ML) to lower the communication overheads of distributed models being trained. The act of transfer gradient updates between nodes during scattered model training can cause a noteworthy block, especially for huge models. Here are some common techniques used for gradient compression:

1. **Mean-centric compression:** Only the mean and the variances from the mean are sent, as opposed to individual gradient values. In doing so, the whole quantity of information is preserved while sending less data.
2. **Quantization:** This entails decreasing the gradient values' accuracy. For example, the gradients can be quantized to lower-precision integers or fixed-point values rather than delivering floating-point numbers, which need more bits for representation. As a result, the transferred data is smaller.
3. **Error feedback compression:** Only the difference between the actual and expected gradients is sent, not the precise gradients. By adding this difference

to the expected gradients, the receiver may then reconstruct the gradients. This method makes use of the overlap between successive gradients.
4. **Sparsification:** With this method, all of the gradients are set to zero and just a portion of the gradients with meaningful values are conveyed. This is predicated on the idea that a large number of gradient values are negligible and have little effect on the model update.
5. **Top-k compression:** With this technique, only the top-k gradients with the largest magnitudes are transmitted. The concept is to keep the most significant gradients and reject the less significant ones.

Gradient compression approaches are very helpful in situations when there is a restricted amount of transmission capacity, such as distributed training over a network or many GPUs. These methods lessen the amount of time and resources needed for gradient updates throughout the distributed system, which helps to speed up the training process.

10.4.2 Gradient Compression Types

In the context of distributed training, a gradient compression model is often used to describe a particular method or technique intended to compress the gradients during the training of machine learning models. The following are some popular models or methods for gradient compression:

1. **Models of gradient quantization:** These models address the quantization of gradients in particular. The gradient values can be expressed with fewer bits thanks to quantization, which decreases the gradient values' accuracy. This reduces communication blocks and helps to send data in smaller sizes.
2. **Communication-efficient SGD (CESGD):** To increase communication efficiency, CESGD is a distributed training methodology that uses gradient compression methods. Sparsification and quantization are combined to minimize the quantity of data sent between devices while training.
3. **Models of low-rank factorization:** The main goal of these models is to use low-rank factorization to approximate the gradient matrices. It is possible to greatly minimize the amount of information that must be sent by breaking down the gradients into low-rank matrices.
4. **Residual quantization approach:** This approach blends gradient quantization with residual networks (ResNets) concepts. In order to provide the model the advantage of compression and allow it to keep more information about the updates, it attempts to maintain the high-frequency information in gradients.

10.4.3 Implementation Details

Gradient compression algorithms must be implemented by changing a deep learning model's training loop to include the compression methods. A condensed example is

TABLE 10.1 Aggregation Models or Methods

METHODS	DESCRIPTION
Weighted averaging	This reduces the effect of underperforming or perhaps malicious devices by giving models varying weights based on their dependability or performance.
Federated averaging	It is a reiterative procedure that involves aggregate modeling, local model training, and subsequent return of the updated model.
Secure aggregation	To guarantee that the aggregation process is completed without disclosing specific model updates, methods such as homomorphic encryption and multi-party computation are used.
Adaptive methods	Adaptive methods refer to strategies that modify the aggregation process in real-time according to the reliability or performance of individual devices.

TABLE 10.2 Stochastic Quantization Algorithms

def stochastic_quantization(x, num_bits=8):
scaled_x = x * (2 ** (num_bits - 1))
rounded_x = torch.round(scaled_x + torch.rand_like(x) - 0.5)
quantized_x = rounded_x / (2 ** (num_bits - 1))
return quantized_x
def train_with_stochastic_quantization(model, criterion, optimizer, data_loader, num_epochs, num_bits=8):
train_losses = []
# Stochastic quantization of gradients
for param in model.parameters():
if param.grad is not None:
param.grad.data = stochastic_quantization(param.grad.data, num_bits)
return train_losses
model = SimpleNet()
train_losses = train_with_stochastic_quantization(model, criterion, optimizer, train_loader, num_epochs=num_epochs, num_bits=8)

detailed in Section 10.4.4 in Python that makes use of the well-known deep learning library PyTorch. Remember that the precise implementation could change depending on the demands of the particular compression technique.

This sample demonstrates a fundamental method of gradient quantization. Remember that more advanced methods, such as adaptive compression or sparsification, call for extra thought and can require more detailed adjustments.

10.4.4 Gradient Quantization Algorithms

Gradient quantization methods use fewer bits to encode gradient values in order to decrease their accuracy. This can hasten the convergence of machine learning models and lower the communication overhead in distributed training.

TABLE 10.3 Gradient Quantization Algorithm

```
# Training loop with gradient quantization
def train_with_quantization(model, criterion, optimizer, data_loader, num_epochs,
  quantization_bits):
for epoch in range(num_epochs):
# Gradient quantization
for param in model.parameters():
if param.grad is not None:
param.grad.data = torch.round(param.grad.data / (2 ** (quantization_bits - 1))) * (2 **
  (quantization_bits - 1))
optimizer.step()
# Example usage
# Assuming you have a DataLoader named 'train_loader' and other necessary
  configurations
train_with_quantization(model, criterion, optimizer, train_loader, num_epochs=5,
  quantization_bits=8)
```

10.4.5 When to Utilize Gradient Compression

Gradient compression can be useful for training models with large fully linked components in their models. Communication costs become important for recurrent neural networks and larger models. Gradient compression has a lot to offer such models. Gradient quantization and compression techniques are typically employed in distributed training scenarios where machine learning models are trained across multiple devices or nodes. These techniques aim to decrease the statement above during the exchange of gradient updates among devices, which becomes crucial as the size of the model or the number of training parameters increases.

It's important to note that while gradient quantization and compression can lead to faster communication and reduced training times, they may also introduce noise or approximation errors. Hence, the choice to utilize these techniques should be complete with consideration for the precise features of the model, the training data, and available resources. Experimentation and validation on a representative dataset are crucial to ensuring that the compressed model maintains acceptable performance.

Here are some situations and considerations for using gradient quantization and compression:

- **CPU versus GPU**
  This gradient compression works best when multi-node (single- or multi-GPU) distributed training is used. Compared to the enormous compute density per compute node on a GPU, training on a CPU would provide a lower compute density per compute node. As a result, during training, CPU-based nodes need less communication bandwidth than GPU-based nodes. As a result, CPU-based nodes receive less advantage from gradient compression than GPU-based nodes do.

- **Latency in the network**
  When employing network-connected nodes for dispersed training, gradient compression offers advantages. The size of the model and the network delay

TABLE 10.4 Gradient Quantization Algorithms and Their Benefits

ALGORITHMS	DESCRIPTION	BENEFITS
Stochastic quantization	Stochastic quantization introduces controlled randomness during the quantization process. Instead of deterministically rounding the gradients to the nearest quantization level, stochastic quantization randomly rounds them based on a probability distribution.	The stochastic element can add noise, which may have a regularization effect and help the model generalize better.
Uniform quantization	In uniform quantization, the entire range of gradients is divided into quantization levels, and each gradient is quantized to the nearest level. This is a deterministic process, and the quantization levels are evenly spaced.	Simple and easy to implement, providing a straightforward reduction in precision.
Power of two quantization	Power of two quantization rounds gradients to the nearest power of two. This can be achieved by manipulating the exponent of the floating-point representation.	Decreases the number of unique values that need to be transmitted, leading to efficient compression
Ternary quantization	In ternary quantization, gradients are quantized to one of three values: -1, 0, or 1. Values close to zero are rounded to zero, reducing the precision.	Highly compressive, reducing the amount of information that needs to be communicated.
Quantization aware training (QAT)	Instead of applying quantization after training, QAT incorporates quantization during the training process. This involves quantizing gradients during	Allows the model to adapt to the reduced precision during training, potentially mitigating the impact on performance.
Adaptive quantization	Adaptive quantization adjusts the precision of the quantization dynamically based on the gradient values. Gradients with larger magnitudes may be quantized with higher precision, while smaller gradients may be quantized with lower precision.	Adapts to the varying importance of gradients, potentially improving compression efficiency.
Incremental quantization	Incremental quantization involves gradually reducing the precision of gradients over the course of training. This can be done by progressively decreasing the number of bits used for quantization.	Allows for a smooth transition to lower precision, potentially mitigating the impact on model performance.

between nodes can both lead to poor performance; in these cases, gradient compression might speed up things. If network communication has low latency, gradient compression might not be something you want to use.

TABLE 10.5 When to Use the Compression Algorithms

ALGORITHM	WHEN TO USE
Limited communication bandwidth	In scenarios where the communication bandwidth between devices is limited (e.g., in distributed training across GPUs or over a network), gradient quantization and compression can significantly reduce the amount of data transmitted and speed up the training process.
Large model size	For larger scale models with a substantial number of limits, the communication cost can become a bottleneck.
Distributed training	Gradient quantization and compression are particularly relevant in distributed training setups where the model is trained across multiple devices or nodes. Examples include training on a cluster of GPUs, across different servers, or in federated learning scenarios
Communication cost dominant	When the training time is dominated by the cost of transmission rather than computation, compression methods become essential for accelerating convergence.
Communication frequency	If the frequency of communication between devices is high, such as in synchronous training setups, the benefits of gradient compression become more pronounced.
Tolerance to reduced precision	When there is a tolerance for decreased gradient update precision in both the optimization problem and the model. While some models may need more thought, others may be more resilient to gradients with less accuracy.

- **Model dimensions**
  Weight synchronization is a requirement of distributed training after every batch. Since larger models require more communication during training, gradient compression will have a greater positive impact on these models. When using gradient compression for distributed training, the OpenMP API is used to parallelize the quantization and dequantization processes on the CPU.

10.5 ADAPTIVE LEARNING AND RESOURCE ALLOCATION IN DISTRIBUTED SYSTEMS

The process of using data-driven education to modify and customize learning experiences to each student's unique requirements is known as adaptive learning. One can foresee potential defects or system breakdowns by using adaptive learning. The system can take proactive measures to mitigate or prevent issues, ensuring high availability and reliability, by using lessons learned from past incidents (Figure 10.2).

The resource allocation process consists of these six fundamental components.

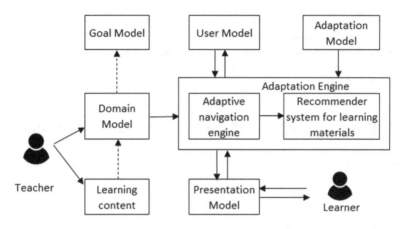

FIGURE 10.2 Architecture of an adaptive learning system

1. Set objectives and goals. The purpose of the mission, vision, and general agency goals helps decision-making. The long range transportation plans (LRTP) and/or transportation asset management plans (TAMP) of an organization may have goals and objectives. The method of allocating resources ought to facilitate the accomplishment of these.
2. Ascertain the limitations. Decide which resources need to be distributed and under what restrictions. Usually, this refers to limitations on the amount of money that is available, but it can also refer to limitations on personnel, contractor capability, equipment, supplies, or other resources. Additionally, there could be other restrictions that are pertinent to the process, including limitations on how precisely particular resources can be used or restrictions on allocating monies among various regions or locations in an equitable manner.
3. Calculate your foals. Convert aims and objectives into precise standards to back up distribution choices. Whenever possible, establish performance metrics that indicate the degree of accomplishment. Set target values for important metrics and determine a desired service level.
4. Distribute resources. Allocate funds and additional resources to the various program categories or job kinds. The distribution of resources among various categories or types of labor is specified by the allocation. The specifics of the resources being distributed, the assets being examined, and the kinds of investments being considered will determine how this process is carried out.
5. Project performance. Assuming the allocated resources and priorities are known, forecast future performance and contrast it with pre-established goals. This might lead to changes being made to the limitations, objectives, or results of other previously mentioned steps. Use the life cycle analysis techniques to forecast future asset conditions, to the degree that targets have been specified for asset conditions.

6. Complete plans and allocation. After allocation is finished, explain to stakeholders the resultant objectives, predictions, and investment priorities by documenting them. After the official procedure is over, more work may be needed, such as creating maintenance schedules based on the list of authorized projects.

10.5.1 Consideration of Risk in Resource Allocation

Decision-makers in the transportation sector must deal with ambiguity. There is always a degree of uncertainty when allocating resources. Elements that face uncertainty include information on the state and performance of assets, projected funding levels and expenses, the performance of a transportation system and particular assets, and potential external events or other circumstances that would necessitate reallocating resources. This unpredictability makes it more difficult to plan for the future and makes agencies more adaptable in order to deal with unforeseen circumstances and changing circumstances.

The transportation sector, along with other industries, has made noteworthy strides in the development of better methods for handling uncertainty in order to reduce adverse effects and maximize favorable ones in recent times. Depending on the sector and application, the word "risk" can have quite varied meanings. For example, the danger of suffering a big financial loss and the unpredictability of financial returns are the two main concerns of a financial analyst. On the other hand, risk management in the nuclear power sector is centered on reducing the likelihood that a nuclear site might sustain catastrophic damage. According to the ISO definition, risk is described in this book as the "effect of uncertainty on objectives". This concept recognizes the potential for both positive and negative effects of uncertainty and encompasses the entire spectrum of applications of risk management.

10.6 CONCLUSION

In this chapter, we summarize the groups of optimization techniques for federated learning that deal with the client drift issue. Future directions for client drift in federated learning may look like this averaging across the ensuing gradients, resulting in an increasingly unbiased estimate of the best update direct. An overview of the issues and driving forces around model optimization strategies for federated learning is given in this review, along with an analysis of the most advanced techniques and algorithms that aim to address these issues. This chapter outlines federated averaging and model aggregation in machine learning, gradient descent algorithms, and resource allocation in federated learning.

REFERENCES

1. Sagiroglu S., Sinanc D. Big data: A review, *2013 International Conference on Collaboration Technologies and Systems (CTS)*, IEEE, pp. 42–47, 2013.
2. Li L., Ota K., Dong M. Deep learning for smart industry: Efficient manufacture inspection system with fog computing *IEEE Trans. Ind. Inform.*, 14 (10), pp. 4665–4673, 2018.
3. Yang H.-F., Dillon T.S., Chen Y.-P.P. Optimized structure of the traffic flow forecasting model with a deep learning approach *IEEE Trans. Neural Netw. Learn. Syst.*, 28 (10), pp. 2371–238, 2016.
4. Abeshu A., Chilamkurti N. Deep learning: the frontier for distributed attack detection in fog-to-things computing *IEEE Commun. Mag.*, 56 (2), pp. 169–175, 2018.
5. Yang Q., Liu Y., Cheng Y., Kang Y., Chen T., Yu H. Federated learning. *Synth. Lect. Artif. Intell. Mach. Learn.*, 13 (3), pp. 1–207, 2019.
6. Rieke N., Hancox J., Li W., Milletari F., Roth H.R., Albarqouni S., Bakas S., Galtier M.N., Landman B.A., Maier-Hein K., et al. The future of digital health with federated learning. *NPJ Digit. Med.*, 3 (1), pp. 1–7, 2020.
7. Du Z., Wu C., Yoshinaga T., Yau K.-L.A., Ji Y., Li J. Federated learning for vehicular internet of things: Recent advances and open issues. *IEEE Open J. Comput. Soc.*, 1, pp. 45–61, 2020.
8. Paleyes A., Urma R.-G., Lawrence N.D. Challenges in deploying machine learning: A survey of case studies. *ACM Comput. Surv.*, 1 (1), 2020.
9. Jordan M.I., Mitchell T.M. Machine learning: Trends, perspectives, and prospects. *Science*, 349 (6245) pp. 255–260, 2015.
10. Cha N., Du Z., Wu C., Yoshinaga T., Zhong L., Ma J., Liu F., Ji Y. Fuzzy logic based client selection for federated learning in vehicular networks. *IEEE Open J. Comput. Soc.*, 3, pp. 39–50, 2022.
11. Konecny J., McMahan H.B., Yu F.X., Richtarik P., et al. Federated learning: Strategies for improving communication efficiency. *arXiv preprint*, 2016.
12. Pappas C., Chatzopoulos D., Lalis S., Vavalis M., Ipls: A framework for decentralized federated learning. In *IFIP Networking Conference, IEEE*, pp. 1–6, 2021.
13. Li T., Sahu A.K., Talwalkar A., Smith V. Federated learning: Challenges, methods, and future directions. *IEEE Signal Process. Mag.*, 37 (3), pp. 50–60, 2020.
14. Li T., Sahu A.K., Zaheer M., Sanjabi M., et al. Federated optimization in heterogeneous networks. *Proc. Mach. Learn. Res.*, 2, pp. 429–450, 2020.

Index

Page numbers in *italic* indicate figure and **bold** indicate table respectively

Accountability, 152–153
Adaptive learning system, *173*
Adaptive methods, 169
Adaptive model updating, 119–120
Adaptive quantization, **171**
Adversarial attacks, 147
Adversarial models, 136
Aggregated data, 141
Aggregation, 141, 164
Aggregator, 163
AlexNet l CNN, 161
Algorithmic bias, 147
Alpha Go., 145
Apache Spark MLlib, **130**
Apple's quick type keyboard, 17
Artificial intelligence (AI), 128, 145, 146
Asynchronous federated learning, 120, 139
Attackers, 135
Authentication and key algorithm (AKA), 131
Automated auditing processes, 153
Autonomous driving, 17
Average of all models (AMA), 118

Backward pass (backpropagation), 36, 37
Batch processing and incremental processing, 114–115
Bengio, Y., 67
Best model environment (BMA), 118
Big Blue, 145
Binary cross-entropy loss, 34
Blockchain technology, 142
Blood pressure, 105
Bulk synchronous parallel (BSP) algorithms, 129

Calculate loss, 35–37
California Consumer Privacy Act (CCPA), 146
Categorical cross-entropy loss, 34
CBOW model, *65*
Centralized database, 163
Centralized synthesis, 124
Chain rule of calculus, 36
ChatGPT, 145

Client devices, 163
Collaborative learning, 4
Collaborative model averaging, 117–118
Collusion risks, 135
Communication cost dominant, **172**
Communication efficiency, 165
Communication-efficient algorithms, 19
Communication-efficient SGD (CESGD), 168
Communication frequency, **172**
Communication overhead, 140
Communication privacy, 122
Communication protocol, 163
Complex machine learning (ML) algorithms, 128
Computational overhead, 140
Convergence monitoring, 164, 165
Convolutional neural network (CNN), 26–27, 112
Convolutional neural network (CNN) VGG-16 model, 161
COVID-19 diagnosis, 104–105
Cross-device federated learning, 19

DALL·E 2, 145
Data anonymization, 156
Data breaches, 147
Data exfiltration, 134
Data heterogeneity, 106–107
Data poisoning attacks, 135
Data possession and governance, 13
Data security and privacy, 107–108
Data sharing, 129
Data traceability, 107
Decentralized computing and model saving, 120
Decentralized data storage, 3
Decentralized training, 164
Deep learning
　activation functions, 41
　background, 23–24
　back propagation, 35–37
　common activation functions, 42–44
　empirical loss, 46–47
　gradient decent, 37–38
　gradient descent, 49–50

177

Index

loss optimization, 48–49
mean square loss, 47
mini batches, 51–52
and neural networks, *see* Neural network (NN)
optimizers, 51
perceptron, 40–41
practice optimization, 50–51
recursive neural network (RNN)
    optimization techniques, 68
    transfer learning (context-based learning), 66–68
regularization, 53–54
stochastic gradient descent, 52–53
word embedding techniques
    Continuous Bag-of-Words, 65
    Skip Gram, 65–66
    Word2Vec, 64–65
Delay differential cell (DD-Cell), 131
Deployment management, 115–116
Detoxification, 149
Differentially private stochastic gradient descent (DP-SGD), 138
Differential privacy (DP), 99–100, 133
Distributed learning (DL), 160
Distributed training, **172**
Drug discovery, 16
Dynamic node selection, 114
Dynamic privacy budget allocation, 139

El Alaoui, I., 59
Encryption, 141
European Commission, 146
EU's General Data Protection Regulation (GDPR), 128
Evasion attacks, 137
Experiments, 157
Explainability, 151–152
Extraction attacks, 137

Fairness, 150–151
Federated averaging, 163, 169
    advantages of, 164–165
Federated differential privacy (FDP), 15
Federated learning (FL), 133
    abundant data, 10–11
    academia and industry, 11
    accountability, 152–153
    advanced algorithms, 14
    applications of
        automotive, 17
        finance, 16–17
        healthcare, 16
        manufacturing, 17
        retail, 17
    for autonomous automobiles, 19
    background and motivation, 1–2
    Bandwidth Balancing Act, 12
    benefits of, 4–5
    collaborative ecosystems, 11
    collaborative intelligence, 2–3
    collaborative learning, 9–10
    communication and computing power, 9
    for custom-designed education, 20
    data and model heterogeneity, 12
    disease diagnosis and prediction
        blood pressure, 105
        cancer research, 106
        clinicians, 105
        COVID-19 diagnosis, 104–105
        healthcare providers, 106
        health data collaboration, 106–108
        patients, 105
    experiments, 157
    explainability, 151–152
    fairness, 150–151
    federated learning frameworks, 13–14
    federated trust algorithm, 155–156
    federation, 153–154
    future trends and advancements, 18–20
    hardware and software advancements, 10
    in healthcare, 19
        background, 95, 97
        objectives, 97
        privacy-preserving techniques, 98–101
    legal and ethical considerations, 13
    legal and ethical frameworks, 14
    ML, in distributed systems, 5–8
    and model aggregation
        algorithm, 164–165
        architecture of, 163
        considerations and variations, 165
        key components and considerations, 163–164
    open-source frameworks, 10
    principles, 3–4
    privacy, 148
    privacy and security
        future directions in, 15–16
        importance of, 14
        secure and confidential data sharing, 15
    privacy preservation in, *see* Privacy preservation
    privacy-preserving learning, 10
    regulatory landscape and ethical considerations, 11
    scalability and efficiency in
        adaptive model updating, 119–120
        asynchronous federated learning, 120
        batch processing and incremental processing, 114–115
        collaborative model averaging, 117–118
        communication and bandwidth optimization strategies, 121–124
        decentralized computing and model saving, 120
        deployment management, 115–116

Index   179

dynamic node selection, 114
federated transfer learning (FTL), 120
modeling compression, 119
multi-device regularization, 118
parallelization techniques, 115
parallel learning/MTL, 118–119
personal information security and network security, 116
refined communication protocol, 116
scaling up, 113–114, *114*
service-oriented architecture, 113–114
security and privacy-related solutions, 14
for smart towns, 19
stability and strength, 148–150
statistics, 156
system and security challenges, 12–13
user participation and incentives
deep learning, 65–68
natural language processing pipeline and system design, 61–64
political framing and narrative extraction, 60
results and evaluation, 68–74
sentiment analysis, 59–60
Federated meta-learning, 19
Federated model aggregation, 166
Federated transfer learning (FTL), 120
Federated transfer studying, 19
Federated trust algorithm, 155–156
Federation, 153–154
Federation Scale, 150
Feedback networks, 25
Feedforward network, 24
FLAME, **130**
Forward pass, 35, 37
Fraud detection, 16, 17
Full homomorphic encryption (FHE), 142

GAN loss, 34–35
General Data Protection Regulation (GDPR), 11, 146
Generative adversarial network (GAN), 30–31
Google Gboard, 18
Google Photos, 103
Gradient calculation, 36
Gradient compression
error feedback compression, 167–168
mean-centric compression, 167
quantization, 167
sparsification, 168
Top-k compression, 168
types, 168
Gradient quantization algorithms
and compression, 170–172
stochastic quantization algorithms, 169–170, **170**
Graph neural networks (GNNs), 8
Guo, Y., 162

Heikal, M., 59
Heterogeneity, 12
Heterogeneous devices, 164
Hidden layer(s), 26
Hinton, Geoffrey, 24
Homomorphic encryption, 15, 100–101, 139, 142
Homomorphic encryption (HE), 132
Horovod, **130**
Hyperparameter tuning, 165

ImageNet, 145
Incremental quantization, **171**
Independent updates, 123
Information exchange, 129
Initialization, 164
Input Layer, 25
Insider attack, 135
Internet of devices (IoD) systems, 131
Internet of things (IoT) devices, 161
Iterative process, 36, 38, 164
Ivakhnenko, Alexey, 23

Joshi, A., 74

Key management, 140

Lapa, Valentin, 23
Leaf, **130**
Limited communication bandwidth, **172**
Local differential privacy, 139
Local learning, 124
Local model training, 3–4, 164
Long short-term memory (LSTM), 28–30

Machine learning (ML)
distributed machine learning (DML), 6
adversarial models, 136–137
background of, 129
existing, 129
threat modeling, 135–136
federated learning and model aggregation, 163–167
gradient compression, 167–172
improvements to, 19
Machine learning/deep learning (ML/DL)
algorithms, 145
McCulloch, Warren, 23
Mean absolute error (MAE), 34, 86–87
Mean squared error (MSE), 33, 87
Membership inference attacks
data exfiltration, 134
data poisoning attacks, 135
Microsoft Federated Learning (MS FL), **130**
Mikolov, T., 64
Model dimensions, 172
Model distribution, 164
Modeling compression, 119
Model inversion attack, 133

180 Index

Model size reduction, 122
Model subdivision, 123–124
Model update aggregation, 4
Model update transmission, 164
MOOC RS
    content-based filtering in, *82*
    course-based filtering in, *85*
    evaluation metrics for
        Mean Absolute Error (MAE), 86–87
        Mean Squared Error (MSE), 87
        Root Mean Squared Error (RMSE), 88–89
    hybrid RS in, *86*
    implication and future research direction, 89
    preliminaries/background study
        collaborative-based filtering, 83–84, *84*
        content-based filtering, 82–83
        data collection and preprocessing, 85
        hybrid approach, 84–85, *86*
        recommender system, 80–81, *81*
    student(user)-based filtering in, *84*
Multi-device regularization, 118
Multilayer perceptron (MLP), 112

Naseem, R., 60
Natural language processing pipeline
    data acquisition, 61, **61**
    data pre-processing, 61–62
    narrative extraction–small training data, 63–64
    text categorization, 62–63
Neural network (NN), 161
    activation functions, 31–33
    convolutional neural network (CNN), 26–27
    feature models, 45–46
    feedback networks, 25
    feedforward network, 24
    generative adversarial network (GAN), 30–31
    long short-term memory (LSTM), 28–30
    loss functions, 33–35
    main components of
        hidden layer(s), 26
        input layer, 25
        output layer, 26
    with perceptrons, 44–45
    recurrent neural networks (RNNs), 27–28
    training, 47–48
Noise injection, 139
Non-IID data, 12, 165
Non-linearity, 31

Optimization techniques, 68
Output layer, 26
Outsider attack, 135

PaddleFL, **130**
Parallelization techniques, 115
Parallel learning/MTL, 118–119
Parameter pruning-based model compression strategy, 162

Parameter server architecture, 7
Partially homomorphic encryption (PHE), 142
Personal information security and network security, 116
Pitts, Walter, 23
Poisoning attacks, 136
Power of two quantization, **171**
Precision medicine, 16
Predictive maintenance, 17
Predictive renovation, 17
Privacy, 148
Privacy preservation, 163, 164
    differential privacy techniques, 137–140
    homomorphic encryption (HE), 132
    privacy attack, in distributed machine learning, 135–137
    secret sharing, 132
    secure-aggregation for, 140–142
    secure multi-party computation (SMC), 132
Privacy-preserving aggregation techniques, 139
Privacy-preserving communication, 4, 15
Privacy-preserving techniques
    data anonymization, 99
    differential privacy (DP), 99–100
    homomorphic encryption, 100–101
    secure multi-party computation (SMC), 100
Process optimization, 17
Pu, C., 131
PySyft, **130**
PyTorch/Federated, **130**

Quality management, 17
Quantization aware training (QAT), **171**
Quantized-SGD (QSGD), 162

Recurrent neural network (RNN), 27–28, 161
Refined communication protocol, 116
Reinforcement learning (RL), 8
Residual quantization approach, 168
Resource constraints, 13
Restricted bandwidth, 12
Ring learning with errors (RLWE), 131
Root Mean Squared Error (RMSE), 88–89
Rumelhart, David, 24

Sala, R.D., 131
Samsung's scene recognition, 18
Scaling federated learning systems
    adaptive model updating, 119–120
    asynchronous federated learning, 120
    batch processing and incremental processing, 114–115
    collaborative model averaging, 117–118
    communication and bandwidth optimization strategies, 121–124
    decentralized computing and model saving, 120
    deployment management, 115–116

dynamic node selection, 114
federated transfer learning (FTL), 120
modeling compression, 119
multi-device regularization, 118
parallelization techniques, 115
parallel learning/MTL, 118–119
personal information security and network security, 116
refined communication protocol, 116
scaling up, 113–114, *114*
service-oriented architecture, 113–114
Secret sharing, 132
Secure aggregation, 15, *141*, 169
Secure multi-party computation (SMPC), 15, 100, 132, 139
Service-oriented architecture, 113–114
SG model, *66*
Sharing model, 129
Simple peer-to-peer network, *7*
Somewhat homomorphic encryption (SHE), 142
Stability and strength, 148–150

Statistics, 156
Stochastic gradient descent (SGD), 36, 38, 160
Stochastic quantization, **171**
Storing and predictive loading, 123
Sybil attacks, 135
SyferText, **130**

TensorFlow Federated (TFF), **130**
Ternary quantization, **171**
Tesla Autopilot, 145
Threat modeling, 135
Transfer learning, 8, 69
True random number generator (TRNG), 131

Uniform quantization, **171**

Vanzo, A., 59
Variational autoencoders (VAEs) loss, 35

Weighted averaging, 169
Williams, Ronald, 24